# Becoming Green Gables

# BECOMING GREEN GABLES

## THE DIARY OF MYRTLE WEBB AND HER FAMOUS FARMHOUSE

ALAN MACEACHERN

McGill-Queen's University Press
Montreal & Kingston • London • Chicago

© Alan MacEachern 2024

ISBN 978-0-2280-2148-3 (cloth)
ISBN 978-0-2280-2149-0 (paper)
ISBN 978-0-2280-2182-7 (ePDF)
ISBN 978-0-2280-2348-7 (ePUB)

Legal deposit second quarter 2024
Bibliothèque nationale du Québec

Printed in Canada on acid-free paper that is 100% ancient forest free
(100% post-consumer recycled), processed chlorine free

This book has been published with the help of a grant from the Canadian Federation for the Humanities and Social Sciences, through the Awards to Scholarly Publications Program, using funds provided by the Social Sciences and Humanities Research Council of Canada. We also acknowledge the assistance of the J.B. Smallman Publication Fund and the Faculty of Social Science, the University of Western Ontario.

We acknowledge the support of the Canada Council for the Arts.
Nous remercions le Conseil des arts du Canada de son soutien.

McGill-Queen's University Press in Montreal is on land which long served as a site of meeting and exchange amongst Indigenous Peoples, including the Haudenosaunee and Anishinabeg nations. In Kingston it is situated on the territory of the Haudenosaunee and Anishinaabek. We acknowledge and thank the diverse Indigenous Peoples whose footsteps have marked these territories on which peoples of the world now gather.

---

Library and Archives Canada Cataloguing in Publication

Title: Becoming Green Gables : the diary of Myrtle Webb and her famous farmhouse / Alan MacEachern.
Names: MacEachern, Alan, 1966– author. | Container of (work): Webb, Myrtle. Diaries. Selections.
Description: Includes bibliographical references and index.
Identifiers: Canadiana (print) 2024031610X | Canadiana (ebook) 20240316460 | ISBN 9780228021490 (softcover) | ISBN 9780228021483 (hardcover) | ISBN 9780228021827 (PDF) | ISBN 9780228023487 (ePUB)
Subjects: LCSH: Webb, Myrtle—Diaries. | LCSH: Webb, Myrtle—Homes and haunts. | LCSH: Historic sites—Prince Edward Island—Cavendish—History. | LCSH: Farms—Prince Edward Island—Cavendish—History. | LCSH: Tourism—Prince Edward Island—Cavendish—History. | LCSH: Cavendish (P.E.I.)—Social life and customs—20th century. | LCSH: Montgomery, L. M. (Lucy Maud), 1874–1942. Anne of Green Gables—Sources.
Classification: LCC FC2614.G74 M33 2024 | DDC 971.7/4—dc23

---

This book was typeset in Minion Pro.

*To Genevieve and Sadie*

# Contents

Figures ix
Acknowledgments xv
Prologue xvii

Introduction 3

**THE DIARY**

| 1924 | 19 |
| 1925 | 31 |
| 1926 | 40 |
| 1927 | 48 |
| 1928 | 59 |
| 1929 | 66 |
| 1930 | 73 |
| 1931 | 80 |
| 1932 | 88 |
| 1933 | 95 |
| 1934 | 102 |
| 1935 | 110 |
| 1936 | 118 |
| 1937 | 133 |
| 1938 | 145 |
| 1939 | 152 |

| | |
|---|---|
| 1940 | 162 |
| 1941 | 168 |
| 1942 | 177 |
| 1943 | 183 |
| 1944 | 190 |
| 1945 | 195 |

Conclusion   203
Notes   217
Index   259

# Figures

1 The Webb farm, Cavendish, Prince Edward Island, undated. Courtesy of L.M. Montgomery Collection, Archival and Special Collections, University of Guelph. | xviii
2 Map of Prince Edward Island, inset map of the Cavendish area, and photomosaic of the Webb farm and surroundings, 1935. Courtesy of Joshua MacFadyen. The photomosaic uses photographs from the Government of Prince Edward Island's Aerial Photographs website, http://www.gov.pe.ca/aerial.survey. Copyright retained by His Majesty the King. | xx–xxi
3 The Webb family, c. 1930. Courtesy of Webb family. | xxii
4 Myrtle Webb diary, December 1926. Courtesy of Webb family. | xxiii
5 Myrtle Webb on the farm, undated. Courtesy of Anita Webb Collection, Parks Canada, Halifax. | xxiv
6 Ada Simpson (née Macneill) and Myrtle Macneill (later Webb), undated. Courtesy of Webb family. | 4
7 Myrtle Macneill (later Webb) at Margaret and David Macneill's home (Green Gables), c. 1890s. Courtesy of L.M. Montgomery Collection, Archival and Special Collections, University of Guelph. | 5

# Figures

8  Myrtle Webb and L.M. Montgomery with cats Lucky and Pat, Ontario, 1936. Courtesy of L.M. Montgomery Collection, Archival and Special Collections, University of Guelph. | 6

9  The wedding of Ernest and Myrtle Webb at David and Margaret Macneill's home, 1905. Courtesy of Webb family. | 8

10  Margaret and David Macneill, with Myrtle, Ernest, and Marion Webb, c. 1909. Courtesy of Webb family. | 9

11  The Webb garden, undated. Courtesy of Webb family. | 11

12  Floor plans of the upstairs and downstairs of Green Gables, 1949. © Government of Canada. Reproduced with the permission of Library and Archives Canada, RG84 vol. 1797, file PEI 56.2, T-10513, images 289 and 291. | 12–13

13  Lorraine and Pauline Webb in front of the Webb home, c. 1925. Courtesy of Anita Webb Collection, Parks Canada, Halifax. | 17

14  Cavendish, Prince Edward Island, 1928. In *Atlas of Province of Prince Edward Island, Canada and the World* (Toronto: Cummins Map Company, 1928), 51. | 20

15  Cavendish Road, from across the Webbs' lane, undated. Courtesy of Webb family. | 21

16  Webb family with horses and wagon, c. 1925. Courtesy of Marion Webb Collection, Parks Canada, Halifax. | 24

17  Pauline Webb and unidentified girl in front of Lover's Lane sign, undated. Courtesy of Webb family. | 27

18  Digging potatoes by the old orchard, c. 1920s. Courtesy of Webb family. | 30

19  Hauling hay, c. 1928. Courtesy of Anita Webb Collection, Parks Canada, Halifax. | 33

20  Webb children with Chester Macdonald, son of L.M. Montgomery, c. 1913. Courtesy of Webb family. | 55

21  Marion, Ernest, and Keith Webb, with Chester Macdonald, son of L.M. Montgomery, Cavendish Beach, c. 1919. Courtesy of

L.M. Montgomery Collection, Archival and Special Collections, University of Guelph. | 56

22 Copy of the Cavendish Beach postcard that Myrtle Webb sent to L.M. Montgomery, 1928. Courtesy of PEIPostcards.ca, https://www.peipostcards.ca/collection/beach-at-cavendish-p-e-island-2550/. | 64

23 Myrtle Webb and L.M. Montgomery in Lover's Lane, undated. Courtesy of Webb family. | 72

24 The Webb girls, c. 1932. Courtesy of Webb family. | 93

25 The Webb girls with Ernest, c. 1932. Courtesy of Webb family. | 100

26 "Lover's Lane" painting, by Helen Haszard, undated. Courtesy of Webb family. | 104

27 Green Gables postcard, 1930s, and handbill for the 1934 film of *Anne of Green Gables*. Collection of the author. | 106

28 Ernest and Myrtle Webb, undated. Courtesy of Webb family. | 113

29 Photo of Lover's Lane by L.M. Montgomery, c. 1900; colourized by her, c. 1920s. Courtesy of L.M. Montgomery Collection, Archival and Special Collections, University of Guelph. | 115

30 Cavendish Road from the Webb farm, 1936. Photo by National Parks Branch site inspectors. Courtesy of Public Archives and Records Office of Prince Edward Island, acc. 5467/14-2. | 123–4

31 "Green Gables" and caption, 1936. Photo by National Parks Branch site inspectors. Courtesy of Public Archives and Records Office of Prince Edward Island, acc. 5467/14-2. | 126

32 "The Haunted Forest," 1936. Photo by National Parks Branch site inspectors. Courtesy of Public Archives and Records Office of Prince Edward Island, acc. 5467/14-2. | 127

33 Map of Prince Edward Island National Park, Department of Mines and Resources, 1940. | 136

## Figures

34 Lorraine and Anita Webb, c. 1930s. Courtesy of Webb family. | 138

35 Two details from Thompson, Jones, & Co's plans for The Links at Green Gables, Prince Edward Island National Park, 1938. © Government of Canada. Reproduced with the permission of Library and Archives Canada, RG84 vol. 151, file PEI 313.7, part1, T-10432, image 435. | 148–9

36 Green Gables tearoom menu, undated. Courtesy of Webb family. | 158

37 Pauline and Anita Webb with servicemen identified only as Larry, Joe, and Ted, c. 1942. Courtesy of Webb family. | 174

38 Pauline, Lorraine, and Myrtle Webb with unidentified servicemen, Green Gables, c. 1942. Courtesy of Webb family. 175

39 Green Gables Golf Course, from *PEI: The Birthplace of Canada* (Charlottetown: Prince Edward Island Travel Bureau, 1942), 28. | 185

40 Wedding of Pauline Webb and Heber Jones, Green Gables, 1943. Courtesy of Webb family. | 186

41 The Webb family, Green Gables, c. 1943. Courtesy of Webb family. | 187

42 Louise and Ina Webb on Green Gables Golf Course, c. 1943. Courtesy of Webb family. | 188

43 Myrtle and Ernest Webb, with dog Nickey, 1940s. Courtesy of Webb family. | 199

44 L.M. Montgomery memorial ceremony, Green Gables, likely 1948. Courtesy of Earle MacDonald. | 204

45 Advertisement for Prince Edward Island National Park seeking furniture for Green Gables. *Charlottetown Guardian*, 30 June 1949. | 205

46 The old parsonage, Cavendish, undated. Courtesy of Webb family. | 207

47 Myrtle and Ernest Webb, undated. Courtesy of Webb family. | 209
48 Myrtle Webb, with cat Peter, undated. Courtesy of Webb family. | 210
49 Photomosaic of the Webb farm / Green Gables in 1935, 1958, and 2020. Courtesy of Joshua MacFadyen, using photographs from the Government of Prince Edward Island's Aerial Photographs website, http://www.gov.pe.ca/aerialsurvey. Copyright for the 1935 and 1958 series retained by His Majesty the King; copyright for the 2020 series retained by the province. | 214–15

# Acknowledgments

Myrtle Webb wrote the diary, entry by entry, over thirty years, with family members occasionally subbing in. I am so grateful that they opened this window to their world.

This book was also a team affair. Having preserved the diary for the decades since Myrtle's death, the Webb family – Elaine Crawford, Bob Crawford, Kelly Crawford, Louise Lowther, Alan Reed, Ina Reed, Donna Burr, Andrew Burr, Pat Jones, Terry Jones, and Brenda Jones – shared it with me, as well as photographs, correspondence, reminiscences, the 1936–40 diary of Anita Webb, the 1937–41 diary of Lorraine Webb, and answers to my endless questions.

Four Western University graduate students pitched in: Robyn Schwarz combed the L.M. Montgomery Collection at the University of Guelph, Sara Poulin researched armed forces personnel stationed on Prince Edward Island during the Second World War, and Blake Butler and Kenny Reilly completed a first pass of the diary's transcription.

Craig MacLeod, Beth Scott, and the web design team at Graphcom created greengablesdiary.ca, which showcases the complete diary with transcription, as well as photographs and other material.

Edward MacDonald and Joshua MacFadyen shared many insights into Prince Edward Island's history – and then MacFadyen did double duty, also creating the book's splendid maps and photomosaics.

Mary Beth Cavert, Lesley Clement, Elizabeth Epperly, and Emily Woster answered many questions about Maud and the *Anne of Green Gables* series of books. Philip Smith, Kate Scarth, and everyone at the University of Prince Edward Island's L.M. Montgomery Institute were warm and welcoming hosts to the Maud world.

Barb MacDonald and Anne Marie Lane Jonah at Parks Canada helped to track down Prince Edward Island National Park material. Staff at Library and Archives Canada, UPEI Library, and the Public Archives and Records Office of Prince Edward Island provided research assistance.

Western University's Samuel Clark Research Fund, Social Science Research Fund, and J.B. Smallman Publication Fund provided research and publication support.

Jeannie Prinsen was her usual wonderful editorial and supportive self. At McGill-Queen's University Press, Kyla Madden championed the manuscript, and then she, Kathleen Fraser, Robert Lewis, and the press's anonymous reviewers much improved it.

For Genevieve Warner and Sadie MacEachern – my family – Myrtle's diary was a COVID-19 lockdown project. While self-isolating in the spring of 2020, Genevieve and I read the handwritten diary out loud while the other corrected the typed transcript. Sadie coded the transcript with hashtags such as #foodgath and #GG that would assist in the writing. Then I wrote.

Thank you all – and congratulations. We did it.

# Prologue

On a sunny Wednesday afternoon in August 1909, Myrtle and Ernest Webb hosted a garden party at their Cavendish farm on Prince Edward Island. If needed, the young couple had ample excuse for such midweek festivities. Family friends were visiting from Massachusetts. Myrtle's aunt Maggie was back home on the Island too, having spent years as a schoolteacher in the Klondike. (On her return, she presented her niece with a locket containing gold dust.)[1] Myrtle herself was six months pregnant with their second child. Also, it was simply summer on Prince Edward Island.

What's more, the Webbs had just taken ownership of the property where the party was being held, a 140-acre parcel of rolling farmland on the Island's North Shore.[2] The farm had everything. There was substantial woodland along the back, field upon field of rich red soil, a stream that threaded its way to a sizable pond, and a line of sand dunes announcing the Gulf of St Lawrence. And at the very centre of the property was a large and sturdy old farmhouse with plenty of barns and outbuildings. Myrtle had lived on this farm for most of the past thirteen years, having moved there when she was twelve. She and Ernest had been married there in 1905, they had returned in 1907, and now it was officially theirs. It was a lovely place to be raising a family.

And if reality were not enough, the Webb farm had recently acquired an unexpected touch of romance. Cavendish author Lucy Maud Montgomery had published her first novel, *Anne of Green Gables*, to great international acclaim just a year earlier, and the farm was becoming associated with it.[3] The novel is about Anne Shirley, a spirited young orphan from Nova Scotia who comes to live with

Figure 1 | The Webb farm, Cavendish, Prince Edward Island, undated.

an elderly brother and sister on their farm, Green Gables, in the fictional PEI community of Avonlea – a farm much like the Webbs' in a community much like Cavendish. Reporting on the garden party, the *Charlottetown Guardian* newspaper described the property in reference to locations from the book: "The tables were spread under the shade of the apple trees in 'Old Orchard' in full view of the Lake of Shining Waters." After the charming hostess had served a "bounteous repast," some of the guests played games while others "enjoyed a walk through the beautiful path known as 'Lover's Lane' now made famous by the author of 'Anne of Green Gables.'"[4] Although the *Guardian* did not say so, Montgomery herself may well have been in attendance; she and Myrtle Webb were cousins and confidantes, after all. The newspaper might not have covered this modest party at all but for the fact that in 1909 the Webb homestead was already being identified as the inspiration – even the actual setting – of Montgomery's 1908 book. It hardly mattered that *Anne of Green Gables* was a novel and that both "Anne" and "Green Gables" were imaginary.

Myrtle and Ernest Webb made the farm their home for the next thirty-six years. They worked its land. They cut and burned its firewood. They stocked and fished its pond. They renovated and maintained the house. They raised five children there and watched them move away.

They became leading figures in their community. As time passed, they increasingly shared their ordinary home with its increasingly famous reputation. In the 1910s, they grew used to having strangers drop in, intent on seeing sites from the book. In the 1920s, with car ownership and automobile tourism on the rise, they welcomed more and more visitors from all over. In the 1930s, they finally surrendered to calling their farm what everyone else did: Green Gables.

But the Webb family did more than just witness their home in the process of becoming what it is today, the most famous house in Canada.[5] The Webbs also participated actively in making Green Gables the most famous house in Canada. In the 1910s, they put up signs for visitors that identified locations associated with the book. Beginning in the mid-1920s, they welcomed literary pilgrims as boarders each summer. They hosted dignitaries and conventions for teas and meals. They even sold *Anne* books and Green Gables postcards. The Webb family cemented the association between Anne's world and their own, to the point that for many readers and tourists from around the world, Green Gables *was* Prince Edward Island.

The Webbs were so successful, in fact, that when Prince Edward Island National Park was being established in 1936, the federal and provincial governments decided that it was natural – indeed, essential – that the Green Gables home and property be made its centrepiece. Facing expropriation, Ernest and Myrtle Webb had no choice but to sell the farm. Yet they were allowed to stay on in Green Gables for almost another decade, living in the middle of the national park as caretakers of what had been their home. Then, in the last days of 1945, they were told on just two weeks' notice that they had to leave. The literary connection with *Anne of Green Gables* that had long enriched the Webbs' lives ultimately upended it.

---

In the years when the Webbs were experiencing many of their greatest changes, Myrtle Webb was keeping a diary. When she first picked up the pencil in 1924, she was a forty-year-old homemaker running a household of eight, and the farm was of interest only to a relatively small number of travellers. By the time she set the pencil down in 1954, she was a seventy-year-old widow who lived alone, no longer occupying the house that was now a major Canadian tourist destination.

In contrast to her cousin L.M. Montgomery – a writer who kept a journal to capture, and later amend, her innermost thoughts in

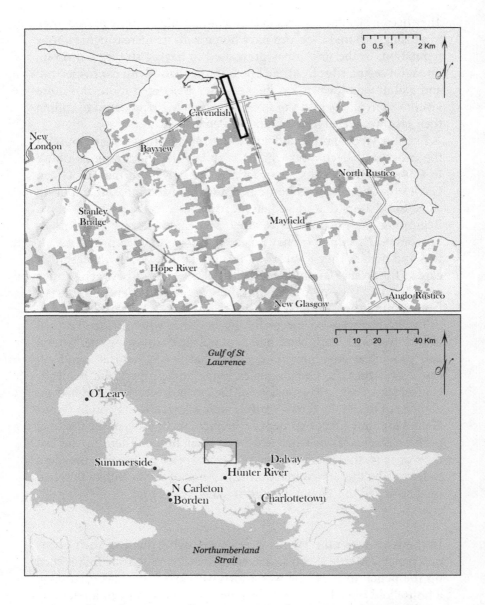

entries that often ran on for pages – Myrtle was content to jot down a short, prosaic review of the day's events. She noted the weather, what work and other activities members of the family were up to, their visitors or people they had visited, news about community births, marriages, or deaths – and often that was it. Few days rated

Figure 2 | Map of Prince Edward Island with place names of major towns and communities mentioned throughout the text (bottom left), an inset map of the Cavendish area (top left), and an aerial photomosaic of the Webb farm and surroundings in 1935 (above). Visible in the photomosaic, from top to bottom, are the Gulf of St Lawrence, sand dunes, Macneill's Pond ("Lake of Shining Waters"), Cavendish Road, the Webbs' house and barns, and the backwoods through which Lover's Lane runs.

Figure 3 | The Webb family, c. 1930. *Back row:* Anita, Ernest, Myrtle, and Keith. *Front row:* Lorraine, Pauline, and Marion.

more than forty words. In the diary's back pages, she recorded transactions ranging from the amounts charged long-stay boarders to a list of which cows had been bred by which neighbours' bulls.[6] Today, we may think of diaries as inherently private, but historically, they have tended to be closer to semi-private, with many left out to be read or even co-written.[7] Myrtle's diary was sufficiently public that it was accessible to the whole family. When she was sick or away from home, Ernest or one of the children recounted the day's happenings in her stead. All in all, about 5 per cent of the diary was written by others. To that extent, it was not just Myrtle Webb's diary but the Webbs' diary – the Green Gables diary.

The brevity of the diary's daily entries ensures that in its entirety it is relatively compact. It is written across seven simple, slim volumes, beginning with a 48-page scribbler and ending with a hardbound 200-page notebook; its thirty years comprise just over 200,000 words on 1,000 handwritten pages.[8] Myrtle's descendants preserved the diary in the decades after her death but never made it public or made it available to researchers. But Myrtle Webb's diary can now be read in full at greengablesdiary.ca. With the Webb family's blessing and assistance, I developed a web exhibit that includes scans and transcripts of the entire diary, as well as family photos, Green Gables memorabilia,

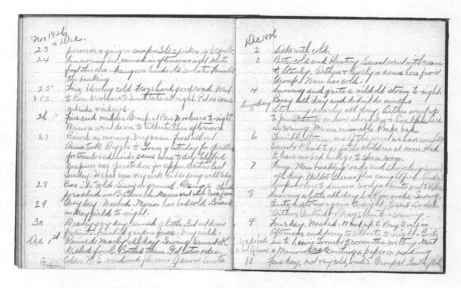

Figure 4 | Myrtle Webb diary, December 1926.

maps, and an introductory text. We launched greengablesdiary.ca on 24 April 2024 – the centennial of Myrtle's first post. I encourage readers to visit the site.

Yet the succinct nature of Myrtle's writing also means that individual entries often benefit from explanation or context. *Becoming Green Gables* explores a selection of the entries as a means of revealing the world of Myrtle Webb and her family, along with the history of Green Gables. It focuses on the years 1924 to 1945, when Myrtle kept the diary faithfully, with a conclusion that covers the decade that followed, when she wrote only sporadically. The entries – about ten for each year – have been chosen because they are both representative and evocative, capturing the rhythm and routine of the passing seasons at Green Gables while marking life's gradual and sudden changes. We learn how the Webbs farmed and worked and socialized and travelled and communicated and played and worshipped and much more. As a means of retaining Myrtle's voice, each of the entries is reproduced in full with its original spelling and punctuation.[9]

Each entry serves as a springboard for elaboration on a topic that it has mentioned. Thanks to daily changes in the diary's interests and

Figure 5 | Myrtle Webb on the farm, undated.

activities, even as the text proceeds chronologically, discussion spirals out in countless directions, from potatoes to Prohibition, from "Aunt Maud" to modernity. Although the foundation of this book is the Webbs' own story, it is also a history of their famous home, the community, the province, the nation, and the world in which they lived in the second quarter of the twentieth century. A belief underpinning the book, and echoed in its structure, is that reducing historical actors or episodes to a single meaning is to miss, and thus to miss out on, their complexity.

But given the diary's content – and my own background and interests – the book is also situated in and speaks to specific literatures.

For one, the book demonstrates the important role of women in tourism development. There exists a substantial international literature on the tourism industry's capacity to empower women, but it overwhelmingly deals with the Global South, and little of it is historical.[10] Conversely, although there is a considerable historical literature related to women and travel in the Global North, its focus tends to be on women as tourists, not as operators.[11] *Becoming Green Gables* shows that the winter planning and day-to-day summer labour of women such as Myrtle Webb, the four Webb daughters, neighbour Katherine Wyand, and members of the local Women's Institute were essential to making Green Gables, Cavendish, and Prince Edward Island major tourism destinations.[12] (And, at least through the mid-1930s, the clear majority of tourists to Green Gables were also women, drawn to this place by the writing of a female author about a female character.) The summer trade provided rural women such as Myrtle Webb a rare chance to build and run a business out of their own home.

The Webb diary also sharpens the picture of Green Gables itself. Considering how closely identified with *Anne* the physical site has become – not to mention how important to Prince Edward Island and Canadian tourism and culture – remarkably little has been written of its history, and this account has been produced mostly by Parks Canada staff for internal use.[13] *Becoming Green Gables* shares new findings about the house and property, such as the degree to which the Webbs maintained and modified their home to accommodate tourists in the 1920s and '30s. It also shows the degree to which the growing celebrity of Green Gables in this era did not just happen but was facilitated by the Webbs and, to some degree, by L.M. Montgomery herself; they were not simply relying on awareness of an existing *Anne* brand but were also helping to build this brand.[14] In this regard, the book makes a novel connection between the literary and the literal Green Gables.

In its later years, the diary also offers a rare account of the history of national parks in North America, providing a compelling behind-the-scenes look at a park's establishment and development. Whereas most histories of parks lean heavily on internal correspondence and reports, *Becoming Green Gables* traces the day-to-day progress of a park's creation from the perspective of previous owners – describing in detail the dramatic physical changes that were wrought to the Green Gables house, grounds, and farm. That the Webbs continued living in their old home, in the middle of Prince Edward Island National Park, makes them especially unusual and valuable witnesses to the park's first years.[15] What's more, Myrtle's diary captures how Green Gables experienced the Second World War, offering arguably the most captivating view of any North American national park in wartime.

The Webb diary also chronicles the unfolding of modernity across rural Canada in the early to mid-twentieth century.[16] In the mid-1920s, the Webbs were still growing and gathering much of their own food, they relied on horses for transportation and wood for fuel, and they were involved in the rural co-operative movement in numerous ways. By the mid-1940s, none of these things were true. To be sure, the family's modernizing arc was not absolute: they engaged with the cash economy at the beginning of this narrative, and they still grew a large vegetable garden and maintained a close-knit relationship with their rural community at the end. Nor was the family's arc at all typical: that they lived in, profited from, and ultimately were forced to sell a home that was becoming increasingly famous greatly accelerated the transformation of their way of life. But the very speed with which Green Gables changed from a largely subsistence farm to a golf course, the centrepiece of a national park, and a major tourist attraction allows readers to easily observe the onrush of modernity in the Webbs' lives.

Although the diary's entries and their stories continually guide us outward – connecting the Cavendish community to the wider world – they always bring us back again to Green Gables, to the Webb family, to Myrtle. My primary motivation in writing this book is to introduce readers to Myrtle Webb's world. Coincidentally, just a few months after Myrtle began her diary in 1924, L.M. Montgomery read and transcribed into her journal a somewhat similar account of everyday life on Prince Edward Island, the 1890s diary of Cavendish farmer Charles Macneill. "I don't think I ever read anything quite so delicious in my life," Montgomery wrote. "[I]t gave me the keen, sad delight of a vanished world."[17] Myrtle's diary does much the same. It opens a window into the life of a family over the course of three decades.

I admit to loving that Myrtle Webb shared the name of the everywoman wife and mother of Thornton Wilder's 1938 play *Our Town*. Yet these Webbs were not characters but real people. They lived a real existence in a real place that they loved. Their existence changed when their home became accepted as the setting of a famous novel. Although their lives grew increasingly governed by this fictional connection, they remained as real as ever, so they grieved the eventual loss of the place. In fact, generations after losing it, the descendants of the Webbs still identify with the farm. They are still the Webbs of Green Gables.

# Becoming Green Gables

# Introduction

Ada Macneill of Cavendish was nineteen years old in 1882, living on her own, and teaching at an unidentified schoolhouse near O'Leary, on the west end of Prince Edward Island, when she became pregnant.[1] Family lore has it that the father was a Rev. Edward Locke. Although there was no minister named Locke on the Island at the time, there was indeed a married farmer named Edward Locke, who would later become a minister, and he was living just a short distance from where Ada is known to have boarded. And there was a schoolhouse on the edge of his farm.[2]

Ada's family may have rejected her because shortly after giving birth to a daughter on 2 August 1883, she packed the two of them up and left Prince Edward Island. They went to Havelock in the interior of the neighbouring province of New Brunswick, where Ada took work as a domestic servant in the home of farmer Charles B. Keith. Given that Locke had a brother who lived not far from Havelock, it is quite possible that he set Ada up in this situation. At some point, Ada gave her daughter the name Myrtle Locke Keith Macneill.[3]

Mother and daughter lived in Havelock for a dozen years before returning to Prince Edward Island. (On 8 March 1935, Myrtle noted the anniversary in her diary: "39 years ago came to Cavendish.")[4] The family situation had changed greatly since they had last lived there. Many of Ada's older family members, including her father, had died, and the children of her generation had moved away. The death of her grandfather had left a family farm – what would eventually become known as Green Gables – in the hands of Ada's aunt and uncle. Margaret and David Macneill were a sister and brother around age sixty, she a brusque, sarcastic woman and he a shy, kind man.

Figure 6 | Ada Simpson (née Macneill) and Myrtle Macneill (later Webb), undated.

The house was more than enough for the two of them, and David needed help around the farm, so it was natural that Ada and Myrtle moved in with them; it was a beneficial arrangement all around.[5] In 1901, Ada married widower Walter Simpson and went to live with him in Bayview, the next community over; they soon had two children together, Cecil and Elaine. Eighteen-year-old Myrtle stayed on with David and Margaret in Cavendish.

Today, Cavendish is a tourist hub to which hundreds of thousands of visitors flock each summer. But at the beginning of the 1900s, it was an absolutely ordinary farming community, indistinguishable from countless others sprinkled across Prince Edward Island. Founded in 1790 by Gaelic-speaking Scots Highlanders, Cavendish was a farming community with a one-room schoolhouse, a post office, and Presbyterian and Baptist churches but no store of its own. With about forty families totalling 150 inhabitants, it was slightly smaller than Bayview to the west and Mayfield to the south and much smaller than the Acadian community of Rustico to the east. Even into the 1920s, Cavendish was insignificant enough that its name did not merit mention on some maps of the Island.[6]

Figure 7 | Myrtle Macneill (later Webb) sitting under a tree at Margaret and David Macneill's home (Green Gables), c. 1890s. Note that the kitchen wing, at the far side of the house, is only one storey; the Webbs would raise the roof to create a second storey in 1914.

Around 1901, Myrtle became friends with L.M. Montgomery, her third cousin, who lived just half a kilometre down the road. Maud had grown up in Cavendish with her grandparents, and as a child, she had fallen in love with David and Margaret Macneill's farm, particularly the woods that ran down the back of the property and the path through these woods that she dubbed Lover's Lane.[7] But Maud had largely been away at university or teaching in the first years that Myrtle was living in Cavendish. Now that Maud had returned, she got to know better this cousin nine years her junior. The age difference was something of a barrier, although it became less important as they got older; Maud later noted that there were others she felt more naturally close to because Myrtle "belongs to a generation a step removed from mine."[8] Nonetheless, they grew close because they had so much in common. Both were avid readers and gardeners. Both felt the sting of caring for a rather caustic, older female relative. Both loved the

Figure 8 | Myrtle Webb and L.M. Montgomery with cats Lucky and Pat, Ontario, 1936.

forests, fields, and seashore of this quiet corner of the planet. Maud considered Myrtle a "kindred spirit."[9]

By now, you may be wondering. A fatherless girl. Arrived in Cavendish from off Island at a young age. Moved in with and helped to care for a stern elderly woman and her more soft-hearted brother. Became friends with L.M. Montgomery in the years just before she wrote *Anne of Green Gables*. Lived at Green Gables.

Was Myrtle ... Anne of Green Gables?

When Montgomery's book became famous, the author bristled at the suggestion that her characters and plots were anything but products of her own imagination. "I have *never* drawn any of the characters in my books 'from life,'" she told her journal in 1911 – before recounting across several pages the degrees to which she was inspired by various people and places she knew. However, she pointedly did not connect Anne to anyone in real life, let alone to Myrtle.[10] Years later, upon hearing that an old Island beau was saying that Anne was a real person named Myrtle Webb, Maud wrote in her journal, "He knows as well as I do that Myrtle Webb is not 'Anne' – that she does not remotely resemble Anne, either physically, mentally or historically."[11]

Yet privately – more privately than she considered the journal that she expected would be published someday – Montgomery recognized that Myrtle shared some commonalities with Anne. "Aunt Maud always told us," Myrtle's son would later say, "that the character of Anne was a combination of her own life and my mother's life."[12] This might be explained away as the author flattering her friend's children, except for Maud's characterization of Myrtle's life story to others. In 1936, when describing the Macneill farm to her pen pal G.B. MacMillan, Maud wrote, "David and Margaret adopted an orphan niece" – framing Myrtle in Anne-like terms although she knew perfectly well that her friend was neither adopted nor an orphan.[13] (If anything, Maud was *more* of an orphan than Myrtle. Both had lost one parent, as Maud's mother had died when Maud was one year old, and Myrtle had never known her father. But whereas Maud's father had left her with her maternal grandparents and moved to Saskatchewan, Myrtle's mother raised her and was a steady presence throughout Myrtle's life.) Regardless of the degree to which Maud was inspired by Myrtle's childhood when creating Anne Shirley, the fact that a real woman lived in the fictional character's "home" would forever muddle the two in many people's minds. Myrtle seems only to have loved the attention that Green Gables drew as it became more

Figure 9 | The wedding of Ernest and Myrtle Webb at David and Margaret Macneill's home, 1905. The groom and bride are at centre. To the left is best man Will MacKendrick. To the right are May MacKendrick (née Webb) and maid of honour Ellice Lowther (née Laird).

and more of a destination in later years. She was annoyed, however, whenever tourists assumed that she was Anne.[14]

In life Myrtle could be mistaken for a grown-up Anne, but in death she has typically been described only in ways that, inadvertently or not, liken her to the childhood Anne. Undoubtedly seeded by Montgomery's misleading characterization, numerous scholars have wrongly claimed that Myrtle was "adopted" by David and Margaret Macneill. A Parks Canada memo from the 1970s casually refers to "the orphan, Myrtle." And through the first five published volumes of Montgomery's complete journals, Webb is identified in the notes *eight times* as "born out of wedlock" – that is, she is characterized in this fashion multiple times even within single volumes.[15] To the small degree that Myrtle Webb is remembered at all for her association with Green Gables, it is for the circumstances of her arrival rather than for the half-century that she lived there.

---

Myrtle's connection with the farm that would become Green Gables almost came to an end early in the new century. A branch of the Macneill family lived in O'Leary, in western Prince Eward Island,

Figure 10 | Margaret and David Macneill, with Myrtle, Ernest, and Marion Webb, c. 1910.

and while visiting them, Myrtle met her future husband. A member of a local farm family, Ernest Cecil Webb was also a salesman for farm machinery who, in the course of demonstrating or installing something at the Macneill farm, cut his finger. He was sent to the house, where Myrtle took care of him.[16] Nothing is known as to what drew them together. Myrtle is remembered as a no-nonsense woman; in photographs, she can look terribly serious, even uncomfortable. Ernest, three years older, is remembered as quiet and steady but warm – and handsome, with a shock of white hair from a relatively young age. They courted, got engaged, and on the morning of 20 September 1905 were married at Margaret and David Macneill's Cavendish home, perhaps so that the elderly siblings could attend.

The wedding ceremony was in the parlour under an arch of greenery. Myrtle wore a white brilliantine gown and carried a bouquet of asters. This wedding is of special interest to fans of L.M. Montgomery because the author's future husband, Rev. Ewen Macdonald, had recently moved to Cavendish.[17] One of her biographers has Ewen officiating and, as she puts it, "quietly eyeing the woman he was hoping might become Mrs. Macdonald," but there is actually no evidence that either was present.[18] Montgomery does not mention attending the event in her journal, and although as a new local minister Macdonald may well have been invited, he certainly did not officiate.[19] In any case, by mid-afternoon, Ernest and Myrtle were husband and wife, and they departed amid showers of rice for a new life together across the Island in O'Leary.

They would live there only for eighteen months. In the spring of 1907, Myrtle and Ernest were drawn back to Cavendish. David and Margaret Macneill were not getting any younger – he was now seventy, and she was sixty-eight and going blind – so an arrangement was made whereby the Webbs would move in and take care of them and in return be given ownership of the farm.[20] For their part, the Webbs may have felt the need to be more securely settled. In O'Leary, a baby daughter, Ina Rosamund, had died in infancy. And now Myrtle was pregnant again. The Webbs got to work fixing up the Macneills' house and grounds, making it their own. Montgomery would later write that she had long been worried about what would become of this farm that she loved so much. But then along came Myrtle, who would become "an intimate friend," and she married "a very fine man ... and he just stepped in and hung up his hat. They both loved the place and were careful to preserve all its beauty spots."[21]

Once settled in Cavendish, Myrtle and Ernest had three children in quick succession: Marion Claire in 1907; Keith Fairbairn in 1909, whose first name honoured the New Brunswick family that had taken in Ada and Myrtle years earlier; and Anita Maud in 1911, whose first name came from one of Ernest's sisters and whose second came from "Aunt Maud" Montgomery. After a pause, two more daughters arrived: Allison Lorraine in 1917 and Pauline Joyce in 1920. The Webbs looked after their great-uncle David Macneill until his death in 1914, and they continued to care for their great-aunt Margaret. Part of attending to the needs of three generations meant making room for everyone, so in 1914 Ernest raised the roof over the kitchen, creating three new bedrooms upstairs.[22]

The layout of the house and barns back then was much as it is today at Green Gables Heritage Place.[23] (But that is only because, having

Figure 11 | The Webb garden, undated.

demolished the barns when Prince Edward Island National Park was created, Parks Canada eventually rebuilt versions of them. Only the Green Gables house itself is original.) The main barn, a two-storey building running west to east, was to the north of the house and situated to shield the farm's human and livestock inhabitants from the winds off the Gulf of St Lawrence. On the barn's main floor, there was (from west to east) a cattle barn, a threshing machine operated by a horse treadmill, a young cattle barn, a narrow feed room, and a horse stable. There was a henhouse just west of the main barn and, perpendicular to the henhouse and running south, a combination pig house, granary, and driving shed to store buggies and sleighs. Sometime in the 1920s, Ernest and son Keith moved an outbuilding – missing from today's footprint of the yard – to the south end of the barnyard, facing the main barn. This building contained a boiler room (for mixing mash for pigs), an icehouse, a woodshed, and a room to store farm machinery. Relocating this outbuilding enclosed the barnyard on three sides and, with the help of a new picket fence, kept livestock out of the "house yard."

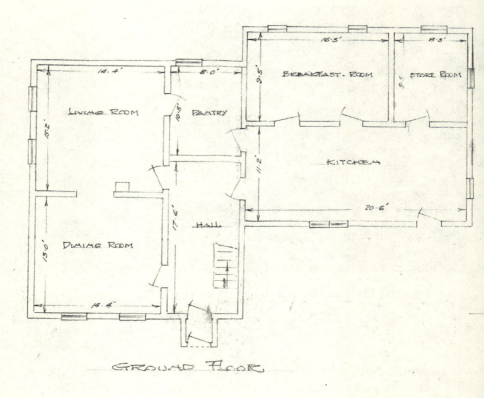

Figure 12 | Floor plans of the upstairs and downstairs of Green Gables, 1949.

To the northwest of the house, across the lane, was what the Webbs called "old orchard." To the west, a few large balm of Gilead trees provided some shelter from the wind. Just north of the house, there were lilac bushes along the fence and a large Manitoba maple, and to the northeast, there was a kitchen garden. To the south, there were silver maples and birch trees on the lawn. And at the entrance of Lover's Lane sat the outhouse.

Today, a waterfront property on Prince Edward Island is likely to be built close to the shore and oriented toward it. But there were different priorities for a Victorian farmhouse. Even if the barn were not blocking the view to – and the wind from – the north, the Gulf of St Lawrence would not have been visible from the house. The Green

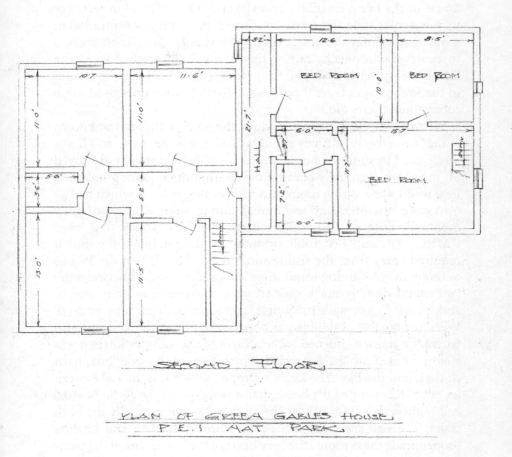

Gables house was oriented east to capture the sun's power. The main lawn sloped gently down to the east until it fell away steeply to the creek, making for a perfect coasting hill in winter. There was an apple orchard here in front of the house too, along with flower gardens and bushes and a large Acacia tree. Rose bushes grew outside the kitchen, and there were pink peonies on both sides of the front door.

The Webb house was well suited to the family.[24] Although already reasonably old, it was in solid shape, with a one-storey kitchen wing that may date to the 1830s and a two-storey south wing that was likely constructed in the 1870s. Myrtle's diary catalogues constant, incremental remodelling over the years, but emergency repairs were rare. The house is restored today to resemble "a typical farm house of the late Victorian period,"[25] and it was typical in terms of its vernacular style and its wood construction, but it was unusual in a way that we may not notice today: it was big. After Ernest created three new bedrooms by raising the roof over the kitchen wing, the house measured just shy of 2,300 square feet.[26] Of the 125 homes in the Webbs' 1921 federal census subdistrict, none possessed more rooms than theirs did.[27]

When one walked in the front door, the room to the left was known as the "front room," fittingly enough. (Today, it is the "parlour.") It was rarely used in summer, but in winter a pot-bellied stove was moved in; the room eventually became the community's quilting hub. The next room was a sitting room (now the "dining room"), which had its own stove in winter. Next was a small dining room, which the family eventually outgrew and converted into a pantry. Today, this room ("Matthew's room") is visible from the front door, but at the time it required entry from the sitting room or kitchen. When the Webbs outgrew the old dining room, they knocked out a wall between the two rooms directly north of it (since restored as the "dairy porch" and "pantry") and made this single large room their summer kitchen. With its big table, it doubled as a workroom in winter and was also where the women churned butter. North of the summer kitchen was a storeroom (now "back porch"), which housed the woodbox, barn clothes, and the like. The kitchen proper, which ran the full eastern length of this wing of the house, had a stove, pump, large cupboards, and – always – two couches. The washing was done under the back stairs. The size and openness of the summer kitchen and kitchen proper made these rooms the very heart of the house – even the community. Forty people could be seated here and often were.

Upstairs, there were no fewer than seven bedrooms. It is not known where everyone slept, but the south wing had four bedrooms, divided among the five children. What is now "Anne's room," the first to the left at the top of the stairs, was always Marion's, the oldest. There were three bedrooms in the north wing, including Ernest and Myrtle's large, long one directly over the kitchen. (A smaller version is now the "hired hand's room.")

As for the farm itself, it was a going concern. A long, thin property of 140 acres, it was one of the largest farms in Cavendish; it took half an hour to walk from its backwoods down to the shore. There were roughly fifteen fields in which to grow potatoes, grain, and hay, as well as to pasture livestock. The Webbs always had three or four workhorses on hand, along with ten or so Holstein and Guernsey cows, a litter of pigs, some poultry, a dog, and a cat or nine.

---

Myrtle, Ernest, and their growing family immersed themselves fully in Cavendish life. This life was made more interesting thanks to L.M. Montgomery's unexpected, tremendous literary success. Her first novel, *Anne of Green Gables*, an overnight bestseller across North America upon its publication in 1908, launched a whole series of *Anne* books and made its author one of the most famous in Canada. *Anne of Green Gables* owed its popularity not only to the indelible portrait of its spirited protagonist, Anne Shirley, but also to the portrait of its setting, namely the farmhouse called Green Gables and the rural community of Avonlea. Although Montgomery herself moved to Ontario after marrying Rev. Ewen Macdonald in 1911, her books enticed readers who wanted to explore the landscape and experience the way of life about which she rhapsodized. As early as the summer of 1909, a *Charlottetown Guardian* reporter spent time as a guest of Myrtle's mother, Ada, in Bayview, with plans to "visit Avonlea and Green Gables and take in the scenes of Miss Montgomery's famous novel."[28] Many from off Island came in search of these sites too – whether they sought the locations that inspired the books or fully believed that they were real places. As early as 1911, *Saturday Night* magazine, in an invented exchange with the author, chastised her for making the Island so attractive that it was sure to be overrun with tourists. "Why, one of the midsummer dreams of the Canadian traveller is to find Green Gables and catch a glimpse of Anne."[29] A trickle of literary pilgrims to the Cavendish area soon became a steady stream.

The Webb farm received some attention from *Anne of Green Gables* fans in the 1910s because Montgomery was known to have modelled the novel's Lover's Lane, a bucolic walk much-loved by Anne, after a path through its woods. But the Webb home was not routinely assumed to be Green Gables because there was another local candidate: Montgomery's own childhood home. She had been raised in her grandparents Alexander and Lucy Macneill's Cavendish home and written her early books there. The house was abandoned but still standing, and so it was a favourite with tourists. When *Maclean's* magazine ran a 1919 feature on "The Author of Anne," it carried a photo of this site and made no mention of the Webb farm at all.[30] But Montgomery's uncle grew tired of gawkers and souvenir hunters, and in 1920 he tore down the old Macneill homestead. If only by default, the Webb farm would now be the unrivalled Green Gables.

The connection did not have much of an effect on the Webb family at first. They were busy making a life from what they could grow and gather on their farm – and sell. In just the first three years of the diary, Myrtle speaks of the family selling cattle, pigs, pork, poultry, eggs, wood, hay, potatoes, tomatoes, and cream. But in 1920s Prince Edward Island, such an existence was getting more difficult. The largely agricultural economy of the province was in a tailspin, with farmers facing postwar inflation alongside deteriorating markets for their goods. Out-migration was hollowing out Island society too. Although other rural parts of the province suffered more, Cavendish's population had dipped from 152 to 125 between 1911 and 1921.[31]

By the spring of 1924, the Webbs were struggling to stay afloat. Myrtle and Ernest were middle-aged – she was forty and he forty-three – and supporting a large family. Aunt Margaret was in her mid-eighties, fully blind, and in constant need of care. None of the five children were contributing financially yet to the household's running, as Marion (often called "Peggy") was just sixteen, Keith fourteen, Anita ("Nita," "Neta," or "Nan") twelve, Lorraine (or "Waine" because of little sister Pauline's early inability to pronounce her name) almost seven, and Pauline (or "P.J.") four. That spring, L.M. Montgomery told her journal of having received a "rather depressing" letter from Myrtle Webb: "They are having very hard times on PEI and she writes as if they might have to give up farming and try something else. Times are hard everywhere."[32]

As a potential source of supplemental income, summer tourism was still in its infancy on the Island. What tourism that had existed along the North Shore since the 1870s had been concentrated a little to the east of Cavendish, from Rustico to Stanhope. There had been no hotels or boarding houses in Cavendish and no calls for them. But the interest generated by *Anne of Green Gables* changed that. In 1921, Jerry and Anna Simpson, who lived two farms west of the Webbs, built a large new home and began welcoming summer travellers to Sunnyacres Farm – travellers who, as soon as they arrived, dutifully trooped over to the Webbs' farm to see the homestead said to have

Figure 13 | Lorraine and Pauline Webb in front of the Webb home, c. 1925.

inspired Montgomery. The Simpsons' venture must have encouraged Myrtle and Ernest to wonder whether they, too, could profit by their providential association with the famous book.

The story of what is now Green Gables can seem an unlikely but straightforward one – the story of an ordinary house consecrated by literature thanks to the genius of its author and the devotion of its readers. But it is also the product of many pieces falling into place in the 1910s and '20s: an especially picturesque property, with woods and field and sea; an unusually large house, able to accommodate many visitors; an alternative site of inspiration torn down; and a family with young children – most of them, importantly, girls – having difficulty making ends meet and willing and able to welcome guests. History happened to the Webbs, as it happens to all of us, but they also made it happen, as we all do.

# The Diary

## 1924

20 April 1924
Wind N.E. Easter Sunday. Snowing until 10 a.m. A lot of snow. Fields covered. Froze hard at night. Up to B.View. Radio Poor. Long day. No preaching.

There is no knowing why, at the age of forty, part way through the calendar year, Myrtle Webb took up a pencil and wrote this entry in a fresh new notebook, beginning a diary that she would maintain for the next thirty years. She never explains. In fact, she only rarely mentions the diary in the diary, namely when observing her first anniversary of writing and occasionally when apologizing for having nothing to say or no time to say it. She wrote most every day but was not above backdating a few days' worth of entries when need be. Although the diary was relatively public, with Ernest or one of the girls filling it in when she was sick or away, she kept it in her bedroom. We might picture Myrtle sitting in bed at night, a kerosene lamp for light, taking a few minutes to capture the day's events.

This first entry, short and pithy and composed of a few sentence fragments, would be the model of almost 10,000 to follow. First came the weather, often with the wind direction and a Fahrenheit temperature above ("A") or below ("B") zero.[1] Then followed a few snapshots of the day, such as where the Webbs visited or who visited them, what work they did, and anything unusual or deemed worth noting. The blunt nature of such diary writing can make diarists appear more stoic and dispassionate than they really are; Myrtle's letter-writing to

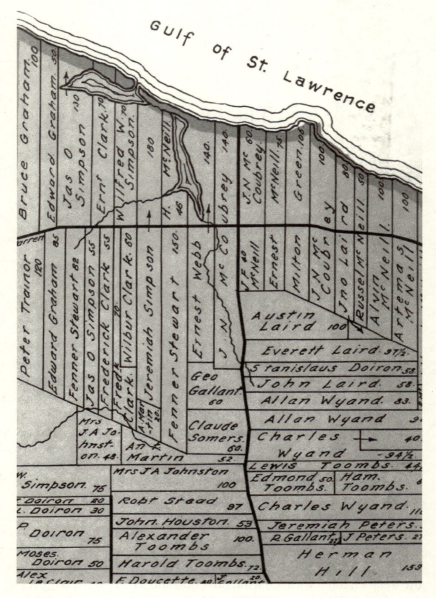

Figure 14 | Cavendish, Prince Edward Island, including landowners, *Cummins' Atlas*, 1928. Many of the Webbs' neighbours feature prominently in Myrtle's diary, including the families of Jeremiah (Jerry) Simpson, Fenner Stewart, H. (Ham) Macneill, J.N. McCoubrey, Fred Clark, Austin Laird, Allan Wyand, and Harold Toombs.

Figure 15 | Cavendish Road, from across the Webbs' lane, undated.

her children is more expressive.[2] She would eventually grow somewhat more relaxed and expansive in her diary writing but not by much. The diary was not a place to reveal her very deepest thoughts – perhaps because Ernest and the girls had access to it and perhaps because such writing was of no interest to her. This was how Myrtle Webb chose to chronicle her life.

*26 April 1924*
N.E. *fine. Ernest went to Creek in* A.M. *Got bag of flour and clover seeds. Did Saturdays work. Broke road from brook to Ham's gate.*

It was a Saturday, so Myrtle did Saturday's work – work that she mentions seventeen times in the diary without ever indicating what it constituted. Not baking bread, which tended to be on Mondays or Tuesdays. Not churning butter or washing clothes, which could be any day of the week – except Sunday. Perhaps she was referring to scrubbing the floors or baking for the weekend or emptying the ashes from the woodstove or any number of tasks that needed regular doing around the household but were not important enough to specify. And, of course, Myrtle undoubtedly performed Saturday's work hundreds of times over the years of her diary without explicitly saying so.

On this Saturday, Ernest went shopping at the Creek, the nickname for the nearby community of Rustico. The Webbs, like all Islanders by the early twentieth century, were immersed in the cash economy and gave their business to several local general stores.[3] For groceries and for household and farm goods – flour, kerosene, paint, everyday clothes, and the like – they alternated between Harold Toombs's store in Mayfield (4.5 kilometres away) and E.C. LePage's store in Rustico (7.5 kilometres). They also travelled 17 kilometres to Hunter River, usually for larger bulk items such as coal, fertilizer, or animal feed, and on occasional visits to Charlottetown (40 kilometres), they shopped for shoes or specialty items. The country stores were typically produce dealers as well, so in the early years of the diary especially, Myrtle writes as often about the Webbs going to a store *with* goods as she writes about them going *for* goods: taking lumber to sell to LePage's store, chickens and geese to Toombs's store, or potatoes and pork to Hunter River. These were always commercial exchanges, never barter, and Myrtle sometimes kept track of the family's accounts with these stores on the back pages of the volumes of her diary.[4]

Yet the very act of writing "Got bag of flour and clover seeds" suggests that the Webbs made purchases relatively infrequently. In the diary's first three months, Myrtle mentions three times that the family bought flour, but this is the *only* grocery item mentioned in this period. Doubtless the Webbs also bought tea, sugar, salt, molasses, and other staples, but for the most part they relied on what they grew, collected, and made on their farm. As Island historian Edward MacDonald writes of this era, "most Island farms were first and foremost subsistence operations."[5] The Webbs grew vegetables, including potatoes for sale. They sold eggs. They raised cattle, pigs, and chickens, and sometimes geese and ducks, for sale or slaughter. Like many Island farm families, they separated milk and sold the cream, keeping the skim milk for their livestock and for themselves.

*29 April 1924*
S.E. *Snowing in* AM. *Ernest and Keith cleaning grain. Up today but pretty crippled. Sent order to Lou S. Darling for seeds $1.00.*

*Letter from Aunt Sadie. She is in Gladstone, getting settled. Ernest up to Wilburs getting glass cut for hot bed.*

That spring, Ernest built Myrtle a hotbed, a glass-covered enclosure heated by fermenting manure. Her plants there would get a head start on the Island's short growing season, before being transplanted to the garden when the weather got warmer. Seeds from the catalogue of Lou S. Darling, a Michigan-based seed company, would sprout in an artificially warmed patch of Island soil – which was nicely emblematic of how the Webbs navigated both global systems and local conditions.

Notably, Myrtle made room in the hotbed not just for vegetables but also for flowers; life was about more than surviving. She was renowned for her flower gardens. L.M. Montgomery recounted in her journal that her indelible first memory of Myrtle was of the younger cousin, new to Cavendish, delivering her a bouquet of Shirley poppies.[6]

*5 May 1924*
*S.W. & S.E. Blowing a gale. Washed regular & bedding. Marion cleaned Anitas room. Keith went to run for smelts. Got 6 & some perch. Raining at 11 PM. Darnley better today. Put manure in hot bed. Saw first carriage come down hill this AM. XYZ*

Spring on the Island is mud season, so the sighting of a horse and carriage on Cavendish Road, the dirt road – now mud road – that bisected the farm, was as sure a sign of spring as the appearance of violets or robins. Spring was the time for cleaning, planting the garden, removing the banking from around the house, plowing and sowing and harrowing the fields, and a hundred other jobs around the house and farm. There was most definitely a distinction between "women's work" and "men's work." Keith did the bulk of the farmwork with his father, whereas the girls did housework with their mother. But the prevalence of Webb girls meant they did a lot of farmwork too.

Spring also meant gathering up what nature provided. The girls' annual search for mayflowers may well be the most regularly mentioned activity in the entire diary. There were also smelt, perch, and gaspereau (or alewives) running in the brook to the east of the house. There were trout to be fished from Macneill's Pond, near the shore, the pond that they shared with neighbour Ham Macneill – and that became identified, wrongly, as the inspiration for *Anne of Green*

Figure 16 | Webb family with horses and wagon, c. 1925. The three children with Myrtle and Ernest are likely Anita, Lorraine, and Pauline.

*Gables*' Lake of Shining Waters.[7] There were clams to be dug along the shore. A few days after this entry, Myrtle wrote that she and Ernest had walked up to get clams off Art Simpson's shore: "Yum Yum."[8]

The five Webb children weave in and out of the diary in these years in much the same way that they travelled around Cavendish: constantly, randomly, on their own, or in small packs. They had considerably more freedom and more responsibility than we would expect of kids today. In October of that year, Ernest and Myrtle would be called away to O'Leary on short notice and leave the children, ages four to sixteen, on their own for three days.

*10 May 1924*
*N.E. Fine but cold wind all day. Very heavy frost in morning. Ernest went to Rustico in AM. Girls cleaned dining room. Ernest to Stanley and Marion up to Mothers at night. Very tired. We can't find Sandy.*

"Very tired." This is the first appearance of what would become a common refrain in Myrtle's writing. In fact, "tired" is one of the diary's most frequent words, showing up more than "supper" or "snow" or "mother."[9] There are variations too, such as "Awful tired" or the sarcastic "Tired? Oh no" – not to mention the more expressive "All in but the boots." Even granted the fact that Myrtle was writing at end of day, her constant reference to being tired is striking. Only forty years old, she is regularly weary and would continue to be for much of the rest of her life.

She was also dogged by ailments throughout her adult years, many of them not identified in the diary or, seemingly, in life itself. She had periods of back pain, indigestion, headaches, peritonitis, and jaundice. She could be "miserable," "mean," "crippled," "sick," "on my back," "not very spry," or "in bed," often for days at a time.

Given all that, it is remarkable how "busy" Myrtle was – a word that appears almost as often as "tired." The two, of course, were undoubtedly related. But Myrtle was busy not only in housework, farmwork, parenting, and soon, keeping boarders but also in community and church activities, music and reading and crafts, long walks with Ernest, and much else. She did not let frequent tiredness or illness prevent her from living a full life.

*29 May 1924*
*s. Finished planting spuds. Digging in garden all day. Aunt M.*
*very miserable. Girls came home.*

For years, Aunt Margaret Macneill had been unwell. Now, she had pneumonia and was surely dying. She had been blind for years; the Webb children's lasting memory would be of her walking through the house, hands outstretched before her. Much of the day-to-day responsibility for her care in recent years had fallen to the children, particularly Marion, the oldest. But even little Lorraine recalled guiding Margaret by the hand to the outhouse at the opening of Lover's Lane.[10]

*1 July 1924*
*Lovely day. Washed in AM and sewed in P.M. A lot of cars on*
*the go today. Two cars went back the lane and had their supper.*
*Class at night.*

What first drew visitors to the Webb property was not so much the house as Lover's Lane. Longer and wilder than it is today, it was L.M.

Montgomery's indisputable inspiration for the wooded trail that the fictional Anne loved.

And, importantly, it was publicly accessible. The Webbs' driveway ran along the west side of the property – rather than winding beside the brook farther to the east, as it does today – so a visitor could drive straight back down this lane and join up with Lover's Lane, skirting the house without disturbing the family or asking permission to trespass. There is no indication, however, that the Webbs were ever irritated that tourists and Islanders alike occasionally strolled and picnicked there. They were proud of their farm's small fame. In fact, early on, Ernest hung a sign directing visitors to Lover's Lane.[11] In October 1923, many of the trees along Lover's Lane were knocked down in a hurricane – one that greatly resembled the post-tropical storm Fiona that would devastate the Island ninety-nine years later. "The poor old lane has some remnants of beauty here and there," Montgomery lamented in her journal the next summer, "but it is sadly unlike what it was."[12] Yet as Myrtle's entry suggests, visitors kept coming.

It was because of this public attention and the need for extra income that the Webbs decided to take in boarders for short and long stays. It was an easy matter to get up and running: have the Webb children give up their bedrooms in the south wing for the summertime, plan for some extra laundry and to feed a few more people at mealtimes, and that was about it. Ernest and Myrtle had the example of their neighbours Jerry and Anna Simpson, who had opened their farm to tourists in 1921. Some sources have the Webbs taking in boarders as early as 1922, but Myrtle makes no reference to tourists staying there in the diary's first summer of 1924. The closest is an early-October mention: "Two men came and stayed the night."[13] Prince Edward Island was just beginning to experience an automobile-driven tourism boom, and the Webbs' business relied exclusively on word of mouth, so their home stayed relatively quiet a summer or two longer.[14]

The Webbs charged a very standard rate for Prince Edward Island rural lodging: in the mid-1930s, it would be $2 per night or $13 per week for room and meals. There was no Green Gables surcharge. In fact, whereas the Simpsons called their boarding house Sunnyacres Farms, the Webbs just told potential visitors to contact Mrs E.C. Webb.[15] They did not use the name Green Gables, and they did not paint their gables green. Such restraint suggests that they did not presume to exploit their home's connection with Aunt Maud's writings,

Figure 17 | Pauline Webb and unidentified girl in front of Lover's Lane sign, undated.

or that she had expressly asked them not to, or that they themselves wanted to preserve a space between her fictional world and their real one. There is in fact no evidence of any of the Webbs referring to the house or farm as Green Gables until 1936. They may well have been the last to start doing so.[16]

*20 July 1924*
*Sunday. Raspberries for breakfast. Just one perfect day. Pres church in AM. Keith & Anita & Waine went. Marion came home at noon. Enid & Reuel brought her. She got her hair cut in town. Mr Mason preached this afternoon and he & Judson Simpson came here to supper. Another busy day.*

L.M. Montgomery had been on the Island earlier that month and was disturbed by what she saw. "One thing depressed me very much," she told her journal. "Cavendish is getting so shabby. Almost all the houses are unpainted and dowdy ... Times are hard, of course, but I fear there are other reasons – indifference, the dying out of the old families ... There is something wrong somewhere."[17] The nostalgic Montgomery was to some degree granting Cavendish a golden age that it had never really experienced outside her own books, but times really were hard.

Yet as Myrtle's entry shows, Cavendish in summertime could also be bliss. She had noted "a magnificent rainbow" on the previous day and began each of the next two entries, "Lovely day." More than that, Cavendish in summertime provided a bounty. Berries were there to be taken, whether cultivated in your garden or picked wild in the woods, fields, or hedgerows, and there to be eaten fresh or made into pies or jams or preserves. You could even sell them, and Myrtle did. And 1924 was a particularly good year for berries. Wild strawberries were first spotted along next-door neighbour Fenner Stewart's barn on 22 June, but for the weeks that followed, the Webbs depended mainly on their own cultivated patch.[18] When strawberry season ended in mid-July, raspberry season began. Myrtle spoke of the family gathering 14 quarts of raspberries one day and 12 quarts another. When raspberry season ended in mid-August, the blueberry harvest began. After blueberry season ended in early September, the cranberries were soon plentiful down near the shore, to be gathered in big bags and stored in the basement for the winter.[19] Remarkably, in 1924, Myrtle wrote of family members or herself picking berries on twenty-six separate days – often for entire days.

> *15 September 1924*
> *Lovely fine day. <u>Aunt Margaret died at 9:15 PM</u>. after a terrible hard day, mother here. Bob & Jennie & Hester here until midnight. The long long watch is over.* XYZ

After months of occasionally noting that Aunt Margaret was "miserable" or "cranky" or "fussy," Myrtle mentioned her almost every day throughout the first half of September, increasingly as "quiet." On the fourteenth, she had what Myrtle believed was a stroke, and the end was clearly in sight. She died the next day.

Margaret Macneill had lived all her eighty-six years at the farm that would become known as Green Gables, the last seventeen under the Webbs' care. The very large funeral took place two days later, and the day after that, Myrtle tidied up. She washed the sheets from Margaret's bed, sorted her things, and burned some of them. "It seems so strange not to hear Aunt Margaret calling," Myrtle wrote. "It is the first day that we have been alone just ourselves for a good many years."[20]

*22 September 1924*
*Perfect weather very warm today. Keith went to North Carleton to pick potatoes. They are paying $2.00 a day. Marion, Anita, and Margaret Johnson went to Rustico for a drive. John Johnson, Mayfield died this morning at 3 o clock. Very bad with asthma and choked to death. Peter Stewart, Mrs. Darley's brother died aged 89 yrs. Started boiling for pigs.*

Prince Edward Island had borne the nickname Spud Island throughout the Maritimes for some time but was in the very first years of being famous across the continent for its potatoes.[21] Not table stock but seed stock. The province's spuds reproduced well and were relatively resistant to disease, so they were becoming popular across North America as seed potatoes. As a result, the acreage under cultivation rose swiftly, which meant that teenage boys like Keith were in high demand and that their harvest workdays were long and hard.

Keith could have hired out at many places along the North Shore, so the fact that he was headed to North Carleton, 40 kilometres away, suggests that he was going to work at the farm of Harry and Ellice Lowther. Ellice was originally from Cavendish and had been Myrtle's maid of honour, and they were still close friends. But spuds are thicker than water: five days after this entry, Myrtle wrote, "Keith came home from Carleton. He has had quite enough."[22] Quitting North Carleton, however, did not mean quitting the work altogether. Keith picked potatoes on two more neighbours' farms that fall, just as he had planted potatoes at three neighbours' farms that spring.

Not all work between farms was paid work. The Webbs and their neighbours regularly worked together at labour-intensive jobs – whether time-sensitive ones such as harvesting crops, occasional ones such as hooking rugs, or one-offs such as moving a building – without money changing hands. Sometimes it was understood that such work would be quickly and directly reciprocated, as when Ernest helped next-door neighbour Ham to harvest his potatoes one week and Ham helped Ernest with his potatoes the next. Just as often, the work was done simply in the knowledge that there would be opportunity for future reciprocation, as when Ernest helped Cecil to saw wood and, weeks later, Cecil helped Ernest to butcher animals. The diary is also replete with instances of the Webbs helping or being helped but with no evidence of reciprocation. For people without

Figure 18 | Digging potatoes by the old orchard, c. 1920s. From left: Keith, Ernest, Lorraine, Pauline, and Anita Webb.

much money, it just made sense to treat such labour as a form of credit and to save money for the purchase of goods. And it made sense to be, and to have the reputation of being, good neighbours.[23]

> 11 December 1924
> N.E. Blowing and snow flurries. Jerry came home. Anna doing fine. Ernest went to Creek, bad road, neither sleighing or wheeling.

L.M. Montgomery described Cavendish in winter as a "snowy prison," and in the worst of storms, it certainly could be.[24] But snow on the roads and fields, like ice on the rivers, actually made travel easier on the Island for most of the winter than it was in the late fall and particularly in the spring, when sleighs, carriages, and cars might all be unable to make their way. The winter was quieter, but because the farm demanded less, it was also a time to get in a lot of visiting and community activities.[25] In the early twentieth century, Prince Edward Island was the only Canadian province to have meteorological observers record the number of days suitable for sleighing.

*24 December 1924*
*Anita at Jerry's. All pretty busy here. Box of books from Maud,
30 books. Made doughnuts and candy.*

There were Christmas rituals at the Webb house in the 1920s and '30s: a flurry of practices for the church concert and then the concert itself, visitors and visiting, baking sweets, going to Ada's for dinner, and on the twenty-fifth, Myrtle telling her diary some variation of "Children had a good day and Santa was very good to all."[26]

There was also always a box of books from Aunt Maud. Thirty books one year, fifty the next, and occasionally magazines. Montgomery picked up a dozen novels – often detective fiction – every time she visited her publisher McClelland and Stewart in Toronto, and many of these books eventually made their way to Prince Edward Island.[27] The entire Webb family were inveterate readers, and occasionally throughout the winter, Myrtle would note that a book had claimed her day. Montgomery's generosity to the Webbs was sufficiently well known that it was mentioned in *Chatelaine* magazine in 1928. The writer of a profile on the author spoke to a local woman who enthusiastically reported – in a broad Acadian accent – "She's so awful good to de people up dere. Efery Chreesmas she sen' Mrs. W– where she stays, twelve book."[28]

## 1925

*18 February 1925*
*Fine but colder. Busy getting ready for Institute at Freds. I was
on lunch committee. Had quite a good meeting, lots of fun.
Anna & Mrs Irving had papers on an ideal home.*

Winter on Prince Edward Island can be predictably erratic. Certainly, 1925's winter was. January was cold, snowy, and blustery, and Keith got a frostbitten face one day when coming home from cutting down trees in the woods. But February turned mild, with so much rain that the brooks and hollows filled, and it was not safe for the children to walk home from school through the fields. The roads, Myrtle reported ominously, were "bad bad."[1]

The Women's Institute was a respite for Myrtle and many Island women throughout the year but especially in winter. Its meetings got them out of their homes to spend time with other women – if only, as on this occasion, to learn how better to maintain their homes. The "WI" did a great deal of valuable work on Prince Edward Island: it maintained local schools, performed home-front work during the First World War and petitioned for female suffrage afterward, and would soon be critical in lobbying for a provincial sanatorium.[2] But although Myrtle often spoke of the institute in her diary, she rarely mentioned such activities. She focused instead on the social time that it gave her with friends and neighbours.

Myrtle's mother, Ada, had been the founding president of the Sterling branch of the Women's Institute in nearby Stanley Bridge. The Cavendish branch had been dubbed the Avonlea branch at its creation in 1920 – an homage, of course, to the fictional community in the *Anne* books. Myrtle belonged to and was even president of the Avonlea branch for a time.[3] To today's reader, for whom early-twentieth-century Cavendish may already resemble late-nineteenth-century Avonlea, the name of the branch is a disorienting intrusion of fiction into reality. One almost expects to read of the election of Rachel Lynde.

> 11 *March 1925*
> *Poured rain in forenoon and about 5 oclock. Cleared up at sundown. The community gave Mr & Mrs. John F McNeil a surprise party on their Golden Wedding day. They presented them with a pretty good program and two very comfortable armchairs. Pretty tired to-night.*

The house must have been bursting at the seams; Myrtle subsequently notes that the celebration drew sixty-eight guests and "over twenty serenaders."[4] We can only envy the degree of community that existed in Cavendish in this era. It was accepted, if not expected, that most everyone regularly interacted with their neighbours. As mentioned, this was often to exchange labour: Ernest could be found working with local men at the woods in winter, on the road in spring, at the hay in summer, and at the potatoes in fall; and Myrtle could be found almost any time with neighbourhood women sewing or preparing food for fundraisers. But it was more than that. Members of the Webb family were constantly off to church or to the meetings of youth groups, women's groups, or community groups, or they were visiting family or neighbours – or welcoming them as visitors. In

Figure 19 | Hauling hay, c. 1928. Lorraine, Pauline, and Ernest Webb on load, with unidentified boy. Keith Webb and unidentified woman standing. The boy and woman may be summer boarders.

March 1925, some or all of the Webbs visited other people's homes or attended church or meetings on twenty-one occasions, and on twelve occasions visitors came to their home.

*18 March 1925*
*S.E. Dark day, thawed like smoke. Ernest cut hole between two big rooms. Went to Institute at Milton McKenzie's at night. Annual meeting, Mrs Ben Woolner new Pres. Mrs Leigh Warren, Mrs Webb Vice Pres. Took a carriage, a lot of bare road. Foggy all afternoon.*

Today, Green Gables Heritage Place has been restored to reflect a rural Island home of the late nineteenth century. Dating it to this period allows visitors to envision the house as they imagine Montgomery did when she drew inspiration for what would become *Anne of Green*

*Gables*. And since this era is when the book is set, it has the added advantage of allowing visitors to imagine (or mistake) the house for the Green Gables of Anne herself.

But the Webbs' home was a constant work in progress. Each spring brought a fresh round of wallpapering, painting, and laying new oilcloth in one or multiple rooms. And the makeovers only increased as the Webbs took in more tourists – and, in turn, had more money for such makeovers. Ernest cutting a doorway between the front room and the sitting room in 1925 may have been to assist flow when tourists were around, but more likely it was just to assist the growing family year-round.

The Webbs may have felt the need to open the house up after the Macneill anniversary party a week earlier. A month later, Myrtle hosted a Women's Institute meeting with a program dedicated to the works of Mohawk poet Pauline Johnson, and sixty women attended. Imagine that the next time you visit Green Gables Heritage Place. Nowadays, the fire marshal has declared that the downstairs can have a maximum occupancy of forty.

*14 April 1925*
*E. heavy white frost but a perfect morning. Mrs. Eustis washed. Wind came around at noon. Dad & I went over to Hazel Grove to see Mrs. Bagnall. Marion & girls over to Jerry's. Keith went up to Herbies for smelts. Got <u>none</u>. Saw a butterfly. Roads wonderfully dry. Cars running.*

After a long Island winter, Myrtle was on the lookout for the first signs of spring. The sheer variety of such observations throughout the 1920s speaks to how aware she was of the natural world on the farm, how much it figured in her life. She at times noted the year's first appearance of wild geese, swallows, blackbirds, and robins or the first collecting of smelts and herring.[5] She occasionally mentioned the first wildflowers, although it is surprising how occasionally, given her love of flowers. Instead, she more often chronicled when her own flowers were planted. Another sure sign of spring was the appearance of people. Warmer weather cleared and dried the roads, increasing mobility. A month earlier, Myrtle had noted that Harry Lowther had made it up from North Carleton with horse and carriage: "First wheeling."[6] Now, the automobiles were blooming.

Myrtle's recording of spring firsts would decline over the course of the diary. It may be that making and recording these observations were more important to her when the children – her fellow observers – were young. Perhaps, as they and she aged, other matters squeezed such sightings off the page. It may also have been that as the family gradually grew less dependent on the farm for their subsistence – in terms both of buying more food off-farm and of relying more on tourism income – the natural world was of somewhat less significance. Yet her attention to the weather did not diminish; she continued to mention it, right down to the diary's final entry.

> 20 April 1925
> NE. 26A *Just a year since I started to keep a diary. Bitter cold grey day. Blowing hard and very cold. Keith & Ernest making a chicken house. Murray Robertson dropped dead at Hunter River this morning.*

With times tight, all of the Webbs looked for ways to bring in additional income. The family always kept chickens, but in 1925 Keith got more directly involved. The day after the new henhouse was built, he got fifty day-old chicks from Charlottetown. Just as the diary that spring chronicled Ernest's sowing of the crops and Myrtle's planting of the vegetables and flower gardens, it also traced the chickens' progress. Within a week, the chicks were "out to-day for a while." Within a month, Keith had forty-nine that were well established, and Myrtle had seventy-eight of her own, presumably hatched from older hens. Keith's chickens went quiet that summer, in the diary at least, but reappeared in November just in time for their demise. Keith killed and sold seventeen of them, a total of 95 pounds, at 25 cents per pound. The year's investment had grossed him about $24.[7] Next spring, the Webbs bought 100 chicks.

But before the chickens came the eggs. In the early twentieth century, Prince Edward Island fully embraced the co-operative movement popular throughout rural Canada. Farmers formed local collectives that bought, graded, shipped, and marketed their goods, and "egg circles" were the most successful of these initiatives on the Island. Consumers got a better, more standard product, and farmers got a higher price; the Island's model was copied across the nation. It was Ernest who attended annual egg circle meetings throughout the 1920s and '30s, but as on many Island farms, it was his wife who cared for the chickens, dealt with the co-operative's "egg man," and spent the earnings as she saw fit. Myrtle refers to selling eight and a half dozen eggs in November of that year and twenty-four and a half dozen in December.[8]

The Webbs were members of a number of such co-operatives. They teamed up with other Cavendish farmers to buy fertilizer at wholesale prices. They sold their cream to the co-op dairy in Stanley Bridge, where they were shareholders. And just as Myrtle was active in the Women's Institute, Ernest was active in the Farmer's Institute, where men gathered to learn from experts about the latest agricultural methods.[9] In fact, Ernest had been president of the local branch through at least the late 1910s.[10] The Webbs provided for themselves but not by themselves. Co-operatives simultaneously relied on and reinforced the tight bonds of rural communities like Cavendish.

> 29 July 1925
> Fine. Ernest & Cecil went to H.R. with poultry. The Misses Harris asked the kiddies to a picnic at shore. They had a wonderful time. Had a fire and roasted hot dogs & marshmallows. Vivian with them. Heavy thunder to-night. Aileen Laird is dead. Heavy hail at Kensington. Mr Myles McDonald and team of horses killed at Darlington.

In the previous diary entry, news of the building of a chicken coop appeared alongside the sudden death of a family friend. Here, fun at a picnic shares space with a fatal accident. The dramatic and the mundane flowed together in Myrtle's brief entries.

When a place first becomes a tourist destination, the relationship between host and guest can be quite personal; in fact, that can be one of the attractions for both parties. Although *Anne*-loving tourists had been dropping in at the Webb farm for as long as they had owned it and although the Webbs had by now opened their home to summer boarders, Myrtle's mention of tourists still tended to be on a by-name basis. Paradoxically, that makes it difficult to identify tourists in the diary's early years, as they blend in with neighbours and family.

The Misses Harris were the daughters in a family visiting from Connecticut who stayed at neighbour Jerry Simpson's farm for part of that summer, dropping in at the Webb home twice during their stay.[11] It was not at all uncommon for tourists to include the five

Webb children in their summer fun, as they do here. The children were taken out on fishing excursions or for car rides – and they, in turn, guided visitors along the North Shore, down Lover's Lane, and through the Green Gables homestead itself. It made them proud of their home. It also gave them the chance to play tourist.

The Cecil mentioned in this entry is Myrtle's half-brother, twenty-three-year-old Cecil Simpson. He lived with their mother in nearby Bayview, and members of their households were always back and forth between the two in these years. Ernest worked with Cecil a lot: at the hay, at the wood, cutting and thrashing grain, transporting and butchering animals, and picking potatoes. With Cecil's father having died a few years earlier, Ernest had become something of a father to him.

*12 September 1925*
*Dark and rained hard in afternoon. Putting roofing on hen house. In bed most of the day. Reading "Emily Climbs." XYZ*

Given the use of SE for a southeast wind, WI for Women's Institute, YPPG for Young People's Progressive Group meetings, and YPS for its successor, the Young People's Society, one could mistake XYZ for just another abbreviation that helped Myrtle to keep her diary entries short.

But this one was different. Myrtle jotted XYZ down every twenty-eight days or so, always on its own, usually in the margin; the diary's final XYZ appears in August 1931, when she was forty-eight. That Myrtle tracked her menstruation is not surprising. All women probably do in one way or another – perhaps especially when they have five children. Nor is it surprising that she coded her periods, given that this was something of a family diary. It would be surprising only if she thought the code unbreakable.[12]

Saturday. Rainy. That time of the month. A just-published book by your cousin and close friend Maud.[13] Plenty of reasons to give the day over to reading.

*27 October 1925*
*Froze hard. Fine day and lovely night. The childrens concert came off very well. They took in over $40. $38.55 clear I think. Short of candy.*

Two days afterward, there was a federal election in Canada, and Ernest served as a poll worker in nearby Mayfield. The Webbs were staunch Liberals, and Myrtle's report in the diary of Arthur Meighen's Conservatives winning the most seats is a terse one. But it was the local children's concert that was the focus of the Webb family's attention that week – indeed, that month. Practices had been held throughout October, sometimes at Mayfield Hall and sometimes at people's homes, including the Webbs' place. On the day before the performance, Marion and Ernest helped to fix up the Hall, and Myrtle reported, "Practice until 11:40. Everybody tired." The day after the concert, she wrote, "[E]verybody near dead."

Why, in the decade beginning around 1925, did the people of Cavendish become consumed with putting on concerts and plays – so much so that they gained a reputation across Prince Edward Island? There was, for instance, no charismatic stage director leading the campaign. Theatre fever seems to have been born in part from a desire to raise money for the community hall. It was also thanks to the support and involvement of adults in the community – including Ernest and Myrtle. But above all, it was due to a close-knit group of young people, of the right age at the right time, who wanted to perform – including all five of the Webb children. Green Gables must have been filled with the sounds of singing and acting in those years. Reference to "practice" appears almost 200 times in Myrtle's diary in the second half of the 1920s alone.

*3 November 1925*
*Cold wind but fine. Keith at Greens, turnips. Ernest helping Jerry this afternoon. Mr Kochaly speak in Pres. C. to-night. 3 kiddies went.*

The world in which the Webbs lived was in some ways a small one. Much of their food and fuel came from what they grew and collected on and around their farm. When they needed other goods, they looked first to buy, borrow, or barter from neighbours or to buy from stores nearby. As they were limited in the ways that they could travel or even communicate long distances, their ability to develop and maintain relations with people was based largely on proximity.

Yet they were also worldwide Webbs. They apparently received the *Charlottetown Guardian* daily newspaper – as suggested by Myrtle's entries referencing what had appeared in it that day.[14] They listened to neighbours' radios and would eventually have one of their own. They received letters from distant family and friends, including boarders from across the continent and around the world who had stayed at their home and who kept in touch. They also attended a great number of talks in churches and halls throughout the countryside and in Charlottetown.

On this occasion, the speaker was Absolom Kochaly, a native of what is now Urmia, Iran, who had come to Canada and become a Baptist minister. He was ministering in New Brunswick in this era but took periodic trips to Prince Edward Island to give talks on matters related to Persia and the Mideast. The "3 kiddies" this night heard him speak on "The Great Betrayal," recounting the Armenian genocide that had happened at the hands of the Turks ten years earlier, beginning in his own home city of Urmia.[15]

*1 December 1925*
*Lovely day, washed in AM. Went to Town afternoon. Terrible rough road. Went to pictures. Harold Lloyd in The Freshman. Good. Stayed at Enids all night.*

Forty kilometres is a significant outing by horse and carriage or sleigh, so trips from Cavendish to Charlottetown were infrequent and often called for an overnight stay. Myrtle had visited the capital only twice previously that year, both times in July: once to attend a Women's Institute picnic at the Experimental Farm (and to enjoy the town all decorated up for Old Home Week) and once just for a jaunt, during which she and Ernest bought arch supports. She had not seen a movie previously that year either; once a year was her average in the 1920s.

Myrtle does not mention Ernest on this occasion, but it is unlikely that she travelled this distance alone. Regardless, she stayed at the home of Enid and Reuel LePage on Fitzroy Street. (Myrtle's mother, Ada, was the second wife of Walter Simpson, Enid's father, making Myrtle and Enid stepsisters.) Enid and Reuel are two of the most constant presences in Myrtle's diary, appearing regularly for its entire thirty years.

The following day, Myrtle went to A.E. Toombs Music Store on Queen's Street and bought a new organ. It was delivered to the house a few days afterward. The purchase of a luxury item a few weeks before Christmas signals that the Webbs' financial situation was improving from the rather dire state that she had described to Maud a year and a half earlier. But perhaps the organ was also expected to pay for itself; Myrtle soon spoke of two people coming to the house for music lessons.[16] If nothing else, the organ suggests that the Webbs were committed to staying in Cavendish.

## 1926

*7 January 1926*
*Fine in AM. Snow storm after dinner. Keith went to Stanley with cream. Marion went to Wesley's to practice. Blowing a gale and bitter cold to-night. Keith and Anita up at the Cosy Corner Rink.*

After a typically enjoyable Christmas 1925 – "Santa extra good to us this year"[1] – the Webbs settled in for what would turn out to be the long, cold, snowy winter of 1926. The snow started and just kept coming. It snowed ten days in January, ten more in February, eight in March, and six in April – including what Myrtle judged to be the worst snowstorm of the winter. On 5 May, Ernest took a horse and sleigh to Hunter River and found that 20 feet of snow still covered Ernie Laird's hill. Two days later, it snowed again. There was still a lot of snow in the woods in early June.

And when snow was not falling, it was drifting, which made travel treacherous. ("Anna and I had quite a tumble out of sleigh backwards on our heads," Myrtle wrote.)[2] The trains that wound through the Island's interior were repeatedly blocked, and the mailman's sleigh might not arrive for days on end. And when the snow was not falling or drifting, Ernest and Keith might spend the entire day shovelling it: around the house, to and around the barn, and in order to make a path to the brook for the cattle to get water. When the men were done shovelling, it would start snowing again. Months of such weather took a toll. The whole Webb family got sick that winter: Marion had earaches and tonsillitis, Myrtle had headaches, and everyone came down with the cold or was "grippy" (i.e., had the flu).

Yet the winter of 1926 saw the Webbs not just making the most of the season but also finding new ways to do so. Marion, now eighteen, was given a new pair of snowshoes and used them to get around. Myrtle started hooking mats (or rugs), an activity that would all but consume her winters in the years and decades to come.[3] She bought her first canvas in February and by April, after completing two mats of her own, was going to neighbours to help them with theirs.

Meanwhile, sixteen-year-old Keith became obsessed with skating and hockey that winter. He would head off to the outdoor rink at "Cosy Corner" or "McCoubrey's" – which may or may not have been the same place – in every sort of weather to clean it of snow and hit the ice. After one cold, windy night, "Keith froze ears bad," Myrtle reported.[4] Yet just two days later, the *Charlottetown Guardian* noted that Cosy Corner skaters had been entertained by "Mr. Cecil Simpson with a radio concert and by Mr. Keith Webb with gramophone selections."[5]

Keith was not the only person who, having been given lemons, made frozen lemonade. All of the Webbs, all of Cavendish, and indeed all of the North Shore seem to have laced up the skates that winter. Myrtle reported fifty skaters at the rink one night. On another occasion, the women of Stanley Bridge held a hot lunch at the rink, in advance of hockey in the afternoon and a skate at night, and raised more than $75.[6] The rink, of course, was an important community gathering place before and after 1926, but that winter's wicked weather made it all the more important to get outside, meet people, and have fun when you could.

> *16 March 1926*
> *Fine. Finished ice. Skating to-night. Hooking. Have sold a lot of wood. There is such a depth of snow people can't get to woods and there is no coal at H.River.*

It was a good winter for ice and a bad one for wood. Each year, the Webbs checked to see when the ice in the pond that they shared with Ham Macneill on the north side of their property was thick enough not just to skate on but also to collect. Thick enough was an inexact measure, but 12 inches was the minimum, and in March 1926, the ice was 30 inches. Large slabs were sawn free, hauled home by horse and sleigh – thirty loads some years[7] – and packed in sawdust in the outbuilding nearest the house, ready for year-round use. Other Cavendish folks also harvested ice from Macneill's Pond, in what was at least on some occasions a reciprocal, communal activity.[8]

It was practically a New Year's Day tradition for Ernest, often with Keith or Cecil, to be in the woods cutting and hauling firewood for the winter a year away, and 1926 was no exception. But the bad weather that started in early January made completing the job difficult: with so much snow in the yard that year, the men had to do the sawing back in the field. It was not until early May, with the help of neighbours, that the sawing of next year's wood was completed.[9]

The Webbs were fortunate to have a surplus of wood from the previous year, enough to supply themselves and neighbours who ran short. They were also fortunate that, like more than four-fifths of Island farm homes, they did not rely principally on fossil fuel for energy.[10] They did have a coal stove, but it was apparently used sparingly in this period: Myrtle mentions Ernest going to Hunter River for a load of coal only every few years. (By 1940, it would be one or more times each year.) To the degree that they could, the Webbs provided for themselves with things from their own land.

> *4 April 1926*
> *Easter. Perfect morning and wretched night. Dad and I had a walk back to woods on crust and K. & Marion went to shore. Started snowing in afternoon and very dirty rest of day and night. Not many out to Church. Mr Tyndalls last Sunday. Mother sick. Radio wonderful.*

In 1931, the decennial census would ask a new question of Canadians: "Has this family a radio?" As late as then, only seven of the ninety-one households in the Webbs' census subdistrict would have one, and their household was not among them. But Myrtle's mother did own one and had for years, so the children and sometimes their parents walked down to Grandmother Ada's to listen to it.[11] There was not much Canadian programming yet, so the Webb children may have been entranced by popular American shows such as "The Ipana Troubadors" or "National Barn Dance." But it was almost always Sunday that they visited, and the only programs that Myrtle mentions explicitly were sermons coming out of New York state. Still, that they arrived home so late – 11:30 one time, midnight the next, even 1:00 a.m. – suggests that they twirled the dial long after the sermon was over. "Radio wonderful" is a fitting recap; the fact that they could listen was almost as important as what they listened to.

*28 April 1926*
*Lovely day but wind cold. Anna getting her baby chicks to-day. Big washing this morning. Finished quilting. Ernest clipped Sport and Daubin.*

Given how suffused L.M. Montgomery's fiction is with rural Prince Edward Island, it is remarkably devoid of farm animals. The rare times when they do appear, they are just a spot of local colour, not living, breathing creatures. For example, although the very catalyst of *Anne of Green Gables* is the Cuthberts wanting to adopt a boy to help out around the farm, Anne is described helping with the animals exactly once. Even then, her driving the cattle home from the back pasture, through Lover's Lane, is just an excuse for daydreaming; the passage is about ruminating, not ruminants. Lover's Lane is a cow path, but Anne need not watch her step.[12]

The Webb farm, in contrast, was teeming with animal life: cows, horses, pigs, chicks, hens, ducks, geese, dogs, and cats. Despite this menagerie, Myrtle seldom wrote about animals in her diary over the decades. She does mention the horse Laddie fourteen times between 1924 and 1937 (almost exclusively when he is sick or being clipped or shod), but no other pet or livestock is referred to more than a half-dozen times. None of the named animals – the horses Laddie, Dolly, Sport, Daubin, Lassie, Queenie, and Mischief; the cattle Girlie, Polly, and Lucy; the dogs Nickey, Chum, Nero, Happy, and Punch; and the cats Polly (another Polly!), Winks, and Tex – make much of an impression. We learn next to nothing of their breed or colour or look or temperament.

To pet-loving people of the twenty-first century, it may be difficult to understand that rural folks like the Webbs enjoyed having animals around but did not necessarily speak much about them. This silence may reflect the diary's form: that the enjoyment of curling up with a cat or the experience of milking a cow simply never rises to the surface in a two- or three-line entry. But the diary rarely even mentions when a pet dies. Much of the Webbs' day-to-day life revolved around growing food for animals, feeding and watering them, generally caring for and interacting with them, and in the case of livestock, eventually selling or killing them. That was a good reason not to get too attached to animals on the farm. A month after this entry, the diary abruptly notes, "Sold Sport."[13]

*30 June 1926*
*Mrs Joe Stewart died this morning at Prince County Hospital after an operation for tumor, terrible shock to everybody. School exam. Webbs all there. Lorraine got three prizes. Anita her P.S. certificate & PJ a box of paints. Mother & Cecil down this evening. Vern's wedding day.*

Students eagerly anticipated and nervously dreaded the annual school exam day. It marked the beginning of summer holidays but only after the teacher had quizzed students orally on every subject, with family in attendance. The twenty-two students of Cavendish School, their answers observed by twenty members of the community that day, "acquitted themselves in a very satisfactory manner," according to the *Charlottetown Guardian*. Prizes were awarded, and the day concluded with the students delivering an address to teacher Miss Jennie MacKay: "Perhaps many times you have found us very trying, but you have always been so patient and kind with us that we hope that if you will be so good as to remain another year in Cavendish, that we may do still better in our studies and also in making your work more pleasant."[14]

The three youngest Webbs all did well that day. Most significantly, fourteen-year-old Anita received her public school certificate for completing grade eight, potentially ending her time as a student. It is nice to hear what the youngest Webb girls were up to. To this point in the diary, Myrtle had mentioned Marion 148 times and Keith 186 but Anita (or Nita or Nan) only sixty-five, Lorraine (or Waine) twenty-nine, and Pauline (or PJ) twenty-three. Whereas the two oldest children worked in the house and on the farm with their parents, the three youngest were still largely expected just to go to school and to play – and, of course, to help out when needed.

*27 July 1926*
*84. Fine, smoky and warm. Cutting coiling and raking. Washed and baked. Miss Edwards has gained 3 ½ lbs.*

Tourism used to be a more tranquil, luxuriating affair than it is today. Rather than rushing around from place to place, more often you went to a place and stayed a while. The automobile changed that, making it easier to holiday for a shorter period, to take daytrips from a central base, and to hop from one destination to another. The Webbs experienced this transition in the 1920s, as they welcomed some summer boarders for many weeks at a time and others for just a night or two.

There is a hint of satisfaction in Myrtle's observation – just after mentioning baking – that one of the summer guests, Miss Edwards of Toronto, had gained weight in her first eleven days staying with them. Myrtle and her daughters took pride in their home cooking, made whenever possible with ingredients grown or collected nearby: vegetables from the garden, eggs from the chickens, and milk from the cows; fresh trout from the pond and fresh clams and lobster from the sea; and bread, biscuits, pies, cakes, cookies, muffins, jams, and pickles from the kitchen. Myrtle does not note what Miss Edwards weighed when she stumbled out of the Webb home five weeks later.

Later that year, upon visiting Cavendish School, a Red Cross nurse declared nine-year-old Lorraine and six-year-old Pauline to be underweight by 3.5 and 4 pounds respectively.[15] These amounts are not substantial and likely speak to the girls being lean and fit from playing and helping out around the farm. But they may also speak to how food was distributed on farms such as that of the Webbs. Cow's milk was separated and the cream sold, leaving skim milk for the family to drink. Eggs were sold rather than eaten. And perhaps the summer guests ate better than the hosts.

*6 August 1926*
*Just a perfect day and a big one for Cavendish. The institute entertained the Federated Teachers Convention of Canada at a banquet at Jerry Simpsons. Over three hundred teachers fed and about 150 others. Warm day, all tired to-night.*

It was indeed a big day for Cavendish. Women from four local Women's Institutes, including Avonlea, had been baking for days in preparation. Men had assembled an outdoor banquet space at Jerry Simpson's place. The weather cooperated, and everything went off without a hitch. The *Toronto Globe* carried enthusiastic news of the event on page five: "The dinner was a delight, the scenery was lovely and the air was exhilarating." Its headline, "Federation Welcomed at Home of 'Anne of Green Gables,'" made clear what the main attraction was.[16]

Prince Edward Island had been trying valiantly for years to attract tourists, but there was a great deal working against it. The province was hard to get to, its roads were terrible, there were not enough accommodations or things to do, and it shut down entirely on Sunday. The popularity of the fictional Green Gables and, increasingly, its real-life facsimile offered a rare beacon of hope. The *Globe* noted that the convention of hundreds of teachers from throughout Canada returned home "enthusiastic 'boosters' for the Prince Edward Island."[17]

Later that year, the editor of the *Charlottetown Guardian* noted that those who read L.M. Montgomery's works fell in love with the Island. "Why not capitalize [on] it?" he asked. "Green Gables is still in existence, the Lake of Shiny Water [*sic*] still glimmers in the sun as Anne saw it ... Avonlea could, with a little enterprise, be converted into a shrine which thousands of tourists would visit, where they could purchase souvenirs, photographs of the author, photographs of 'Anne Shirly' [*sic*]."[18] What the editor failed to notice was that such work was already well under way. The teachers' convention was a big day for Cavendish – and for the Webbs, Green Gables, and Prince Edward Island – not only because it suggested what might be done to encourage tourism but also because it demonstrated that people, particularly women, were already doing it.

> *1 September 1926*
> *Mother, Aunt S. and Mr. Macdonald started for Ontario, interesting trip to station, a dark morning, cleared later. Finished shingling barn roof. In to Wyands at night. Arthur here.*

"Mother" here is not Myrtle's mother, Ada, but Myrtle herself. For the next month, the diary is written in her daughter Marion's hand. That Myrtle did not take the diary with her to catalogue her trip to Ontario and that Marion maintained it in her place show the extent to which it was the family's diary.

Earlier that summer, L.M. Montgomery had written to Myrtle with an invitation to visit, enclosing a $100 cheque. Whereas Maud lent a considerable amount to her Island relatives in Park Corner over the years, most of it never repaid, this is the only time she is known to have given the Webbs money. "[S]he has worked hard there for 20 years," Maud explained in her own journal, "and brought up a fine little family so she deserves a bit of a party."[19]

Whether Maud could provide one was another matter. Her husband, Rev. Ewen Macdonald – the "Mr. Macdonald" of Marion's entry – had accepted a new parish earlier that year, and they had relocated from Leaskdale to Norval, Ontario. It had been a somewhat distressing move for Maud, and it was she more than Myrtle who needed cheering up.

Maud kept Myrtle and herself busy that September, as they whisked off to Niagara Falls, to the old parish in Leaskdale, and to the beauty salons of Toronto. For Maud, the high point of the visit was simply the chance to take long walks in nature with a woman she considered a kindred spirit. "It is one of the grievous lacks in my life that Ewen has no feeling whatever for beauty in nature, art or literature."[20] But what Maud called "pin-pricks" kept her from being entirely happy throughout Myrtle's stay. She despaired when her dog Dixie had to be sent away after chasing sheep. She suffered constantly from toothaches and earaches. She complained that it was the rainiest September she had ever known. After Myrtle had headed home, Maud concluded in her journal, "I think I gave her a nice time, too, and these three weeks will always shine pleasantly in my memory, despite these pin-pricks."[21]

How Myrtle judged the visit is unknown. She did not, of course, keep her own diary during the trip, nor did she discuss it afterward in the family diary, which was for daily retrospection, nothing more. It was left to Marion to give a verdict of sorts. In her final entry before handing the diary back to her mother, she wrote, "Mother looks pretty good to us; she's gained 6 lbs."[22]

*14 September 1926*
*Richard Stevenson died this evening at 8. Dad in Mayfield at the Poll all day. Keith ploughing. Not doing much. Nan home. A fine cold day. Mailed Miss E's things, wrote to Maud & Mother. Letter from M. from Norval. Anna Mrs Blackmire, & Margaret over, Gertrude here about Rally Service. Robbie & Arthur in. Yes and so are the Liberals! King is going right back to where he's supposed to be. SMW!!*

While Myrtle was in Ontario, Canada went back to the polls for the second time in a year. William Lyon Mackenzie King's Liberals won a minority government and three of the four seats on Prince Edward

Island, and Marion was over the moon about it. What she means by "SMW" is anyone's guess. "Says Marion Webb"?

*23 November 1926*
*Fine day. Keith took grist to Roller mill. Ernest banking. Made doughnuts, marmalade, pumpkin preserve & ginger snaps. Sold 2 porkers, 14 ½ cts per lb.*

Just an ordinary autumn day, with everyone busy. The kids in school, presumably. Keith off to Wheatley River, 15 kilometres away, with a wagonload of grain to be crushed into feed or flour. A little late in the season, Ernest finally getting the banking in – that is, piling seaweed around the base of the house for insulation in winter.[23] Myrtle baking and baking. (And with no word of a community event forthcoming, at that. This food seems to have been for the Webbs.) And two pigs doing their part too.

## 1927

*21 January 1927*
*29A. Fine but bleak wind. Dad out on line again today. All fixed from here to Central. Was badly smashed in the ice. Group at Mrs. Paynters in Rustico.*

The Webbs were not early adopters of most modern technologies of this era; some of their neighbours bought radios and automobiles well before they did. But in 1927 they were already among the one in four Prince Edward Island households that owned a telephone, and they appear to have owned it for years. Each June, they dutifully attended the annual meeting of the Cavendish Rural Telephone Company, a co-operative that was one of the almost fifty telephone companies operating across the Island.[1] They shared their phone too, taking calls and delivering messages for Myrtle's mother and their friends nearby.

The downside was that when the lines were down – literally – it was up to members of the co-operative to fix things themselves. On 17 January, Prince Edward Island received what Myrtle called "One of the heaviest silver thaws we have ever had." The ice made everything "gorgeous beyond words,"[2] but it also took the phone out, and Ernest spent at least two days getting it up and running. Over the next decade, Myrtle tells of Ernest spending almost twenty days out on the line, almost always in the dead of winter.[3]

> 15 February 1927
> 12A. Snowing a little all day. Dolph Flemings baby girl died last night. Rev & Mrs Peter Jackson arrived to-night. Everybody tired.

Myrtle's diary is teeming with ordinary mysteries. For her purposes, writing a few words or a short sentence would be enough to recall an entire incident or conversation later. But for the reader, it may not be enough to understand what happened.

That winter, the Webbs agreed to board the new minister of the Cavendish United Church while a new manse was being built. It would help the church, which the Webbs often attended, but it also paid them $10 per week, a welcome wintertime windfall.[4] "The Jacksons are very nice," Myrtle was pleased to note on the day after their arrival. But in the weeks to follow, her references to them grew uncharacteristically tart. She noted in her diary when "Mr. J" had a boil on his face, and when it burst, and when "Mrs. J" had one on her nose. In mid-May, the Jacksons moved out – although still awaiting the completion of the manse – and Myrtle wrote, "No one sorry here."[5] However, he was their minister, so they continued to hear him preach. But that November, out of nowhere, Myrtle wrote that "Rev Jackson through a bomb into the group" and, the next day, that "[e]veryone sore at Jackson for the way he has acted."[6] Seven months later, Jackson gave his farewell sermon in Cavendish and took over a parish in New Brunswick.

There is no knowing what was at the root of this rift and the Jacksons' departure. Perhaps it was a personality issue. Or perhaps it was a doctrinal matter brought about by the union of Canadian Presbyterians, Methodists, and Congregationalists, which had transformed the Webbs' Presbyterian church into a United Church congregation. At least initially, the Cavendish church had overwhelmingly supported the change – but L.M. Montgomery, in her journal, said that many had come to have second thoughts.[7] Myrtle did not explain, and after the Jacksons left, she never spoke of them again.

*10 March 1927*
*Lovely day. In bed all day until 6 PM. Hard job to get upstairs again. Girls went to practice at Lewis's. Keith at Freds thrashing. No foreign mail, ice in straits.*

Myrtle's back had been troubling her for a couple of days – neuritis, an inflammation of spinal nerves, she said. But it worsened, and she spent the next four days in bed. (As luck would have it, she got back on her feet the day that five little girls arrived at the house, having been invited by Pauline for her seventh birthday party. Pauline had not cleared this with anyone.) When Myrtle's back improved, she developed a headache that lasted for days. It would be a full two weeks before she would write, "Feeling better."[8]

According to her diary, between the spring of 1924 and the end of 1929, Myrtle spent all or part of seventy-six days in bed. On ten occasions, she spent multiple days there. Progress was making it down to the couch in the kitchen, where she spent another six days. It was usually back pain or headaches – the word "migraine" never appears – that kept Myrtle laid up.

Meanwhile, the world carried on. Except, on this occasion, for the mail. With ice jamming the Northumberland Strait, "foreign mail" – that is, mail from anywhere in the world beyond Prince Edward Island – could not arrive by boat.

*28 April 1927*
*Pouring rain all day. Got Eaton order and papered our bedroom.*

Flip through the Eaton's catalogue, mail in an order, and receive it in the mail – often within the week. What could be simpler, more modern? The Webbs were apparently starting to feel more financially secure in this period because Myrtle submitted ten orders to the T. Eaton Company of Toronto between 1926 and 1927, more than she reports doing during the rest of the diary combined. Of course, it may be that shopping by mail was still something of a novelty for Myrtle, so she mentioned it more than she would later. The diary is ultimately a chronicle of what she chose to write about, not an account of all that happened.

There was nothing unusual in and of itself about the Webbs buying wallpaper. Papering one or more rooms was a regular spring chore throughout Atlantic Canada.⁹ For the Webbs, it was always done between the planting of the farm fields and the arrival of the tourists. Indeed, there were only three years between 1924 and 1945 when no wallpapering went on at Green Gables. Wallpapering was a relatively cheap and easy way to freshen up a room – and with kerosene lamps, as many as three woodstoves, and a coal stove all emitting smoke throughout the year, it needed to be done regularly to keep the walls and ceilings presentable. In 1927, it was Ernest and Myrtle's bedroom, the front porch, and "Mother's room" (that is, Ada's guest bedroom) that got papered. Also, new oilcloth was laid in the kitchen and the "big room" (presumably, the sitting room), and at least some of the exterior was whitewashed.¹⁰ Green Gables is renowned today for its timeless quality, but during its life as a home, it was constantly changing.

*26 May 1927*
*Pouring rain all morning, beautiful in PM. Miss Rodd here to tea. Keith to H.R. for oats. Mrs Gordon Wright lectured in Mayfield Hall splendidly. WCTU organized Mrs. Woolner, President. Mr McLeod Mrs Wright and Mr Howes here to see "Green Gables." Practice tonight. XYZ.*

Prince Edward Island was soon to hold a provincial election that had become essentially a referendum on Prohibition. Conservative premier J.D. Stewart was vowing to repeal the alcohol ban that the province had enacted in 1901 and to bring in government-regulated sale. It seemed a reasonable gamble: other provinces were doing away with their bans in this era, and the Ontario Conservatives had won an election on just this promise a few months earlier.¹¹

But Prince Edward Island was not Ontario. Prohibitionists were galvanized by the threat of repeal, and the dynamic Sarah Wright, national president of the Woman's Christian Temperance Union, gave a stirring series of talks across the province. Swept up in the excitement, those who attended the Mayfield talk formed a WCTU branch of their own, with twenty-year-old Marion Webb its treasurer.¹² That Wright asked to see Green Gables afterward, joined by dignitaries of the provincial Temperance Alliance, must have made the Webbs very proud.

This is one of only two times in the entire diary that Myrtle refers to her home as "Green Gables" – and this in quotation marks. The other time was a week later.[13] Although the Webbs were accommodating – figuratively and literally – to people who associated their home with Montgomery's book, they did not work to strengthen this association. They were careful to ensure that their home maintained its own identity, presumably so that they could too. But with the Island's tourism on the increase, the pressure to be Green Gables was growing. That same summer, the *Charlottetown Guardian* carried an editorial, "Green Gables Land Should Be Named." It argued that the well-read tourists who were flocking to Cavendish should learn not only of its literary connections but also of its real-world settlement and heritage. For this reason, the newspaper believed it worth indulging tourists' interest in what it twice called "The House of the Seven Gables."[14]

> 25 June 1927
> Very fine. Blowing hard. Prohibition <u>Liberal</u> & Government Control <u>Conservative</u> Provincial Election. Prohibition has a big majority 23 sure 5 lean & 2 not heard from.

As Liberals – and Marion, at least, a Prohibitionist – the Webbs were undoubtedly happy with the outcome. The lesson that both Island political parties took from the election was that when it came to mixing alcohol and politics, it was better to abstain. Prohibition would stay on the books until 1948, making Prince Edward Island the last province in Canada to repeal it.[15]

> 14 July 1927
> Fine and very warm. About all I can do to feed the crowd. Maud great. Marion has been pretty miserable.

July 1927 was the first real harbinger of what summers would be like for the Webbs for the next decade. The tide of boarders, and tourists generally, was steadily rising, with regular farmwork and housework threatening to get squeezed out of the diary and out of life itself. There were meals and beds to be made, dishes and laundry to be washed, visitors to be picked up or dropped off at the Hunter River train station. The Webbs appear to have been averaging only a half-dozen or so short- or long-stay boarders per night at this stage, but these numbers occasionally swelled. Later in life, Lorraine would recall once serving twenty summer guests herself when she was ten years old.[16]

Nor was the bustle thanks only to the paying guests. There were also the random tourists who dropped in at all hours, asking to see Lover's Lane and Anne's room and Anne. And there were the expatriates, whose return all Islanders were learning to view with a mixture of welcome and dread each summer. The visit of L.M. Montgomery and her family made things even busier that month. Although they do not seem to have spent any nights at the Webb farm on this trip, they were regular visitors during the day – Maud, in particular, taking long walks through its fields and down Lover's Lane.

Montgomery's biographer Mary Rubio, who paints this trip as another occasion when the author lamented all that Cavendish had lost, sees such misgivings an indication of her growing fixation on the past.[17] And certainly, Maud was nostalgic for the old days and the old places. She mourned the loss of trees along Lover's Lane to old age and to the 1923 hurricane. But she largely reconciled herself to this reality, understanding that if she loved the "old beauty spots" more than the new growth that was regenerating, it was "[b]ecause I am a stranger to them and them to me." On Maud's last walk of this trip, she told her journal, "I went across the fields to Myrtle's and we had supper out on the front lawn under the blue evening sky with all the beauty of the old hills and trees and meadows around it. Oh, there is no place like my own bonny land."[18]

Myrtle's simple analysis of her friend and cousin was "Maud great." And indeed, Maud had a special reason to be great on 14 July: she had received a letter that day from British prime minister Stanley Baldwin, saying that he wanted to meet her and to visit Green Gables during his upcoming visit to Canada. Wistfulness over the loss of past haunts did not diminish Maud's delight on learning this news.[19]

Meanwhile, twenty-year-old Marion was "miserable." Since Myrtle used the word to mean both sick and morose – perhaps what we would recognize today as depressed – the exact nature of Marion's misery is unclear. This is not a criticism of Myrtle's writing. It was a society that had a limited vocabulary to express psychological suffering and limited ways to treat it.[20]

*1 August 1927*
*Raining in AM. Cleared up at noon and Myron took Marion to Kensington and brought Alice Grey home. Marion going to Toronto with Maud.*

Prince Edward Island's summer sea air was always promoted to tourists as a restorative. But Myrtle and Maud agreed that what Marion needed, to snap out of whatever illness or funk was bothering her, was a change of scenery. She returned with Aunt Maud to Norval for a two-month stay. It would end up being an important trip for Marion; it was then that she met Murray Laird, the man she would marry.

It was also an important trip in terms of the relationship between L.M. Montgomery and the Webbs. Early in the century, Myrtle and Maud had become friends, if not of the closest kind. Myrtle, for example, rarely shows up in Maud's journals of this era. But they were drawn closer by having children of roughly the same age; Maud's sons Chester and Stuart were born in 1912 and 1915 respectively. If nothing else, it meant that the children of the two families were thrown together on the Macdonalds' visits to the Island. And when the kids were of the right age and inclination to be compatible, such play dates were successful. While on Prince Edward Island in 1923, for instance, Maud noted that Chester and Keith were getting along well and that Stuart and Lorraine were "cronies."[21] This socializing did not turn into deep, long-lasting friendships between the Webb and Macdonald children, but as Montgomery's boys caused her increasing worry and as the Webb girls matured, Maud grew more attached to them, and they became like daughters to her.[22] "I guess she had always wanted a little girl," Marion said late in life, "so I fitted in all right."[23]

The other thing, of course, that drew the Webbs and Montgomery nearer to one another in this era was the crystalizing identification of their home with her books. This association was proving mutually advantageous. Besides giving the Webbs an annual income from tourism, it gave Maud a PEI base for her PEI brand – making the authentic literary also helped to make the literary authentic. And it turned them into confederates of a sort in an unexpected, dizzying development, which simply gave them more to talk about with one another. For all these reasons, Maud and Myrtle's friendship deepened in the 1920s and '30s.

Figure 20 | Marion, Anita, and Keith Webb, with unidentified cat and Chester Macdonald, son of L.M. Montgomery, in front, c. 1913.

*3 September 1927*
*Fine, very warm, muggy weather. Very busy all day.*
*Mr MacFarlane came at night so I have six now. Miss Moore &*
*Anna over.*

Figure 21 | Marion, Ernest, and Keith Webb, with Chester Macdonald, son of L.M. Montgomery, in front, Cavendish Beach, c. 1919.

August had been even more hectic with tourists than July. There were ninety cars at the beach one Sunday. The Webb homestead was full up one day, so a family from Massachusetts camped in the orchard. The diary was at times little more than a listing of boarders coming and going. It was a summer of "Big crowd out," "Every bed full," and "Did a whale of a wash."[24] The form of Myrtle's diary and her own busyness mean that the specific details of how she handled the day-to-day running of the tourist operation are unfortunately not available. Did long-stay guests pay a deposit in advance? How did she organize check-ins and check-outs? How much of the winters' canning and preserving was done with the summer trade in mind?

The busyness flowed into September. A group of nurses from Montreal arrived, followed by Mr MacFarlane, the brother or husband of one of them – "so I have six now," Myrtle noted.[25] The "I" is striking. Although the Webb girls were certainly helping out and would take on more and more responsibility as they grew older, Myrtle thought of the tourist operation as hers.

*22 September 1927*
*Fine day. At potatoes all day. Good crop.*

Everything on a farm has a time of year when it demands your full attention, but on the Island, potatoes were practically a season unto themselves. Having been planted in June and sprayed with a natural fungicide in July and August, they were ready to be harvested come September.[26] This work called on the whole family – so much so that many rural school districts, including Cavendish, set aside a two-week fall "digging vacation," knowing that students would be absent anyway. In fact, picking potatoes called on the whole community. In 1927, the Webbs got all their Irish cobbler and Green Mountain spuds picked across four days in late September, but their harvest season was not over. Immediately after finishing their own potatoes – presumably with neighbours' assistance – Ernest and/or Keith spent seven of the next nine days away at the farms of a variety of neighbours, helping to harvest their potatoes or grain.[27]

Then they got back to grading their own spuds and delivering them to Hunter River over four days in late October. Myrtle notes that Ernest received 55 cents per bushel on one shipment and 60 cents on another. The bushel is a unit of volume, but in potatoes it corresponds to a weight of 50 to 60 pounds, so the potatoes were priced at approximately 1 cent per pound. Myrtle also notes that one of the shipments was 41 bushels. If this was an average-size load, then the crop earned the Webbs roughly $100 that fall.[28]

*25 October 1927*
*Finer to-day tho' it rained at noon. Ernest on road in AM & he and John Laird went around with petition for railroad to Rustico. WCTU at Holden McLures.*

It is ironic, to be sure, that prior to drumming up support for the railway, Ernest spent the morning working on the road. Prince Edward Island had, in the words of historian Edward MacDonald, "flung itself into highway construction" in the 1920s.[29] It was a means of landing federal funds and from there distributing work – and patronage – throughout the province. (Myrtle has Ernest "on road" ten times that decade.) Roadbuilding was also, not incidentally, a means of improving infrastructure for Islanders and tourists alike. The number of tourists to the Island roughly doubled between the mid-1920s and mid-1930s, the great majority arriving by automobile, and improved roads were both a cause and an effect of that.[30]

Nothing came of the North Shore's attempt to convince the Canadian government to build a spur line from Hunter River. Rustico was one of the main fishing ports on the Island, and it was in the middle of an important agricultural area, but the same was true of any number of places around the province. The North Shore petitioners did not think to mention, let alone to foreground, what did in fact set their area apart: that it was the backbone of the Island's burgeoning tourism industry.[31] The province still saw itself as one built on farming and fishing, not yet grasping the growing importance of tourism.

> *31 October 1927*
> *Fine to-day. Ernest shipped a barrel of spuds to Maud and a Geddie chair. Dug out dahlias and went to Alberts in evening. Did some repotting of flowers.*

Just as Montgomery shipped the Webbs a box of books each fall, so too did they occasionally ship souvenirs of the Island to her: barrels of potatoes, turnips, or fish, as well as pine saplings from Lover's Lane.[32] This year, they also sent a chair. John Geddie was a nineteenth-century Cavendish pastor who became the first Presbyterian missionary to Polynesia.[33] A full or partial set of his chairs had been given to David Macneill, who in turn passed them down to Myrtle. Maud clearly must have admired the heirloom – enough for Myrtle to be willing to break up the set or break it further. And Maud did cherish the gift; it was among the list of items that she bequeathed to her son Chester in her will.[34]

> *24 November 1927*
> *Finer day but very cold. Anita washed. Hester and Anna here this evening. The girls went to Mrs Buotes with Marions coat. Will Gray in Alberton shot himself and accidentally his wife early this morning.*

Many of those who appear in Myrtle's diary do so for the first and last time in death. Death was not just newsworthy but also demanded memorializing, so after noting a death in the entry, she typically jotted the deceased's name in the margin, where it would be easy to find later. She did the same with births.

According to the *Charlottetown Guardian*, farmer and fox rancher Will Gray had grown despondent: "His crop was a failure and he worried greatly over debts incurred." At daybreak, he had taken a gun and killed himself. His wife, it was said, had been "shot by her husband while trying to take the weapon away from him." She survived to raise their nine children.[35]

Rural Prince Edward Island in the early twentieth century was the kind of place one can easily romanticize – a place whose residents were close to nature, to their work, to their food, and to one another. But it could also be a place of grinding poverty and desperation. There is no knowing whether the Webbs knew the Grays, but they knew such families. They were not far removed from them.

## 1928

*3 January 1928*
*Fine day but cold. 3A zero this morning. Washed. Lonesome to-night. Have radio in to-night.*

After a busy Christmas season – "Santa was very good to all"[1] – Ernest set out for O'Leary on New Year's Eve to visit family and friends, leaving Myrtle alone with the kids for the next ten days. She tells of doing very little. Other than church, she largely "stayed home and kept on fires" as winter raged outside.[2] A radio, perhaps her mother's, was brought to the house for her to listen to. She read Temple Bailey's romantic bestseller *Wallflowers*, undoubtedly part of Maud's annual gift.

"Lonesome" is about as expressive as Myrtle ever gets in her diary as to her feelings for Ernest. Perhaps that was because the family had access to the diary, but more likely it was simply because it was not in her nature to write about such things. She was not Maud. Her feelings for her husband would have to be expressed in what they did together through forty years of marriage. Raise five kids. Work side by side on the farm and in the house. Attend most everything together. Take long walks to the shore, through the fields, and down Lover's Lane.

*7 February 1928*
*Fine. Had Dr. Fleming overhaul me. Practice for senior play at night.*

Myrtle's health problems in the winter of 1928 were a harbinger of the problems that she would face for much of the next five years. In the first few months of the year, she suffered from headaches, back trouble, indigestion, and gallstones. And just generally, she was "feeling bum," "awfully mean," "fierce," or "doubled up." The family relied on house calls by Dr James Fleming of Stanley Bridge, brother of their neighbour Dolph. Although Myrtle would note later in the month that he "gave me a lot of dope," there is little evidence in the diary that she was overmedicated – or alternatively that he ever really got to the heart of her problems.[3]

*6 March 1928*
*Just a perfect day all day and a finer night could not be wished for. The Play, Mrs Briggs of The Poultry Yard came off with a bang. Anita was Mrs Briggs, Lorraine Melissa, and Marion Virginia. They made $103.15c. Sold candy. We packed it here in afternoon. Pretty big day and all very tired at night but very satisfied with success of play.*

For the previous few years, Cavendish had come down with a relatively mild case of the drama bug, but in 1928 it flared into a full-on fever. The catalyst was the reopening of the Cavendish Hall after it had been renovated and enlarged, as it provided a venue and, to pay off its debts, a beneficiary for ticket sales.[4] "The young people" had selected *Mrs. Briggs*, a three-act comedy, and had their first practice on New Year's Eve. Cavendish's Senior Dramatic Club met at Jerry Simpson's on 12 January and chose *Among the Breakers*, a two-act drama. Both plays were turn-of-the-century works by now-forgotten American playwrights; the Cavendish troupe did not favour the classics. But they took these productions seriously. Myrtle makes note of seven practices in January, eight in February, eleven in March, thirteen in April, one in May, and two in June – forty-two practices all told, between the two plays.

The three oldest Webb girls performed three of the seven parts in the youth production and became stalwarts of the local drama scene in the coming years. Somewhat surprisingly, their parents were heavily involved in the senior production too. Surprising for Myrtle, given that she had nagging health issues all that winter and spring. And surprising for Ernest, given that he was known for his calm, quiet demeanour; "lovely" is an adjective that has followed him down through the years. But Ernest loved to perform and starred in a number of subsequent Cavendish productions. (In the twenty-first century, Lorraine would fondly recall a play that required she put a fish down her dad's collar, which meant catching a fresh brook trout every night.)[5]

After the successful first performance of *Mrs. Briggs*, the communities of Hunter River and New Glasgow invited the Cavendish youth to perform it again "on 50-50 basis," raising almost $31.[6] *Among the Breakers* ran for three nights, including once in Rustico, and brought in over $140.[7] We know these precise amounts because Myrtle invariably recorded them – suggesting that it was she who managed the proceeds, which in turn suggests that she was important to the running of their troupe. There is no indication that the shows were ever for profit; although the concessionaires may well have kept their sales, ticket sales were apparently all poured back into the hall. Yet Myrtle writes of the money with clear pride, without ever referencing where it was going. It was the ability to organize and execute an artistically *and* commercially successful community venture, in tough times, that she and the Webbs took pride in.

*5 April 1928*
*59A. Just a wonderful day. Sitting out on saw most of afternoon.*
*Just a delightful warm wind. Snow almost gone. Very mild*
*to-night, looks like rain. Thyra here.*

The Webbs either owned or shared with neighbours a portable sawmill to cut their wood. Placed on a sleigh or built with its own runners, it would be parked beside the pile of logs that had been cut that winter. Two men would grab the ends of a log, toss it onto the sawmill's bench, and run it through the large circular saw, cutting off a block at a time that, later in the year, would be split into firewood small enough to fit in the stove.

Myrtle's job was to sit on each log so that it did not roll on the bench as the saw began cutting into it. After each cut, she had to jump up so that the men could pull the log another block's length down the bench, and then she would sit down again. It sounds undignified, but it was an important job – and an oddly enjoyable one that she could do out in the spring air while moving continually and while in constant conversation with family and friends working together. Just stay well clear of the saw.

> *10 May 1928*
> *Lovely day all day. Marion came home. Mr Saint, Fuller man here to dinner. Albert Kayes Syrian here in afternoon. Play at New Glasgow to-night Jimmy Jousons Job. Albert a little better. Sowed mixed grain across brook.*

Ethnicity, let alone race, rarely makes an appearance in Myrtle's diary. That was not because only British stock inhabited rural Prince Edward Island. After all, only 10 kilometres from Cavendish was Rustico, a significantly larger Acadian community. And it was not because Myrtle was blind to ethnicity, as she would casually specify "a Frenchmans horse" or "two Irishmen selling cloth."[8] Rather, it rarely appeared because there were few times when members of the Island's white Anglo-Saxon majority interacted with ethnic minorities. This was a society where even Protestants and Catholics were somewhat segregated, having their own hospitals, elected legislators, and *dentists*.

A rare instance of diversity at your doorstep was the periodic visit of a peddler with a pack full of goods. Most of the Island's peddlers were Lebanese. Albert Kays had been born in the village of Kfeir, Lebanon, early in the century and had joined the chain of migrants from that area who had made their way to Prince Edward Island. They were Christians who had escaped oppression by the Turks – much like Absolom Kochaly, whom the Webbs had heard speak on the Armenian genocide – and they were looking for a better life. Kays was a peddler who would soon become a Charlottetown store owner. There is no reason to suppose that the occasional contact with Kays or Kochaly greatly broadened Myrtle's worldview. But she did mention her family hosting Kochaly for supper two years after his talk. Similarly, a year after this visit by Kays, she noted that he was back and "here all night."[9]

*1 July 1928*
*Lovely day, very warm. Wyands started their tea room. Took in over $30. Mr. Pearse play violin at church to-night.*

Dominion Day in 1928 was the day that Cavendish officially went to proverbial hell in a tourist's handbasket. The Webbs' friend and neighbour Katherine Wyand, arguably the first person to recognize Cavendish's true commercial potential, opened a lunch counter, the Avonlea, down on Cavendish Beach – on a Sunday. (She would later say that her shift to tourism was done of "dire necessity": five kids at home, sickness in the home, and the family's best horse and two cows dying the same week.)[10] Although a letter to the editor would appear in the *Charlottetown Guardian* complaining that the restaurant not only violated the Sabbath but also enticed great crowds to do the same, Wyand persisted.[11] And the crowds came. Three Sundays later, Myrtle noted that there were more than 120 cars at the shore.

When Myrtle sent L.M. Montgomery a postcard of the crowded beach, the author was appalled. "It is with bitter regret that I perceive that the beautiful sandshore at Cavendish is becoming commercialized – and therefore ruined!" she told her journal. "Every Sunday hundreds of automobiles are there. Stands for the sale of pop and hot dogs do a roaring business. Lots are being sold for the building of summer bungalows. The automobile has made this possible and there is no way of preventing it." Montgomery was even more appalled the following year to hear that Wyand had ideas for the writer's childhood home: she "is full of a crazy scheme to *rebuild* the house, exactly as it was."[12]

For their part, the Webbs delighted in the growing fame of their community and their home. In fact, 1928 may well have been, from Myrtle's point of view, the best tourist season ever. Her diary is brimming with happiness about that summer's guests and about everything that their stays meant for her and the family: money, of course, but also company, variety, approval, and even a measure of celebrity. The *Guardian* wrote of a small group of women spending all August "at Green Gables ... the guests of Mr. and Mrs. E.C. Webb, at their comfortable homestead."[13] Amid berry picking and the hay and the normal rounds of visitors and visiting, Myrtle also informed her diary, "First four of our boarders left. We were very much in love with all of them." "The Macneills very nice." "All very nice people. The nurses are great." And day after day, she noted, "Lovely day."[14]

Figure 22 | Copy of the Cavendish Beach postcard that Myrtle Webb sent to L.M. Montgomery, 1928.

This was also the first time, however, that Myrtle could not keep up her diary. She had made daily entries faithfully for years, but for a three-week period in August, she wrote just a single, consolidated entry that began "Have been so busy that I have not had time to write."[15] It was a sign of what the crush of tourism would be like for her and the family in the years to come.

*13 July 1928*
*Same old thing.*

Ernest was succinct.

Myrtle spent two weeks in early July visiting the home of her half sister, Elaine Brinton, in Tryon.[16] In Myrtle's absence, Ernest and one or more of the girls maintained the diary. He took the task seriously – in fact, just a few days before this, he offered one of the only entries in the entire diary that mentioned the activities of all five kids. But he tired of it. Life was life; what more was there to say?

Yet Myrtle always did find things to say. She was committed to the diary and to keeping it as regularly as life allowed. It was an accumulating account of the Webbs' activities and social world, a first draft of a family history.

*9 September 1928*
*Blowing a gale to-night. Will be hard on the garden. All the Macneills of O'Leary were down to-day also Will Dyment & wife. Tired to-night. Had to play in church.*

In 1969, in celebration of its centenary, Cavendish Baptist Church would dedicate a set of new bibles to the memory of the late Myrtle Webb, who had been church organist for almost fifty years.[17] Yet in her diary, Myrtle hardly ever alludes to playing the organ – and this is one of the only occasions when she ever writes that she "had to" do anything. There is no indication that she took much pleasure in the task. Of course, that did not stop her from criticizing understudies who did the job poorly. Of the music at a special service the following summer, she would note, "Vivian murdered the accompaniment."[18]

*19 December 1928*
*Stomach bad and xyz at night. Keith got up in afternoon. Pretty weak. Ernest at Cemetery for awhile.*

Ernest was at the Cavendish Cemetery that day digging a grave for Albert Macneill, who had died the day before. Although a generation older than Ernest and Myrtle, Albert and his wife were among their closest friends. The first years of the diary are filled with references to them visiting one another, working in the woods together, or going to egg circle meetings together; Albert had even accompanied Ernest on his trip to O'Leary the previous winter.

But even if Albert had not been a friend, Ernest would likely still have been digging the grave. He regularly tendered with the community to maintain the cemetery. For about $50 per year, he (and quite often Keith) seeded, fertilized, and cut the grass, and they likely cleaned and straightened tombstones too. Whether gravedigging was part of the job is unclear; local men may have volunteered to do it anyway.

The autumn of 1928 had been quiet in the Webb household but for the bouts of illness that swept through. Lorraine and Marion had been sick for a spell, and Keith was down for almost ten days in December with a serious illness that, after five visits from doctors, was diagnosed as pneumonia. Myrtle's stomach issues persisted. She spent four days in bed in October – "Don't remember much" – and was down sick again for three separate periods in November.[19] In mid-December, she was prescribed morphine. She stayed sick well into the new year.

L.M. Montgomery rarely worried about the Webbs – she appreciated that they were much steadier than many other facets of her life – but she was worried now about Myrtle: "She has been miserable for a whole year now. It may be only the menopause. And it may be some organic disease."[20]

## 1929

*6 February 1929*
*Just a perfect day, cloudless all day. Ernest help the crowd haul Andrew Paynters house down from Clifton. Keith helping Lorne with ice. Up nearly all day and had dinner and supper in kitchen. Marion & K. went to New Glasgow to Hockey game. Anita has gone over to Austins for a while.*

The bustle of family life swirled around Myrtle Webb throughout the winter of 1929, but she was a bystander to most of it. Her stomach continued to bother her. A few days earlier, she noted that she had gotten dressed for the first time in three weeks. A few days later, she noted that she had not left the farm for almost two months.[1] It got to the point that being well enough to have a relatively normal day like this one, rather than being sick, was what merited mention. Marion and Anita meantime took over the housework. Keith, having recovered from pneumonia, worked with Ernest in the woods. Snowstorms, school, sleighing, and skating went on as they normally did in a Cavendish winter.

Myrtle's sick spell finally broke a month later. She got up, served breakfast for the first time since Christmas, and stayed up for the day. It would not be the end of her health issues, but it was the end of one of her worst periods of sustained illness.

*5 April 1929*
*Fine. Not feeling well. Mrs Fenner & Mary here to tea hooking and sewing. Bunch gone up to Wilburs to-night. XYZ.*

Even before Myrtle was back to full strength, she was back hooking, sewing, and quilting. The front room at Green Gables was fast becoming Cavendish's hooking hub – the place where, each winter, local women came to learn the craft and to work on their mats while the Webb women worked on theirs.

Not so clear is whether these hooked mats were going on the floor or out the door. A full-fledged hooked-rug craze swept through the Maritimes in the 1920s, driven not only by tourists and commercial dealers intent on purchasing a folk handicraft but also by local women intent on contributing to the family earnings – and on replacing their rugs with a more modern floor covering, namely linoleum.[2] On Prince Edward Island, the Women's Institute ran the Handicraft Exchange in downtown Charlottetown, which in 1927 helped eighty women to sell almost 200 mats to the tourist market at an average of $20 each.[3] Although the Webbs, and Cavendish women generally, were well positioned to take advantage of the tourism market, there is no indication in Myrtle's diary that they were doing so – at least, not yet.

*9 May 1929*
*Lovely fine day and night. The Road Back play came off with a bang. Made $102.65c. Full house. Everybody pleased.*

Three months earlier, the troupe had decided to perform *The Road Back*, a three-act comedy-drama that was popular at the time. Two months earlier, they had begun practices and had held close to twenty since then. Now, it was opening night. The *Charlottetown Guardian* wrote that Ernest was exceptional in the lead role of Pa Fowler, "the discouraged head of the household," who must "stand up for his rights." Seventeen-year-old Anita co-starred as his daughter – in the newspaper's words, a "flip flapper," "a pretty, peppy kid."[4] Myrtle was nowhere to be seen. Thanks either to illness or threat of illness, she had attended only one practice.

Considering all the time and energy invested and the fact that proceeds went to paying off the debt on the Cavendish Hall, it is a surprise that there was only one performance there. But the show toured small towns throughout central Prince Edward Island, with Myrtle often noting in her diary how things went, artistically and financially: Clifton ("a big crowd" and $37.50), New Glasgow, Hunter River, Cornwall, Rustico ($36.30 and "a great time"), and Harrington ("a big crowd" and $35.60).[5] These figures suggest a successful season for the troupe, who were now advertising themselves as the Cavendish Players.[6]

> 3 June 1929
> Cold as charity. Cutting sets. Keith at Charlie Wyands. Ernest & I went to Harolds etc. Wyand girls & Margaret here to-night. Anita got home from Wilmot.

Just the facts. If you are going to boil down the day's experiences of a family of seven into just a few lines – fitting eighteen months of daily entries into a forty-eight-page scribbler – there is scarcely space for editorializing, let alone literary pretensions. Yet Myrtle allowed herself an occasional touch of flair when discussing one and only one topic: the weather. Perhaps it was simply because she was beginning with the weather and felt that she still had the space to be expressive. Or perhaps the subject lent itself to the literary. Weather shaped what you could do in the world and how you would experience the world – it *was* the world – yet it could also be reduced to a single word ("fine") or even a number ("10B"). And Myrtle described the weather in such prosaic fashion thousands and thousands of times.

But sometimes she felt such simplification unsatisfactory. Expressions like "Cold as charity," "Boo but it's a sneezer," "Glorious rain," "Fine day, a regular pet," "Thawing like smoke," and "A good old-fashioned spill" were Myrtle's way of recording not just what the weather was but also how the world felt.[7]

*28 June 1929*
*Pretty warm day but nice. Quilting in afternoon. Alex and May up to-night. YPS in church. Took Lemmie Wyand to S'Side Hospital.*

Sometimes what is most interesting about Myrtle's diary is what she does not include. On this day, fifty members of the Canadian Women's Press Club were taking a trip around the Island and stopped at the Webb farm. This visit to "the old home of L.M. Montgomery" made the front page of the *Guardian*.[8] But for Myrtle, such group tours were growing almost commonplace, so in the diary this one was bumped by quilting.

*Undated [August 1929]*
*In Aug we have Miss Hiscox & Harvey Mr Gillings, The Odell girls Lyle MacF, Anderson, The Misses Norris. Had a very dry July but a splendid rain Aug 4th.*

It was getting so that, each year, Myrtle maintained her diary every day until a great tourist wave overwhelmed her, transforming the entries into so much flotsam, and it would take a couple of months for her to resurface to a calmer world. In 1929, she held on until 8 July, and then the diary becomes a jumble of names punctuated with the rare observation, like "Raspberries good."[9]

What made this summer particularly hectic was that the Webb women, who did the preponderance of managing the tourists, all came down sick. Myrtle took to bed again for a while. Twenty-one-year-old Marion was in bed for three weeks. And, for good measure, seventeen-year-old Anita developed pneumonia. The Webbs hired a girl for a time, and Myrtle's mother pitched in, but the relentless crush on the family – with members housebound in a boarding house that was also becoming an international tourist attraction – must have been exhausting. "Have had a pretty busy summer," Myrtle wrote on 28 August, as normalcy was returning, "Everybody very tired."

But buried in a back page of this volume of the diary is a reminder of the primary reason the Webbs went to all this trouble. It is a list of what their long-stay boarders paid in 1929. The Webbs relied heavily on such boarders in this era, but they also took in visitors for a night or two who do not make it into this accounting.

| Mr and Mrs Cobb | July 1st to 12th | 42.00 |
| Miss Comer | July 2nd to Aug 3rd | 65.50 |
| Mrs Smith | July 3 to 30 | 56.00 |
| Miss Stewart | 2 weeks & 4 days | 34.00 |
| Miss Odell | | 40.00 |
| | | 50.00 |
| Mr. Gilling | | 24.00 |
| Misses Norris | | 91.50 |
| Misses Hiscox | | 56.00 |
| Miss Harvey | | 56[.00] |

Total 515[.00]

In just two months, the Webbs were bringing in the equivalent of a PEI teacher's annual salary from long-term stays alone.[10]

*22 September 1929*
*Just a lovely day. Maud came in afternoon. Alvin Webb and*
*Miss Phillips came too and three other cars came from O'Leary.*
*Roy Stevenson, Keith, Anita and Jean Casely went to O'Leary.*
*Preaching at night.*

L.M. Montgomery's 1929 return was a reminder to her of everything that she loved about the Island, Cavendish, and the Webbs' home. Driving in, she was initially nonplussed to see that the Prince Edward Island Travel Bureau had erected two large signs at the entrance to Cavendish, "one to 'Avonlea Beach' and the other to 'Green Gables' – i.e. Ernest Webb's place," as she told her journal. "It seems of no use to protest that it is not 'Green Gables' – that Green Gables was a purely imaginary place." However, Maud appeared to bear no ill will that "Myrtle turns an honest penny selling picture postals of Lover's Lane etc. etc."[11]

During her stay at the Webbs' home, all Maud's old feelings for the place came rushing back. "And I was beginning to think I loved Norval almost as much as Cavendish! Never! ... I was <u>home</u>." The fifty-five-year-old author took long nighttime walks in the fields and along the roads. She found Lover's Lane to be regaining some of its lost beauty. Growing captivated with the antics of two of the Webbs' cats, she wrote, "This has always been a wonderful place for kittens and flowers."[12] (She would soon immortalize these two cats, making them the models for those in *Pat of Silver Bush*.)[13] Montgomery even slept better than she had for months: "The wind is snoring around the old house and the trees on the western hill are singing an old, old song I heard in youth and had half forgotten. It is the music of the old gods and I recall that I belong to them."[14]

> *24 September 1929*
> *Finished potatoes. Marion & Miss Campbell collecting for Sanitorium. Mr Bonnell gave Ernest a $5.00 gold piece.*

Whereas Maud exulted in her visit, Myrtle said little of it. She did refer to Maud eight times over the two weeks but without a measure of detail or commentary; she had more to say about the cranberry season ("small crop") and her flower garden ("wonderful") than about her cousin and friend. Perhaps, as she told her diary five times in these two weeks, she was just tired.

Of this particular evening, Myrtle wrote nothing. Maud, by comparison, told her journal,

> This evening I had a "home" evening of the kind I thought had vanished from the earth. We all sat in the "sitting room" as it is still called there. The chill of the autumn evening was banished by a cosy wood fire. I did a bit of embroidery, Myrtle sewed, Ernest read, the girls wrote letters, the kittens frolicked – we talked when we felt like it and kept silence when we did not. And there was a friendly "kerosene" lamp on the table, casting a mellow glow over all.
> 
> I had expected to miss the hydro. I do not. I like the old kerosene lamps. They seem to fit into this life better than any modern illuminations.[15]

This passage is a lovely precis of life in the Webb home in the 1920s. It is sad, of course, that across thousands of diary entries Myrtle herself never captured the same level of detail, never evoked the same level of feeling about an evening of her life that Maud did in a few sen-

Figure 23 | Myrtle Webb and L.M. Montgomery in Lover's Lane, undated.

tences. That is another way of saying it is sad that Myrtle was not one of the nation's most accomplished writers ever. But it is sad, too, that Maud never wrote such passages about home life in Ontario but had to return to Prince Edward Island to experience such peace.

> *29 October 1929*
> *Still cold. The girls & K went to Town with Margaret. Anita & Keith got new coats. Tired to-night.*

Black Thursday, 24 October. Black Monday, 28 October. Black Tuesday, 29 October. The stock market crash, the opening convulsion of the Great Depression, did not immediately register with Myrtle. In fact, the term "stock market" never appears in her diary; the only "stock" is livestock, and the only "market" is of the garden kind. "Depression" – of either the financial or emotional sort – never makes an appearance either.

When Myrtle initially read the news of what was happening in New York, Toronto, and elsewhere, she probably thought her life immune. Unlike L.M. Montgomery, who lost terribly in the crash – including the entire settlement from her successful lawsuit against her publisher, L.C. Page – the Webbs were not investors. They had grown more enmeshed in the wider world in the 1920s – they were listening to radio programs, they were buying catalogue goods more often, and their very home had become a tourist attraction – but they still grew and gathered a lot of their own food, relied largely on their own wood for heat and their own animals for transport, and depended on those around them for much of what they could not provide. But the great unravelling would soon make its way to Prince Edward Island and demonstrate to the Webbs the degree to which the world had become connected.

On 12 December, Myrtle fell ill with what was diagnosed as congestion of the liver – a dysfunction typically the product of congestive heart failure – and was very sick for a week. She struggled for the rest of the month, and the forty-six-year-old spent the last days of the Roaring Twenties in bed.

## 1930

*29 January 1930*
*Snowing, drifting, and colder. Nothing strange or startling happening these days.*

The 1930s began for the Webbs much as the 1920s had ended. Myrtle was still not very well, but she was improving and getting up and out more. Ernest was his dependable self, mentioned mostly in reference to work or taking family members somewhere. Marion and Anita, twenty-two and eighteen years old respectively, were doing much of the housework, especially when Myrtle was not up to it. Keith, now twenty, was usually seen working with or for neighbours – at this time of year, cutting wood or gathering ice. (Truth be told, it is surprising that none of the three oldest had left home yet. At least one of the girls might be expected to have gone to Prince of Wales College or to "the Boston States" – New England – by now. As the only son, Keith was likely waiting to inherit the farm.) Lorraine and Pauline, twelve and ten, still ethereal presences in the diary, only occasionally appear around the edges of the pages.

As for Green Gables, it sat with its back to the winds coming off the Gulf of St Lawrence, patiently waiting out another winter on Prince Edward Island.

*28 February 1930*
*Lovely day. Keith & Ernest in woods in AM. Dad went with Clarence on telephone line. Dora Smith quite sick. Debate in YPSociety at Freds. Miss Mathesons side won. Miss M here for weekend. Resolved that the Maritime Provinces are more essential to Canada than the rest of Canada is to the Maritimes.*

Who could possibly speak against such an obvious resolution?

*3 March 1930*
*Blowing hard but not very frosty. Anita in bed with a bad sore throat. Ernest and I went to Creek to see if we could get a place in EC's store for Anita. Nothing doing. Hockey again at Stanley. Bible Class at Jerrys.*

Asking at the local general store about work for your daughter and being turned away sounds like an archetypal story of the Great Depression. But in the winter of 1930, Prince Edward Island was not yet feeling the full effects of the global economic downturn – in part because it had not been flying particularly high in the 1920s and in part because its agriculture-led economy was still coasting on pre-Depression exports. That Ernest and Myrtle sought to place Anita at E.C. LePage's store in Rustico speaks instead to her faltering first steps toward independence. After graduating from Cavendish School in 1928, she spent the autumn at the Charlottetown Business College but returned to the farm for 1929. She attended a course in Cape Breton in the winter of 1930 and was back on the Island for only two days when her parents visited LePage's store. Turned down there, she helped at home for the summer, worked for a while at a store in York (35 kilometres away), returned home again, and took shorthand lessons early in 1931, but nothing stuck – by which point, the employment and financial situations on the Island were becoming as fraught as elsewhere.[1] It would take Anita a little longer to find her way.

For Myrtle and Ernest, parenting in the 1920s had been relatively straightforward because their children had been, for the most part, fully dependent on them. The 1930s would be more difficult. They would come to experience the stings that came first when their children did not fully launch and again when they did. Most parents, of course, know this experience. But the Depression years complicated matters further, giving the Webb children more reasons to stay at home and making it harder for them to leave.

> 31 March 1930
> Lovely fine day. Big day for me up at 7:30 and helped with work. Anita washed. Marion up but feeling miserable. Pauline miserable all day. Ernest & I went over to Jerrys in a carriage this evening. Elmer down on horseback. Had letter from Miss Collier, Johanasburg.

Tourism continued to expand Myrtle's world well beyond the summer season. Lodgers typically began as correspondents, writing to ask about availability, and many continued to correspond after their stay. Joyce Herd of New Zealand sent a magazine. Miss Collier wrote from South Africa. Miss Marshall, knowing Myrtle to be a reader, sent a parcel of books. "The Windsor girls," two regulars from Windsor, Ontario, regularly sent big boxes of Christmas chocolates.[2] L.M. Montgomery told of regularly receiving mail directed to "Anne of Green Gables, Avonlea, PEI." One wonders whether similar mail was delivered to the Webb home too.

> 5 May 1930
> Fine and cold. Trying to finish satin dress. Got word in afternoon that Harold Toombs and Thyra Clarke had disappeared. There's a heartache in Cavendish to-night. Went down to shore with Mrs Wyand and Blanche. Practice to-night.

A scandal in Cavendish. Thyra was the eighteen-year-old daughter of Wilbur and Nellie Clark, who lived three farms west of the Webbs. She and Anita Webb were the same age and close friends; Thyra often stayed over at the Webb house. Harold Toombs was the thirty-four-year-old owner of the general store that the Webbs frequented in nearby Mayfield. But this was not an elopement: Harold was married and a father of two. After a frantic search, the runaways were tracked down in Hartland, New Brunswick, near the American border. Five days after their escape, they were back, Myrtle wrote, "at their respective homes."[3] Rectitude had been restored.

Myrtle never wrote of the incident again. She noted when Thyra married Fred Bingham in 1935 and when they had a girl the following year. She also mentioned when Harold and his wife, Lena, had more children of their own, and the Webbs continued shopping at Harold's store and selling livestock to him.[4] In 1933, the *Charlottetown Guardian* reported that the friends of Harold and Lena had thrown them a housewarming, at which the Mayfield Women's Institute proclaimed, "[W]e cannot let this opportunity pass without showing in some way our appreciation for you in our community. You have always been ready to help in every good cause."[5] It was as though the entire episode had been forgotten – at least by most people: it may have been bad blood when Thyra's first cousin George tried to rob Toombs's store in late 1930.[6]

The temptation is to judge the aftermath of Thyra and Harold running away together as a classic case of repression. This rural, Christian social order required that the families involved, the community, and life itself return to normal as swiftly as possible. But perhaps that is not giving the people of the community sufficient credit. Maybe they understood that people fell in and out of love, made poor decisions, changed. Maybe they knew that you could not see inside another's marriage. Harold and Lena Toombs were married for another fifty-two years and are buried next to one another.

*3 June 1930*
*Fine very warm. Everybody tired this morning. Got a bag of gaspereau last night at the shore. Clam bake at Bayview to-night. First bunch of tourists for supper.*

"First bunch of tourists" testified to the changing of the seasons as surely as "first blackbird" or "first snowfall" did. The third day of June was quite early for a first sighting, a welcome sign that not even the Great Depression was going to stop the Island's summer trade. Whereas tourist numbers and revenue dipped sharply in Canada in the early 1930s, they held firm on Prince Edward Island. That there were fewer Americans making it to the Island was offset by more visitors from central Canada, and if they were not spending quite so much time and money, at least they were still coming. Interest in Cavendish generally and in the Webb farm specifically kept growing rapidly, uninterrupted by the global downturn. Within just a couple of weeks of this entry, Myrtle noted "big crowd at shore" and that restaurants – plural – had opened on Cavendish Beach.[7] With agriculture and fisheries income plummeting, tourism was gradually becoming accepted as an indisputable, even indispensable, part of the Island's economy.[8]

Myrtle's phrasing in this entry is actually ambiguous as to whether these tourists even were the year's first or rather the first who stayed "for supper." It was relatively common in the early days of automobile tourism for travellers to seek food and even shelter wherever they happened to be. The 1926 edition of Prince Edward Island's tourism guide assured readers, "At most of the farm houses throughout the island meals or lodging can be secured when necessary at reasonable rates." Every word of the 1927 guide was identical except that "most" farmhouses had become "many."[9] Did such guests often appear at the Webbs' doorstep? Did Myrtle typically feed them? Did they eat with the family? None of this is known. Whereas tourists who boarded are named and described, often with affection – and, in some cases, became like members of the family – the many more tourists who spent just an hour or two at Green Gables are invisible to us.

The health of the Webbs' tourist operation would offset the slump in their farm income during the Depression, but there is no evidence that they devoted less effort to farming as a result. If anything, the opposite was the case. They would end up planting larger gardens in the 1930s than they had in the 1920s, and they may well have kept more livestock to feed not just their growing family but also the many boarders who would be coming. And they continued to gather food from forest, field, and seashore. Late May brought the saltwater gaspereau up estuaries to spawn, where they could be caught in great number. Clams were an easy, all-summer treat; just look for small holes in the wet sand, and get digging.

*11 June 1930*
*Fine and very hot. Ernest & Gordon started the cottage. Sewing, etc. Went up to Bayview for clams. Play Mummy and the Mumps.*

Each spring, the Webbs gave their house some upkeep – wallpapering, painting, laying oilcloth, and so on – wherever it was most needed. But 1930 saw a more concerted push. Work went on for well over a month. The kitchen was fixed up, with a new door cut in its eastern wall to the outside. The kitchen and front porch were papered, the floors varnished, and walls whitewashed and painted.[10] And the Webbs built a cottage – not down near the shore, as one might expect, but just to the south of the house. Ernest worked at it throughout June, a flue was installed in early July, and by the end of that month, Myrtle could report that it had welcomed its first visitors.[11]

The cottage was not meant for the family but was a further investment in tourism, a space for overflow when all the beds in Green Gables were filled. Presumably, the cottage was built close to the house to make feeding and taking care of guests easier and because Green Gables homestead was the real attraction of staying at the Webbs, so guests would want to be close to it. Much of the fixing-up of the house and grounds in this and subsequent years was done principally to meet the needs of tourists. The Webbs were committing more of their time, resources, and selves to the summer trade.

*Undated [September 1930]*
*Had a very busy summer. For first two weeks of Aug, had 16 extra and had Miss Sargent until Sept 12th.*

Between the seven Webbs and sixteen guests that August, there were twenty-three people staying in the house and the new cottage every night. Twenty-three breakfasts, lunches, and suppers to be made. An unfathomable amount of laundry out on the line. Little wonder that the diary got set aside.

Myrtle did pick up her pencil later to fill in a few more details about the summer of 1930. It was a hot one, with everything burned up, and there was no apple crop as a result. Ernest's sister Louise died in O'Leary, and Ernest went to the funeral alone – everyone else evidently being needed at home to manage the farm and the tourists.[12] Come September, when the holiday season was over, Myrtle and Ernest themselves holidayed, travelling to western Prince Edward Island to spend ten days with his family.

*14 September 1930*
*Pouring rain all day. Lowther kids home to-day and over here.*
*They are going to PWC. Just a little tired after our trip. Got a new*
*coat for Lorraine and myself. Expecting Murray Laird and his*
*friend any day now.*

When visiting Aunt Maud in Ontario in 1927, Marion Webb had met Murray Laird, whom L.M. Montgomery described as "a very nice chap, well-off, nice looking, quite the pick of the Norval young men." The two young people got along well, and the author tried to encourage a match, but nothing much came of it. Marion returned home to Prince Edward Island. The pages of Myrtle's diary slowly began to be sprinkled with references to "Elmer Fyfe down" from Stanley Bridge for a visit or going to a movie or a play with Marion. Soon, he was just "Elmer." The oldest Webb girl had a beau. Marion and Elmer were engaged in 1930.[13]

But that September, Murray Laird and his friend, Maud's son Chester, drove to Prince Edward Island and stayed with the Webbs. Murray wanted to see if he still had a chance with Marion.[14] Whereas Elmer often arrived at the Webb farm on horseback, the Ontario boys took the Webb girls sightseeing by car around the Island. At the end of their stay, Myrtle wrote, "The boys left this afternoon, and we all boo-hooed like babies." Almost two weeks later, Marion and Lorraine set off up west to visit their O'Leary relatives. But before leaving, Marion called off her engagement to Elmer.[15]

As ever, the diary's dispassionate account of events only hints at the underlying drama. When Marion was away in O'Leary, Myrtle wrote, "Elmer down this evening and we had quite a talk." Marion was not referred to again until four days after her return, when her mother noted that she was "feeling a little better."[16]

*18 November 1930*
*Lovely day. Went down to mail box in morning then lay in the*
*sun for an hour and a half down in the hollow below road. Pretty*
*good for November. Marion got a letter from Maud and has*
*decided to go away Dec 4th.*

Myrtle, forty-seven, walks down her country lane to pick up the mail and finds the autumn day too beautiful to return to ordinary life just yet. After years of bad health, she has been well all year. She recently celebrated her twenty-fifth wedding anniversary. Her children are growing up. She lies down in the field. The sky rushes by, but she is rooted.

This entry is about as evocative as Myrtle will allow herself to be. By comparison, the journal of L.M. Montgomery was always willing to tackle the drama head on. That fall, Maud tells of having received word from Myrtle about Marion's deep unhappiness. Seeing Murray Laird, whom she loved, had made Marion realize that she could never be happy with Elmer, and she had broken off the engagement. But now Murray was back in Ontario and Marion's prospects were far from certain. "Myrtle asked no favors but I knew what was back of it": Aunt Maud was to step in. She invited Marion to live with her for the winter – and thus to be close to Murray. Marion accepted. "What a tangled web life can be!" Maud writes.[17] The author liked the phrase "a tangled web" enough to make it the title of her next book.

*30 December 1930*
*Just a grand day. All went skating in the afternoon. Even to me.*
*Young Folks skating at night. Ernest went with them. Letters*
*from Marion & Elaine.*

Fall became winter, and 1930 ended with Myrtle enjoying the same good health that she had enjoyed all year. Whereas she had spent the last days of the previous year in bed, today she was up skating with the crowd. She and Ernest had paid off some bills. The family enjoyed another nice Christmas – "Just a perfect day. Santa pretty good to all" – with the traditional box of books from Maud and dinner at Ada's. Marion was in Norval now, having been sent off in style by the ladies of Cavendish with a handkerchief shower. Even Elmer Fyfe had come to say goodbye; he and Marion parted on good terms. However, it was bittersweet for Myrtle to see her oldest child leave home. "Feeling pretty blue," she admitted.[18]

## 1931

*12 February 1931*
*Storming worse than ever to-day but not very frosty. Train got*
*through to Borden this AM and from S'Side to Town. No other*
*trains moving. No school. Roads terrible. No mail.*

Winter on Prince Edward Island did its thing of shrinking the world. Whether Bobby the mailman and his horse and sleigh could make it through their appointed rounds was the Webbs' most trusted barometer as to the weather and the state of the roads. This was a bad storm in a winter full of them. It had started snowing on the ninth, and on the tenth, there was no sign of Bobby. He did not make it to the Webbs' until the thirteenth – and only after the local men had broken a track. Then the weather turned bad again, and they did not see him again until late afternoon on the sixteenth. Myrtle jotted down "no mail" thirteen times that winter. "Not doing much but keeping on fires," the storm-stayed diarist noted at one point.[1]

*3 March 1931*
*Ernest went with hogs to Hunter River. Got the enormous sum of 6c per lb. Terrible road and pitches. Practice here at night. Anna fell this evening and broke her leg. Keith went for Stevenson.*

The Depression arrived late on the Island, but it did arrive. In the fall of 1930, farmers discovered that they could not sell their harvest because the export market had entirely collapsed. Ernest had received 12 cents per pound for pork two years earlier and now had to settle for "the enormous sum" of half that. A year later, the price would be down to 5 cents per pound. The story was much the same for all of the Webbs' farm outputs. They had sold chickens at 25 cents per pound in 1928; in 1932, they would get 12 cents. The price for potatoes had fluttered above a dollar per bushel in 1930 but would plummet to between 50 and 60 cents in 1934, bottoming out at 45 cents in 1936.[2]

Yet life for the Webbs did not change all that much. One can read all of Myrtle's diary without realizing that there was a global economic failure. That was in part because the revenue from summer tourists softened the impact of the collapse of agricultural prices. But it was also in part because misery loved company: most everyone in Cavendish, and in all of Canada, was struggling to a greater or lesser degree, and there was a consolation in that. In mid-March, Ernest attended a nearby "poverty social," where prizes were given out to folks with the best ragged costumes. Poverty socials had been around for decades, but the Depression popularized them once again.[3]

*7 March 1931*
*Fine day. Ernest and Jerry went to Rustico for mud for Lems. Austin Laird has egg hauling. Half through with McGarry mat. Keith went to town.*

This was a winter of hooking for Myrtle. She put her first mat of the season in frames on New Year's Eve and started to work on it on New Year's Day. By the end of March, she had mentioned hooking twelve days – sometimes "hooking all day" – and had completed four mats. But this entry is the first evidence that hooking was more than just a hobby for Myrtle; it was also a source of income. The previous summer, a couple named the McGarrys had boarded at Green Gables and evidently had commissioned a mat.[4] Some or all of the other mats that Myrtle made that winter were likely also to sell, and there would be more references to her hooking to order.

What was especially impressive about Myrtle's dedication to hooking that winter was that her bad health had returned. She was sick on numerous occasions throughout January and February: headaches, sore legs, side, and stomach, "miserable." There was more to come.

*15 March 1931*
*Sunday. Fine. Preaching in afternoon. Took Mother home in evening. Roads very pitchy. Sing song here at night.*

"Jesus" never appears in the diary. Nor "Christ," "God," "Satan," or "hell." That Myrtle never discusses her spiritual beliefs – the few lines of a diary entry were hardly conducive to it – can make it easy to miss just how important church was to her and her family. Churches, in fact. On many Sundays they attended both the United Church, where Ernest taught Sunday school, and the Baptist Church, where Myrtle played organ. And beginning in 1931, they also often went to or hosted a Sunday evening singsong. Members of the community gathered and sang hymns in a neighbour's kitchen or in a church manse. Community singsongs became something of a craze across Canada in the 1930s, but it is difficult to determine whether it was a new activity or a new name for an old one. For the Webbs, it was another opportunity to express their Christian faith – and to socialize with friends and neighbours.

*27 March 1931*
*Fine day, but cool wind. North Shore YPS held banquet at Webbs. Fifty seven here. Big time. Toasts and speeches. Keith and Reg Webb came out from Town. Got home at 5 AM. Ernest & K have bad colds.*

Another evening with Green Gables bursting at the seams. The Young People's Society banquet was of sufficient local significance that it was covered in the *Charlottetown Guardian*. The newspaper recounted that the night opened with a discussion about "The Motives of Jesus." The fifty-plus guests then enjoyed a chicken dinner and a singsong. The society's president, nineteen-year-old Anita Webb, acted as "toast-mistress" for a long string of toasts. There was a reading from the youth group's monthly newspaper, "The North Shore Ripples." The evening ended with contests and games and "Auld Lang Syne," sung around the friendship circle before the crowd headed home on heavy roads.[5] The next day, Myrtle reported, "Everyone tired."

*31 March 1931*
*Nice spring day. Washed in am. Dr Fleming down to see Myrtle pretty sick. Congestion of liver. Keith and Reggie went to Mayfield.*

A shift in handwriting in the diary always signalled that Myrtle was either travelling or ill. Here, it is likely Ernest who took up the pencil for the first but not the last time in 1931. Indeed, Myrtle would not be the diary's regular author again until June.

Having felt sick for two days, Myrtle was diagnosed with jaundice, the same condition that had troubled her in 1929. Concerned family members in the following weeks catalogued her high fever, severe pain, and acute indigestion, noting repeatedly that she was "miserable." She was also "sick from morphine," a medication whose side effects can include headaches, sluggishness, and stomach pain.

L.M. Montgomery watched with alarm from Ontario. Hearing that Myrtle had jaundice, she was convinced that the illness had been brought on by disappointment over learning that Marion and Murray Laird had recently broken up in Norval. "Jaundice is often induced by unpleasant emotional disturbances and Myrtle is of the type in which such effects follow," she told her journal.[6] (There is no sign in Myrtle's diary, however, that she had yet learned Marion's news.) Maud also worried that a recent dream of hers had been a portent of this illness and that, "if it is[,] Myrtle will not recover."[7] Later in April, Maud wrote that Myrtle was over her most severe symptoms but was not recovering very well. "I feel worried about her all the time. I am so afraid of – cancer! There, it is out." That Maud's forty-word passage in her journal about her friend's illness followed 800 words about the health of her cat, Lucky, does not necessarily measure the pain that she was feeling for Myrtle. Perhaps it shows that the author was unable to face her fear of losing Myrtle and found it easier to project her anxiety onto her beloved pet.[8]

As for life at Green Gables, it continued much as usual that spring, as mother lay sick in bed. The only real news was that Keith took a job on the other side of Charlottetown and would be away for much of the rest of the year. Meanwhile, Ernest, Anita, and then Marion – home from Norval to help take care of things – kept up the diary, telling of the wood hauled and sawed, the garden planted, and the singsongs sung. The degree to which the Webb girls adopted Myrtle's writing tics when taking over the diary is rather sweet. "Are we tired?" one of the girls asked three times in two weeks.[9]

They *were* tired. And worried. Myrtle, now forty-seven years of age, had been sick for almost two months when one of the girls recorded, "Mother sitting up for few minutes for the first."[10]

6 July 1931
*Fine blowing hard. Cecil took me to Rustico for a drive and in afternoon I went with Ernest hunting for a girl. Girls did big washing. Everybody tired to-night.*

Slowly, Myrtle recovered. She made it as far as an outdoor couch one afternoon in early June. She walked down to the shore one day mid-month. On Dominion Day, she had a car ride, her first of 1931.

And the next week, she and Ernest went looking to hire a girl to help with the summer boarders. It was shades of *Anne of Green Gables* with a tourism twist. This was not the first time the Webbs had hired someone to assist with the cooking, cleaning, and laundry that their tourist business entailed, nor would it be the last: Annie Simpson became a steady summer presence later in the decade. But this was a year when it was clear that Myrtle would be able to do little, and the Webb girls needed help – in part because Lorraine and Marion themselves had bouts of sickness in late June, Marion's bad enough for the doctor to make repeated house calls. Alas, the diary is silent about whether the search for a girl was successful.

> 16 July 1931
> Poured rain at times. Miserable day. Wind NE. Ken arrived about eleven. A good many cars here. Stayed in cottage all day. Sing song at night. Miss Moore & Mrs Webb called in eve.

The cottage that the Webbs had built the previous year to accommodate overflow guests became Myrtle's convalescent ward throughout that summer.[11] Staying there gave her some welcome privacy from the hubbub of Green Gables' guests and gawkers – and, presumably, ensured that the sight of sickness did not dampen their holiday enjoyment. Members of the Webb family often spent the night in the cottage throughout the summers that followed, and they were no doubt glad to have this quiet refuge. But if they were getting away from it all, they were also getting away from their own home; there is an inescapable sense that the Webbs were slowly losing their hold on Green Gables.

That Myrtle was less involved in tourism in 1931 paradoxically meant that she was better able to document it in her diary. This was the only summer between 1928 and 1937 that she sustained a daily accounting of events. There was the steady stream of boarders coming and going – all "very nice people," she twice noted. There were occasions for swimming and fishing, as well as moonlight campfires and clambakes and marshmallow roasts at the shore. This seems to have been the first summer when the Webbs made a concerted attempt to entertain the guests, not just accommodate them. Perhaps this effort was a response to two guests at the beginning of the season having left because, according to Myrtle, "They found it too quiet."[12]

> 15 September 1931
> 80A. Very hot this AM. Marion & Waine washed. Thunder squall about 2 PM. Everybody got wet. Corn for Supper. Oh boy. Knitting a sweater for Pauline. Newt McClure raided & liquor seized.

Recalling summers spent in rural Prince Edward Island in the 1920s, historian William H. McNeill writes, "Meat was exceptional, usually eaten only Sundays."[13] We forget that North Americans of a century ago typically ate less meat than we do today. We may forget this fact especially when reading about a farm with a menagerie of cows, pigs, and chickens that were ultimately destined for the dinner table. But it was not necessarily the Webbs' own table: they sold some livestock and slaughtered others, selling the meat. To be sure, the Webbs ate meat too, but it was not a major part of their diet. The diary, for example, contains only one reference to eating turkey and none to steak. Much of the meat that they ate was beef and chicken that Myrtle had canned or "potted" – although, over time, chicken dinner was increasingly on the menu for special occasions.

Now that corn is a side dish – or a harvest decoration – we also forget that it was once a main course. The first corn of the season, even "cow corn" grown primarily as animal feed, was a real occasion. Picked that day in your own garden, slathered with butter, it dominated the plate, and rightly so. Oh boy.

*29 September 1931*
*Worse than yesterday but cleared up in evening and we had a gorgeous sunset. District Convention of Women's Institute at Mayfield. Ernest Lorraine and PJ went. I set the bread, wonder of wonders.*

"Wonder of wonders." This is Myrtle's wry way of noting how little she has contributed to family chores during this year of illness. But it is only the fifth time since she began keeping a diary in 1924 that she has referred to baking bread, which was surely at least a weekly activity when feeding her large family and summer boarders. In healthy times, baking bread was too ordinary to merit mention.

*2 October 1931*
*In bed all day. Reading Mauds new book The Tangled Webb.*

A telling typo? L.M. Montgomery's new book was *A Tangled Web*, an intricately plotted novel with a love story that her biographer Mary Rubio sees as incorporating elements of Marion's complicated courtship with Murray Laird.[14] But if it is difficult to imagine

Maud poaching Marion's real-life intrigues for literary purposes, it is more difficult to imagine her advertising the fact with such a baldly punning title – and impossible to imagine Myrtle accepting that she had done so, to the point of making light of the title herself.

> *2 November [to early December] 1931*
> *Lovely morning. Very bright rainbows. Anna came over before dinner. Mr Bishop took me to S Side to Hospital. Had operation on the 7th and came home the 28th. Not feeling good. Too much fever.*

"Friends will regret to learn," reported the *Guardian* in one of its quotidian community notices, "that Mrs. Ernest Webb of Cavendish has entered the Prince County Hospital last week for an operation. She is doing as well as can be expected."[15]

In Myrtle's diary, there is little in the way of lead-up to this episode. Just a day earlier, she had written, "Not too bad a day. Feeling rather blue." Yet by this point, Maud had already received a letter from Marion saying that her mother had suffered "another very bad spell."[16] The operation involved draining Myrtle's gallbladder – a procedure typically performed when the patient is deemed too sick for the organ's removal. A doctor supposedly told Ernest that his wife had pancreatic cancer and only a few months to live.[17] Myrtle returned home in early December to convalesce. She wrote little about how she was feeling. But as Christmas approached, she wrote a letter to Maud, who told her journal, "She is home but disheartened – she is no better than before the operation."[18]

> *25 December 1931*
> *Mild and dirty all day. Snow and rain and snowing and blowing at night. Santa good as per usual. Got so many boxes of fruit. A Kimona from the family. Annie Lowther and the Ling girls here in afternoon and Margaret here in evening. Had my dinner in the Kitchen. Tired at night.*

Given Myrtle's illness, Christmas 1931 must have been a bleak one. But Myrtle presents it, and that entire winter, as largely "per usual." Keith had moved back from his job in Southport, and all the family were back under one roof. Ernest and Keith did the outside chores, and the four girls handled the housework.

But Myrtle herself did very little. Her weight had dropped to 115 pounds.[19] For the most part, she stayed on a daybed downstairs, where she could rest but still be part of the family. The only activities that she mentioned doing regularly that winter were reading books, reading and writing letters, receiving visitors, and writing a few lines in her diary. She did not set foot outside the house until mid-April.[20]

## 1932

*1 March 1932*
*Northeast gale, thawing. Anita sick and I had fever again.*
*Lindburg baby kidnapped.*

Myrtle was housebound, but the wider world still intruded. Like millions of people, the Webbs were fans of American aviator Charles Lindbergh – enough that they named one of their cats Lindy. It was tragic when Lindbergh's toddler son was stolen from his crib and more tragic still that May when, Myrtle reported, the "little chap" was found brutally murdered in woods 5 miles from his home.

Unlike with most bits of international news that she recounted and never returned to again, Myrtle followed up in this case. She recorded in 1935 that Richard Hauptmann was to be sent to the electric chair for the killing, in 1936 that he had been granted a forty-eight-hour reprieve, and finally, "Hauptman electrocuted."[1]

*19 March 1932*
*Fine, milder. Keith got three loads mud. Oliver Bernard and Elva here to supper. Up all day.*

Prince Edward Island fishermen enjoyed a rich bounty of seafood from the Gulf of St Lawrence. But the world's largest estuary offered farmers of the Island a bounty almost as rich if they just did the work of retrieving it: free fertilizer. Oyster shell beds along the province's rivers and estuaries were rich in calcium carbonate, which was spread on fields to increase the acidic soil's pH level and so its productivity. Farmers had been collecting "mussel mud" along the shore since at least the early 1800s, and by the middle of that century, they were dredging it up through holes in the ice. Collecting it became a long-standing winter tradition.[2]

In this sense, Keith's retrieval of more than thirty sleigh loads of mussel mud over the winter of 1932 was unexceptional. He travelled all along the North Shore to obtain it – from New London to Cavendish and perhaps as far as Rustico. On his return, he presumably spread it directly on the snow-covered fields that needed it.[3]

The odd thing is that the diary speaks of mud gathering twice as much in 1932 as in all the other years put together. This frequency is especially odd because, by the 1930s, most Island farms were moving away from mussel mud since it was labour intensive, its use was denigrated as archaic by government scientists, and it produced an unsightly, if harmless, scab on potatoes. So why was this winter so mud-filled? It may be that Ernest and Keith had suddenly decided that their fields needed the shot of lime that the mud provided. It may be that they could not afford to buy the chemical fertilizer required to give the soil a nitrogen boost, as Myrtle mentioned them doing annually throughout the late 1920s. Alternatively, Keith may have gathered the mud mostly to sell. Or it may simply have been a matter of opportunity: Keith was at home and an inveterate worker, so he may have chosen to make the most of the "free time" provided by winter on the farm.

*28 April 1932*
*Ground white but not for long. Blowing a gale all day and so cold. Ernest went up to Ced Simpsons for saw and to Austins for load of straw. Cemetery meeting at night. Clive McNeill has job of cemetery again $43.00. Was $49.00 last year. Fever. Set goose eggs under hens.*

The Webbs were hit not only by the fall of farm prices during the Depression but also by the fall of wages. Even the potential remuneration for a year's maintenance of the Cavendish Cemetery shrank. Whereas in 1925 Ernest had been paid $50 for the work, by now a neighbour was willing to do it for $43. In a year's time, the job would go for $34.[4]

With the three oldest Webb children now grownups – all living at home, all willing and able to contribute to the family economy, but all also wanting to start independent adult lives of their own – the Depression affected even their smallest prospects for work on the Island.

*8 May 1932*
*Miserable cold day again. Dr Claude down. He told me a good deal that I didn't know. Alf Simpson and Jerry here after dinner and Mr. Green Margaret and Annie here in evening. Marion went to new Glasgow with Mr Bishops.*

In the six months following Myrtle's surgery in late 1931, L.M. Montgomery wrote more often in her journal about her friend than in any other period of her life. Maud was prone to worry anyway, and Myrtle's unresolved health problems became a constant source of it.[5] And her fears were fanned by her Cavendish contacts, who were convinced that Myrtle was dying. In March, Katherine Wyand visited Maud in Toronto and reported having heard from Myrtle's doctor what he would not tell Myrtle's own family: she had "so many things the matter with her" that there was no chance of recovery. Maud was determined to get all the news but called it "a martyrdom" to sit listening to Wyand. "She would really talk the hind-leg off a cat."[6]

On 13 May, five days after seeing Dr Claude Simpson, who had performed her gallbladder operation, Myrtle wrote Montgomery to share the news that she definitely did not have cancer. But Maud was not comforted because her friend's health was still no better. That her ailment remained undiagnosed seemed almost worse. "Whatever it is," Montgomery told her journal, "I fear she will not recover now. Well, we must face these things."[7]

Yet just five days later, Myrtle proudly shared with her diary that she had "made cookies, a washington pie and custard and creamed beans for supper."[8] Coincidentally or not, from the moment that Myrtle met with her surgeon, her health began to transform. After having only left the house twice so far in 1932, she started taking the occasional walk or drive. She sewed, baked, and made dinner. She was getting back to her old self.

*1 July 1932*
*Lovely day. Big crowd at shore. Girls busy busy. Went back lane for strawberries. Gertrude went home.*

A few years earlier, Myrtle had referred – in unusually possessive terms – to "my boarders."[9] It was a legitimate claim because in the first years of taking in guests, it had largely been her corresponding with, cooking for, and cleaning up after them. But by 1932, she no longer made such pretense. While she continued to recuperate, her four daughters – Marion at age twenty-five, Anita at twenty-one, Lorraine at fifteen, and Pauline at twelve – ran the household. They had been handling all of the domestic duties for months and now spent weeks preparing the house and cottage for the summer tourists: washing, cleaning, papering, varnishing. "Girls ready for boarders," Myrtle wrote.[10]

When the Webbs had started their tourist operation, they had done so with no training or guide: they had simply picked it up as they went along. But they had grown more adept over time. For example, the Webbs and Katherine Wyand, who also kept guests, now traded food all summer when one house was running short; Myrtle's diary contains a summer's accounting of lending cream and borrowing bananas, of lending eggs and borrowing oranges.[11] The Webbs' cottage gave them more flexibility in renting beds. And they better understood that tourists wanted more of an idyllic, Avonlea-like experience, so they provided more opportunities for crafts and clambakes.

*Undated [September 1932]*
*Lorraine went to Charlottetown Sept 6th is boarding at*
*Mrs Aflecks.*

Myrtle's diary gives just fleeting glimpses of the Webb children when they are young. They are whirling apparitions, occasionally spotted catching trout or catching cold. Only when they grow older do their lives and personalities emerge more clearly.

Marion was the oldest, and by 1932 she was a sweet, well-liked woman who had suffered heartache, had lived away from home and moved back, and was likely to leave again when her mother was fully recovered. Keith, above all else a worker, flung himself at jobs on and off the farm. Anita, who was strong, funny, and competent, had already taken jobs and courses away, but for the moment, she was resigned to helping out at home.

Lorraine was just coming into her own. In 1924, when she was six years old, "Lorraine got her first beating in school" had been one of her very first appearances in the diary, but now she was working to become a teacher herself.[12] She had taken the exams for Prince of Wales College in the spring and moved to Charlottetown.

And Pauline? She remained largely invisible, still in the process of taking corporeal form.

> *15 September 1932*
> *Another lovely day. Everybody tired out. Cleaned the cottage up and Dad and I spent the night here. There <u>was</u> a <u>cricket</u>.*

After the tourists had departed and before the potatoes were harvested, Ernest and Myrtle always took a little time for themselves around their September wedding anniversary. Sometimes they travelled for a few days. But this year, with Myrtle improving but still recovering, a holiday closer to home was in order. Unfortunately, their night's sleep was disrupted. Myrtle's entry the next day began, "More or less wrecks."[13] Jiminy.

> *11 October 1932*
> *Cloudy and raining. Maud came about 8:15. Quite foggy to-night. Made Hams preserve.*

L.M. Montgomery had travelled to the Island by train a week earlier. It had been a somewhat difficult trip for her. In a financially straitened situation from bad investments, she opted to travel "on the cheap": rather than getting a sleeper, she had spent overnight on the day coach, hoping that no one recognized her.[14]

She was delighted to arrive at "the friendly Webb farm" and to see for herself that the recent reports were true: Myrtle was fully recovered and looking her old self, if a bit thin. Maud was also happy to be greeted by the cats of Green Gables. "For there are always beautiful cats there," she wrote, and listed the five who welcomed her, including two named Anne and Gilbert.

Maud wrote in her journal of an indelible evening – perhaps the one of this entry – spent with the Webbs:

> Myrtle and I sat in her cosy living room and read and talked and did fancy work, with a couple of cats to do our purring for us, while the rain splashed against the panes and the wind made wild music and afar off the gulf boomed. Even a wild wet night like this was

Figure 24 | The Webb girls, c. 1932. From left: Marion, Anita, Lorraine, and Pauline.

delightful on this beloved farm. It all tasted good – all the sweeter because I feared last spring that it would never be so there again. Myrtle's recovery is little short of miraculous ... When Myrtle was ill I persistently "healed her mentally" according to the suggestions in that old book *The Law of Psychic Phenomena*. Every night before I went to sleep I commanded my subconscious mind to cure her.
Did it?
No, I cannot really believe it.[15]

Just a few months after resigning herself to Myrtle's death, Maud was musing whether the recovery was all thanks to her.

*14 October 1932*
*Blowing hard and quite cold. Maud & I went to shore and M. took some pictures of the waves. Had a quiet evening. Marion sick.* YPS *at Mrs Paynters, over fifty there.*

Myrtle's recovery was nothing short of remarkable. She had been unwell, more often than not, for going on five years and seemingly at death's door for much of the first half of 1932. But now she was taking walks to the shore, cooking meals, and going on drives and to church. She was living her life once more. She would certainly be sick again – "miserable," "mean," and similar descriptors would continue to pepper the diary – but she would not again have the sustained bad health that she had known in these years.

Maud had taken a movie camera with her to the Island. A month later, she sat alone in her parlour in Norval, Ontario, and ran the film through her Kodascope projector. "I seemed to be looking through a window right on P.E. Island," she wrote. "For there was Myrtle walking along the shore with the waves splashing high on the rocks around her – there were the trees waving in Lover's Lane – Marion and Pauline giving the five cats their dinner – 'Lindy' perking up her saucy gray head ... When the film ended I came to myself with a spiritual jerk as if I had at one bound crossed a thousand miles."[16]

4 November 1932
*Ernest doing house work to day. In bed all day.*

The quiet man. Quiet in life and quiet in the diary, too. In a diary largely absent of expressed emotions and opinions, Ernest and Myrtle's relationship must be intuited by what they did. The winter walks in the woods. The time away together that they stole every September. And here the housework that Ernest folded around the barn work.

24 December 1932
*Perfect day, wind cold 10A to-night. Practice at Wyand.*
*Everybody busy all day and everyone well for the first time in years at Christmas.*

It had been a gloriously routine fall at Green Gables. Ernest found a whiskey jar in an alder bush while ploughing. Myrtle received a parcel of books from a boarder, as well as her regular box from Maud. The women spent many days quilting. The family sold pork at 5 cents per pound, chickens at 10 to 14 cents, and geese at 11 cents. There were multiple practices for multiple concerts.[17] The most unusual thing, as

Myrtle observes, was that everyone was healthy this year, even her. And the next day, she noted, "Santa very good to all."[18]

## 1933

*16 January 1933*
*Lovely day, mild. Girls washed. Hung out clothes bare hands.*
*Pauline in bed all day. Anita and Lorraine over at Austins.*

We live in a warmer world than the Webbs did – warmer inside and warmer out. And life less often calls us outside. Having no electric clothes dryer – or electricity, for that matter – the Webb women hung clothes on the outside line year-round and hoped that everything dried fully before the weather turned so cold that nothing could dry and before rain or sleet or snow came and caused the whole process to be restarted. Windy days were best for drying, of course, so the women often found themselves hurriedly trying to attach clothespins to freezing wet fabric, while wearing mitts, as the cold wind off the Gulf of St Lawrence sliced through them. It was noteworthy when a winter's day was warm enough to do this work barehanded.

Inside, Green Gables was a drafty, poorly insulated old farmhouse. The Webbs did what they could to keep it warm. Besides banking the base of the exterior with seaweed, Ernest and Keith installed "hurricanes" – storm windows – each fall.[1] In winter, the family used three wood- or coal-burning stoves throughout the house to supplement the kitchen's big woodstove, which burned every day of the year. In the very coldest of weather, sawdust was packed around the water pipes to keep them from freezing.[2]

And still the house was cold. Once that March, Ernest had business in Charlottetown and stayed the night. "Marion and I <u>didn't</u> sleep together," Myrtle informed her diary.[3] Does she mean that they shared a bed and were unable to get to sleep? Or that it was a novelty that they chose not to share a bed? Either way, it suggests that on cold winter nights, the norm was to double up.

*18 March 1933*
*Lovely fine day and we were all to the wedding. Elmer brought*
*Mother down. Keith & Margaret looked very nice and everything*

went without a hitch and they got away about three. Arthur Woolner here all night.

Keith's courtship happened gradually and then suddenly. In 1929, the diary begins to mention the name "Margaret Lowther," a seventeen-year-old girl tagging along to events with the Webb daughters. Margaret's mother was Myrtle's dear friend Ellice, whose husband had died young that year. The remaining family had moved from their North Carleton farm back to the family home in Cavendish.[4] Soon, "Margaret Lowther" became just "Margaret," soon Keith joined outings with Margaret and his sisters, and soon Keith and Margaret were going to places on their own. There was no word of marriage until 10 March, when Myrtle wrote, "[T]he word is out there is to be a wedding soon."[5] It is unclear whether she had kept it a secret until then or whether she was just learning of the engagement herself.

Amid showers of confetti, Keith and Margaret left for North Carleton, where they would run the bride's family farm.[6] That this was a convenient match all around, with the Lowthers getting a farmer and Keith Webb getting a farm, made it no less of a love match. But the marriage dramatically altered the dynamics in the Webb home. Until then, it was assumed that Keith would take over the farm. This was a major reason why Aunt Maud had invited Marion to Ontario. "There is nothing there for her," Maud had written. "In a few years Keith will be bringing in a wife."[7] But now he would not. The Webb farm might end up with one of the girls or with no one.

*9 May 1933*
*Very fine all day. Heavy white frost at night. Valley Farm play in Cavendish. Good crowd made $45.80. Alvin & Alton Webb came down. Everybody satisfied and tired.*

The Cavendish Players put on a play every spring, but some years it seems to have especially dominated community life. One such year was 1933. The troupe gathered on 17 January to choose the production and selected *Valley Farm*, a "rural play" – one expressly designed for rural companies to present to rural audiences – that they had performed previously. They then held, according to Myrtle's diary, a whopping thirty practices over the next hundred days.

It was worth it: the play was a hit. "This is considered by critics to be one of the best plays of the season," raved the *Charlottetown Guardian* – although one might reasonably wonder how many plays were in this competition and how many theatre critics 1933 Prince Edward Island possessed.[8] The troupe toured throughout Queen's County, performing *Valley Farm* nine times between May and September and making almost $200 in ticket and concession sales.[9]

As usual, the Webbs were well represented in the production, with Ernest and Marion playing two of the lead roles. Marion was Hettie Holcomb, "a country flower, transplanted to city soil," and Ernest was her father, "a typical farmer, true to life."[10] Three years later, the Webb sisters attended an unimpressive performance of *Valley Farm* in a nearby community. "Some show!" Marion wrote, "We are nearly convinced that we are fairly good actors."[11]

> 26 May 1933
> *Very cold North East wind. Big day for Webbs. Lemmie Wyand took us in to Convocation. Lorraine 9th in list of 154 names. I had dinner at Reuels. Got home for supper. YPS at North Rustico. Girls went with Mr. Paterson.*

Lorraine was not graduating from Prince of Wales College, but it was occasion enough that she had completed her first year of study there – and done so well, coming ninth in her class. Within a week, she and her father were off to nearby Mayfield to try to secure a teaching position for her in the one-room school there. They were unsuccessful, so Lorraine returned to college in the fall.

> 13 July 1933
> *All a bit tired. Italian Air Fleet passed over the Island on way to Chicago from Italy. Ernest saw 7 planes. There was 24 planes and 97 men.*

Rarely did happenings in the wider world intrude so visibly on Green Gables. Until a day earlier, only about two dozen aviators had ever flown across the North Atlantic. In a single day, four times that many did. It was the first mass flight in aviation history and a great propaganda victory for fascist Italy. The Crociera aerea del Decennale (Decennial Air

Cruise) fleet of twenty-four seaplanes was on its way from Italy to the Chicago World's Fair. The fliers were on the fifth leg of their journey, hopping from Cartwright in Labrador to Shediac in New Brunswick. When they landed in the small New Brunswick town of almost 2,000 that evening, an estimated 10,000 people were there to greet them. The Canadian Press called this a "new Armada ... sworn not to the conquest of men but to victory over nature's barriers."[12] In the not-too-distant future, Canada and Italy would be at war.

> *Undated [September 1933]*
> *Mrs Irwin, Kathleen and Norah came the 12th. Mr & Mrs Reese the 8th to 18th. Mr and Mrs Gillings the 5th to 18th. Misses Norris the 3rd to the 24th, Mrs Timmins, Adele and Mrs Baker here until August 21st. Mr & Mrs Logan came the 18th and stayed until the 4th Sept. Had a Mrs & Miss Ivy Monroe over night, a Miss Wort, and Mrs. Morler [?] and Margaret Morler [?]. Mrs Kennear and Miss Kinnear of Montreal. Mr & Mrs Anderson of Toronto. Miss Hazel Alward and Maisie Mitten of Moncton. The whole month terribly dry and the last week very hot. Had Miss Jean Richardson for a week and the Gouch [?] family were here for a week. Everybody mighty tired when the busy season is over. Had a nice time with the Logans. Mr. L gave me his lovely white sweater. Lorraine went back to college Sept 7th.*

With Myrtle back on her feet in the summer of 1933, she was once again too busy to maintain her daily diary. The tourist season had started on 1 July, with the Webbs getting the grocery order and lobsters that they would need to feed guests. Within a few weeks, they had to run out and buy extra dishes to accommodate all the visitors.[13] Within a few more weeks, the diary had become its annual summer blur.

Yet even an entry such as this one tells a great deal. It shows that a considerable percentage of the Webbs' boarders were regulars. The Irwins, Gillings, Norrises, Timmins, and Logans had all stayed there a year earlier – in fact, the Gillings stayed every summer between 1929 and 1937. It also indicates just how many of the guests were women: single women, female friends, mothers, and daughters. Seaside tourist resorts tended to attract more women anyway, so it is hardly surprising that a place famous for inspiring *Anne of Green*

*Gables* also inspired women to stay.[14] But it is still worth considering the degree to which summertime Green Gables – run by a woman and her four daughters, assisted by a quiet man who appeared largely at mealtimes – was largely a female space in this era.

> *14 September 1933*
> *Fine but quite cool. School fair at Mayfield. Ernest & I went. Reta McLure here in afternoon. Marion packing her suitcases for Norval.*

Marion had written Aunt Maud after the tourist season, asking if she might visit her in Ontario for a while. But, of course, Maud herself was not really the attraction: Marion's on-again, off-again courtship with Murray Laird was back on. They had been corresponding and gotten over a major obstacle, namely that she wanted children, whereas he, initially, had not.

There is danger in reading too much into the spare words, let alone the silences, in Myrtle's diary. But it may have been that she did not much approve of Marion and Murray's tempestuous romance. Since his initial visit to the Island in 1930, she had not mentioned him again. In Norval, Marion rushed into Aunt Maud's room to show off the engagement ring Murray had just given her. Maud wrote on 14 October, "We laughed and cried together and for a little while I was almost as happy and excited as Marion herself."[15] Myrtle made no mention in the diary of receiving a letter from Marion that fall, let alone one with such memorable news. However, if Myrtle did not warm to Murray when he was a suitor, she would when he was a son-in-law.

> *20 September 1933*
> *Wedding anniversary 28th. Ernest & I went to Carleton in AM. Had a lovely drive. Mr Wright took us to Borden and thro' the Car Ferry "Charlottetown."*

Celebrating a special occasion by taking a tour of the ferry feels like a very Prince Edward Island thing to do. The new *Charlottetown* was something to see. It was the largest icebreaking car ferry in the world at the time and was the first Island ferry equipped to carry automobiles.

Figure 25 | The Webb girls with Ernest, c. 1932. From left: Lorraine, Pauline, Ernest, Anita, and Marion.

Earlier that month, a thousand revellers had enjoyed a moonlight excursion on the *Charlottetown*, dancing on deck under strings of electric lights to music furnished by a nine-piece orchestra.[16]

> *7 December 1933*
> *Colder and snowing a little. Ernest sawing wood at Jerrys this afternoon. Heard that Fred Clarkes has been raided and 147 gallons of rum and two cases whiskey found. Too bad for the community to say nothing of Freds.*

The Clark family lived a few farms west of the Webbs and were by all appearances upstanding members of the community. They regularly held meetings of the Women's Institute, Women's Missionary Society, and Young People's Society in their home. So there was undoubtedly reason for the Webbs, who in the late 1920s had supported Prohibition (or at least the Liberals who supported Prohibition), to be disappointed in Fred Clark.

But why "too bad for the community"? Either Myrtle meant that Fred's actions sullied Cavendish's reputation or that local folks would feel the loss of an arrested bootlegger and his seized bootleg. If the latter interpretation seems far-fetched, consider that there is no sign that Clark's criminality changed how the Webbs felt about him. They kept associating with the Clarks – even soon attending a dance at their house.[17] Prohibition was by definition to be an absolute, but in practice it gave birth to compromise.

*14 December 1933*
*4B. Still very cold. Had a letter from Maud telling of Chesters marriage in Nov 1932. Pretty blue worried letter which made us all feel bad.*

When L.M. Montgomery's son Chester and his girlfriend, Luella, told her that they had married secretly a year earlier, the author was devastated by the news. It was not just that she was already concerned about her son's mental state, or that he, having been expelled from the engineering school at the University of Toronto, had no clear prospects, or even that, despite all this, she thought the girl not good enough for him. It was also that she assumed the backdating of the wedding was meant to legitimate a pregnancy – which it was. Luella was three months pregnant.

Montgomery had an irrepressibly vivid, imaginative inner life; it was what made her a great writer. It was also what could make her highly sensitive and even obsessive. She bore Chester's news as a personal humiliation and largely set aside her journal for the next three years. But she felt obliged to tell her closest friends. That included Myrtle, who in reply sent Maud a comforting letter. Less comforting word came a few months later when Myrtle felt obliged to warn her that Chester's news was all the talk of Cavendish.[18]

*29 December 1933*
*14B. Carrying in wood and keeping fire going all day. Blowing and drifting and bitter cold. No group.*

Winter could be a marshmallow world at Green Gables, with skating on the pond, the sun shining on snow-covered fields, and steam rising off trotting horses. But it could also be a popsicle world, with everything and everyone frozen stiff, waiting for warmth to return.

After a string of relatively warm winters, the winter of 1933–34 was breathtakingly cold across northeastern North America. The cold settled in on Boxing Day, and by 28 December, Ernest was waking at 4:40 a.m. to light the fires. The day of this entry was the coldest day *ever* in Ontario, and new records were set throughout eastern Canada. On the thirtieth, the weather moderated enough that some neighbours were able to visit the Webbs – "Good to see somebody," Myrtle wrote – but by the new year things had frozen over again, and the Webbs were keeping four stoves burning nonstop. There was a short reprieve later in January, but February brought another sustained cold snap. The weather was chilly enough and the farmhouse drafty enough that Myrtle reported one night, "Wind froze my nose in bed."[19]

What could one do in such weather? Some jobs, such as milking the cows, could not be put off. Only one job, gathering ice for the icehouse, was especially suited to the cold. The ice in the pond was between 28 and 31 inches thick that winter. For the most part, when the weather was at its worst, the Webbs hunkered down in the house, doing only what few chores they could, such as churning butter or canning meat. The women hooked mats – seven that winter, a record. Beyond that, they hibernated. "A dandy day for resting and letter writing," Myrtle wrote of one stormy Sunday.[20]

## 1934

*12 March 1934*
*12A. Cloudy in AM but finer in afternoon. Letters from Waine Maud and Miss Moore. Anita started Mrs Boas' mat. Practice at Jerrys at night. Marion painted shells.*

For a time, Marion and Lorraine and perhaps all the Webb girls painted seascapes on seashells in the wintertime, selling their work in the summer to tourists. Insert tongue twister here.

Today, the early- to mid-twentieth-century seashell paintings of Helen Haszard are still remembered on Prince Edward Island. Born in Charlottetown and trained in Boston and Toronto, Haszard was an artist who painted hundreds, if not thousands, of Island seaside scenes on canvas or shells. Her work was "tourist art" but of a good quality.[1] Haszard was a regular summer guest at Green Gables in the 1930s and into the 1940s. She became a good friend of Myrtle, whose diary is replete with references to "Miss Haszard and Miss Moore," likely Haszard's aunt.[2] In 1938, Lorraine Webb would take an art course and spend most of her year drawing and painting. The following summer, Lorraine wrote in her own diary, "Went sketching with Miss Hazard in afternoon."[3]

Haszard was likely the Webb girls' unofficial art teacher, but what she unquestionably taught them, by example, was the commercial value of selling a one-of-a-kind, assembly-line craft to summer tourists. Or, rather, the value of selling another one; Myrtle and company were already making hooked mats in just such a fashion for just such a trade. It was not that hooking mats and painting shells were "invented" traditions, as one could find evidence of such works before tourism on the Island. It was that crafters such as Haszard and the Webbs were monetizing folk art – monetizing their culture's "simple life" – at a scale and in ways that they never had in the past.

*10 April 1934*
*Ernest & I went into Earls for Nellie & Harold. Pretty hard place. Spent the afternoon with Ellice. Ernest away to a private meeting of leading citizens at Mrs. Wyands to see what if anything can be done to better conditions at Earls.*

Tourism earnings insulated the Webbs from the worst of the Depression; their finances improved markedly in the 1930s. But poverty was never far from view. Earl and Annie Simpson's family were in an especially bad way. The sheriff seized their property for a time in 1930, and although they got it back, they never stopped struggling.[4]

The Simpsons were an old Cavendish family, so the "leading citizens" did what they could to help. For the Webbs, that meant taking in Simpson children for a time. Two weeks after "Annie Earl" gave birth to the Simpsons' seventh child in late 1932, seven-year-old Nellie was brought to Green Gables. She was clearly a handful; Myrtle at one point wrote, "Nellie went home to-night to stay. What a relief." But the Webbs had her back again soon after, and she stayed, on and off, for almost half of 1933, including over Christmas.[5] In April 1934, a day after Annie had given birth to the family's eighth and final child, the Webbs took in Nellie and three-year-old Harold once again. The girl stayed for a week on this occasion and the boy for two.[6]

Figure 26 | "Lover's Lane" painting, by Helen Haszard, undated.

The other thing that the Webbs could do was give the Simpsons work. In the years that followed, Ernest occasionally had Earl working with him around the farm. Much more frequently, Annie came to help with the washing and cleaning during the tourist season; she became a fixture at Green Gables in summertime. The situation at the Simpsons' never really improved. The neighbours met in 1936 to discuss getting relief for Earl. "Folks up there not very good," the diary noted. Three years later, the *Charlottetown Guardian* advertised a concert in New Glasgow, all proceeds going to Earl Simpson of Cavendish.[7]

*8 June 1934*
*Went to Rays. Elmer Harris and Dr. Jack Jenkins here taking moving pictures this week.*

*Anne of Green Gables* appeared at the dawn of the film age and has had a relationship with the movies ever since. There had been a silent film adaptation of it in 1919, and now, in 1934, Anne Shirley was to be played in an RKO Pictures talkie by an actress who had changed her name to Anne Shirley especially for the role.

But Elmer Harris was not involved in that production. He was an American playwright who divided his time between Broadway and Hollywood – and Fortune Bridge, Prince Edward Island, where he had a vacation home (today, the Inn at Bay Fortune). Harris was on the Island that summer shooting landscape footage for *The Inner Silence*, a prospective movie, which he had written, that was set in nineteenth-century Prince Edward Island. Jack Jenkins, owner of the Upton airfield (the province's first), was assisting Harris with aerial footage. Sadly, the film that Harris and Jenkins shot that week at and above the Webb farm has long since disappeared. Harris failed to get *The Inner Silence* made at the time, and none of this footage was used when it was finally produced in 1948 as *Johnny Belinda*.[8]

Still, Harris's instinct to shoot footage at the Webb farm for a film that was not based on Montgomery's book is telling. The farm was already becoming the recognized, real-world manifestation of *Anne of Green Gables* – so much so that some of the posters and promotional material for the 1934 *Anne* film include sketches of the Webb homestead, despite the film not being shot on the Island.[9] More than

Figure 27 | Green Gables postcard, 1930s, and handbill for the 1934 film of *Anne of Green Gables*. Note that the sketch of Green Gables on the right-hand side of the handbill is of the Webb home, although the movie was not filmed there. The home was becoming the real-world embodiment of the book's setting.

just the living embodiment of Montgomery's novel, the property was coming to represent picturesque Prince Edward Island more generally, and an old-fashioned and otherwise lost interpretation of the province at that.

*25 June 1934*
*Lovely all day and heavy rain at night, thunderstorm. YPS. Sports night in Webbs field. Quite a number here. Made $5.60.*

Was "sports night" a kick-off to the summer? Did only the Young People's Society take part or adults too? Did they play baseball or softball perhaps?[10] Did Myrtle sell ice cream or lemonade?

The lack of detail makes the reader fill in the scene. Warm sunshine and its promise of the coming summer. A pasture – watch where you run. Gleeful shrieks. Adults talking about the state of the country and the state of the hay. Getting one last game in at twilight, the clouds to the west threatening.

*31 July 1934*
*Fine day, very warm. Washed, baked, churned, and went to Rustico at night. Myron & family returned. Four tourist cars before noon. Girls not feeling very good. Ernest shingling barn. Finished hay. Very light crop.*

It was an ordinary 1930s summer at Green Gables, which meant a little busier and a little longer than the previous one. The growing pervasiveness of the automobile meant ever more tourists – and, this entry suggests, more who were touring earlier in the day. The house was full up with boarders at times, the cottage was in steady use, and at one point two women were camped behind the cottage.[11] Add to that all the normal duties entailed in running a household and a farm. Myrtle's diary – when she had time to write in it – was, besides everything else, a safety valve to release some of the pressure that she felt: "Been a rather trying day," "Have been too busy and tired to write," "very tiresome," "Pretty busy day. Everybody kept moving," "Just a busy day like all the rest."[12] Graphing the frequency of the word "busy" throughout the diary shows the word rise precipitously each summer, before plummeting each September.[13]

Yet the fact that Myrtle could be so busy was amazing. Just a couple of years earlier, she had been unable to wash or bake or churn or travel to Rustico, let alone do all that in one day. She was once again her busy, tired self.

> *13 August 1934*
> *Lovely day, quite cool. Very busy. Canned nine qt bottles of beans. Baked. Churned etc and washed dishes in between. Jerry Simpsons house caught fire and about 200 people gathered there in a short time. They got it out before any serious damage was done.*

That a place is truly a community is most evident when calamity strikes, but Cavendish proved itself a community all the time. Not just in the egg circle meetings and church services and singsongs but also when a farmer bought seed enough for neighbours as well as himself to save them a trip to town or when travellers stayed over because they could get no farther in a winter storm.

The Webbs were fully a part of this community, but they were also part of a growing subcommunity of tourism operators. By the mid-1930s, there were eight summer boarding houses in Cavendish, not only those of Myrtle Webb and Jerry Simpson and Katherine Wyand but also "McCoubrey House," W.A. Graham's "Seaside Farm," Mrs C.F. Stewart's "Kirklawn," and those run by Austin Laird and by Mrs Lorne McNeill. They worked together as they could. The Webbs and Simpsons had held a joint "weaner roast" on the beach for all of their boarders the previous month. Similarly, the Webbs and Wyands swapped groceries when needed during the busy season.[14] They saw every reason to cooperate and little reason to compete; there were more than enough tourists to go around.

> *12 September 1934*
> *Lovely day all day. Had a tremendous shower for Marion at Jerrys. About 150 there. Arthur and Keith and Margaret up.*

With this entry, word of Marion's impending wedding appears as abruptly in the diary in 1934 as Keith's wedding had in 1933. Myrtle – who made note of every birth, death, and wedding in the community – did not note when she first learned of the engagement.

Murray Laird was coming to the Island and was to wed Marion there on 22 September. But then Murray's father died. Since the groom had to stay and take care of his mother, the plans were changed: the wedding would take place in Norval, Ontario, where the couple were to live anyway. L.M. Montgomery wired Marion, offering her own home – and her minister husband – for the ceremony.

On 4 October, Marion and Murray were married at last. Rev. Ewen Macdonald performed the service before just two witnesses, Murray's mother and, as the *Guardian* put it, "Mrs. Ewan MacDonald, cousin of the bride."[15] What the newlyweds did not know was that they had almost had a runaway minister. Ewen suffered from severe depression and had told Maud just the night before that he could not go through with the ceremony; he, and she, barely held it together on the big day.[16] Ewen was forced to retire a few months later, so this wedding service was likely the last one that he ever performed.

One wonders why no Webbs had travelled with Marion to the wedding. True, Ernest had the daily barn work and it was potato-digging season, but it was not an especially busy time of the year for Myrtle. Regardless, she was certainly sad to see her daughter go – the first of the girls to leave home and the first of the children to leave the Island. "Went with Marion to Borden," Myrtle wrote. "Keith and Margaret got on train at Albany. Alvin took the rest of the family to Borden and we saw our dear girl on the boat." Intensifying the sense that the family was scattering, Lorraine and Anita opted to stay down at Keith's farm; just Myrtle, Ernest, and Pauline returned to Green Gables that day. "Will I ever forget that home coming."[17]

> *24 December 1934*
> *Grey day and snowing most of day. Girls washed and scrubbed etc &. Parcel from Marion & 29 cards. Annie & Edward over.*
> *Keith and Margaret arrived at 9.15 and were we glad to see them.*

It had been a quiet autumn. This being Marion's first Christmas away, Myrtle was intent on making it feel as normal as possible. Having Keith and his wife arrive on Christmas Eve helped. So did hearing from others. By virtue of boarding tourists each summer, Myrtle connected with a remarkable number of people from all over. She had mailed fifty-three Christmas cards and thirteen parcels earlier in the week, and now every day she was receiving a bunch in return.

They were reminders that she, the Webbs, and Green Gables were in others' thoughts.

"All kids again on Christmas morning," she recorded the next day. "Santa very good as per usual. Aunt Mauds books on the way." The Webbs were visited by Keith's in-laws and by Irving Green, a young man who would appear regularly in the diary in 1935. On Boxing Day, Myrtle put a quilt in frames and started to work. The day after Maud's box of books had finally arrived, there was a snowstorm, and Myrtle reported, "Everyone reading or sleeping."[18]

## 1935

*11 January 1935*
*Went to town on a desperate road. Mud, bare ground over dykes and snow banks but such a lovely day over head. Saw the picture Anne of Green Gables. It was wonderful. Stayed at Reuels.*

Picture it. The couple bundle up for a winter's evening and step out of their house, an ordinary house that has become famous since they moved into it, a house thought to be the inspiration of a beloved novel or misunderstood to be the author's or, somehow, the protagonist's childhood home. The book has once again been made into a motion picture, and the manager of the Prince Edward Theatre in Charlottetown has sent the Webbs a special invitation to see it. Ernest harnesses the horse and hitches it to the sleigh, and the couple head off. It has been raining to the point of flooding in recent days, and the roads are terrible. But the night is clear and beautiful. They travel through the quiet countryside, up and down hill after hill after hill. Well over two hours later, they arrive. They stable the horse and walk to the theatre. Like every showing of the movie on the Island, this one is packed. Ernest and Myrtle sit in the dark as the make-believe story set in their real-life home unspools. "It was wonderful."[1]

*8 March 1935*
*6B. 10B & 20B at different places. Another perfectly fine day. Wind came around N E. Cold. YPS at Webb's. Over thirty here. Busy day had treasure hunt so there was some stir. Very cold night.*

Two of the Webb children had already moved out, and the youngest child, Pauline, was about to turn fifteen, but the house was still very much a mainstay for Cavendish youth activities. On this occasion, Rev. W.A. Paterson led the Young People's Society's Bible study, and Pauline read a paper on prayer. Anita convened the fellowship program, and Irving Green was selected to head a committee for a planned oratorical contest. The treasure hunt, in the words of the *Charlottetown Guardian*, "led six groups a merry chase from one end of the house to the other many times before the treasures were found."[2] Green Gables was a house laughed in, as well as lived in.

> 6 April 1935
> Nicer to-day but still very cold for time of year. Letter from Marion. Ellice over in the morning to tell us the good news of the arrival at Keiths of baby Ina Austina. Dad & PJ went to Hunter River to Dentist. Planning to go to Carleton to-morrow.

Myrtle and Ernest had felt their world shrinking in recent years, but it was growing too. They had not lost a son and a daughter but had gained a daughter-in-law and a son-in-law – and now their first grandchild. It took them a little while to find someone to do the barn work – "Mother miserable" by the delay, according to substitute diarist Anita – but once they had succeeded, the new grandparents hurried down to meet Ina.[3] Ernest stayed for three days before the cows called him home; Myrtle stayed for three weeks.

Ina Austina's middle name was given in honour of her mother's brother, Austin Laird. Ina herself does not know the original source of her first name, and she had not known or had forgotten that her father's parents had a daughter named Ina who died young.

> 16 April 1935
> David Johnson here hauling wood. Mounties came for Irving Green, everyone feeling bad. Girls washed. Rained in afternoon.

Life was uneventful while Myrtle was away in North Carleton. Just a few days earlier, Anita had written, "Nothing exciting happened today except for the first time for months the family went to bed at 8 PM."[4] Irving Green's arrest ended all that. The young man, a friend of Anita's, had first appeared in the diary on Christmas Day and had become a regular presence at the Webb farm all that winter; he had been at work repairing the hall floor just a day earlier.

Green was initially arrested for having received goods at a Charlottetown store on the pretense of acting on behalf of E.C. LePage's North Rustico store. He was then found to have been the perpetrator of a string of break-ins at local stores, including that of LePage. A constable had ridden throughout the countryside on horseback looking for the stolen goods, ultimately finding more than $50 worth buried in a hay mow.[5] Myrtle visited Irving once in jail, a week before he was sentenced to two years in Dorchester Penitentiary in New Brunswick, but she did not say in her diary how he was or what they talked about.[6] She never wrote of him again.

Anita did, however. In 1936, she would begin keeping a diary of her own, and in October she wrote, "18 months for a friend of mine is up today. What will become of him?" She spent an evening talking with a friend about Irving. "It brought back a heap of memories."[7]

*6 May 1935*
*King's Jubilee celebration. <u>Sports</u> out from Town for first time. Dad working at Cemetery in afternoon straightening monuments. Girls cleaned sewing room and landing. Bon fire on Austins hill tonight.*

The British Empire had reached its greatest geographical extent only a decade earlier, so it was difficult as yet to register its decline – especially on a day when people around the world were celebrating, or at least recognizing, King George V's twenty-fifth year on the throne. At Green Gables and elsewhere in Cavendish, it was an ordinary day filled with the usual spring cleaning – of houses, brush, and frost-heaved tombstones.

"Sports out" was another sure sign of spring. Myrtle occasionally still provided phenological information in her diary – that is, indications that the seasons were changing. She might cite the appearance of a common bird or flower species, such as a robin or a violet. But she most routinely noted the year's first appearance of automobiles on the Cavendish road. Between 1924 and 1935, she mentioned the first car almost every year, typically in early May.[8]

What made this year's first sighting so impressive was the appalling state of the roads. With federal assistance, Prince Edward Island had

Figure 28 | Ernest and Myrtle Webb, undated.

invested heavily in road improvement during the Depression; it was far and away the largest relief project undertaken in the province.[9] The paving of some roads and rebuilding of many more clay ones paid huge dividends in the long term, but it greatly disturbed things in the short term. The previous summer, Myrtle had written, "Everyone up in arms about the way the road has been left" – although Ernest himself was one of the men being hired to widen it.[10] Conditions were even worse in the spring of 1935. "Roads all shot," Anita wrote.[11] Returning from seeing her granddaughter for the first time, Myrtle wrote, "Dad brought me home over the worst road either of us have ever travelled on. Nearly dead at night."[12]

Road improvement eventually resulted in improved roads. And when it did, the spring cars came earlier. On 25 March 1936, more than a month earlier than what used to be normal, Myrtle would record, "Cars running on pavement."[13]

*22 July 1935*
*Blowing a gale. Washed. Mrs. Rogers & party left. Scrubbed "Bideawee." Party from Winnipeg here, travelling in a bus. Big day. All the house people went to Town. Anita made a birthday cake for Mrs Timmins and Mr Young.*

It was becoming a truism to say that each tourist season felt a little busier than the last. But each did, and it likely was. Myrtle had noticed in mid-June that the number of letters enquiring about boarding was on the rise. By late June, the Webbs had already welcomed guests from New York, California, and Ohio. On 2 July, with the season already upon them, Ernest went out and bought lumber for a second cottage. He built it over the next two weeks, furnished it on 15 July, and had it ready to rent on 16 July. It was rented its very first night.[14]

The Webbs dubbed the new cottage Bideawee – "stay a little." Although it is a phrase that appears in L.M. Montgomery's *Anne's House of Dreams*, it was not a reference to the book but simply the sort of saccharine faux-Scottishness popular in the Maritimes tourist industry at the time.[15] Given the degree to which Cavendish had become *Anne*-land in the 1930s, one wonders why the Webbs did not give their cottages names from the extended *Anne* universe. The Webbs continued to set self-imposed limits on their home's association with Montgomery's works. Yes, they accepted the PEI government putting up signs identifying their house as Green Gables. But no, they had still not painted their gables green.

*23 July 1935*
*Big day. Election, provincial. Conservatives wiped off the map of Prince Edward Island. Mr & Mrs Mason here last night and again to-night. Mr Alan Longstaff and family came to-night to Bidawee.*

The provincial Conservatives had had the misfortune of getting elected early in the Depression, failing miserably for years to free the Island from it, and now, just as the economy was finally starting to improve, they were routed by the Liberals. The federal political scene followed the same script. But the election on Prince Edward Island was particularly decisive: Walter Lea's Liberals won every seat, purportedly the first shutout in the history of the British Empire. As long-time Liberals, the Webbs must have been over the moon.

Figure 29 | Photo of Lover's Lane by L.M. Montgomery, c. 1900; colourized by her, c. 1920s.

Just one day old, "Bideawee" cottage was now "Bidawee" in Myrtle's spelling. Either way, the name did not stick. A family of Haydens stayed at one of the two cottages much of that summer, and soon the Webbs were differentiating between what they called "the small cottage" and "the Hayden cottage."[16] The Webbs did not advertise, relying instead on their home's association with Montgomery's books and then on word of mouth. So they did not have to be marketing whizzes.

> 4 September 1935
> *Perfect day and Nan started on her trip to Marion. Annie Earl here washing. Had a supper party of six. Tired?*

The summer rush was winding down. It had been a busy season again, with guests staying from a single night to five weeks and everything in between. It been a hot one too. One day in August, the temperature had risen all the way to 95 degrees Fahrenheit in the shade. The weather got so warm that the Webb women served supper outdoors for three evenings – unheard of.[17]

Amid the busiest part of August, Myrtle sent a postcard – bearing a photo of her own home – to her son-in-law, Murray. "I have stood the work wonderfully well," she wrote, "but my hand is shaky this morning." It was Murray she was writing to because Marion had been sick. "Glad Peggy is feeling better and I know you have had an anxious summer as well as a happy one."[18] Marion ("Peggy") was expecting, and Anita ("Nan") was off to Norval to help in the later stages of the pregnancy, just as Lorraine had travelled to North Carleton to help Keith's wife, Margaret. Anita could be spared now that the tourism season was over.

> 3 October 1935
> *Got a telegram from Murray. A new girl arrived at 2 AM.*
> *So glad its over. Lovely day. Dad gone to funeral. Lois very sick.*
> *Marion Elizabeth <u>Pat</u>.*

"Marion" after the baby's mother. "Elizabeth" after Murray's mother. And "Pat"? That is less clear. Coincidentally, L.M. Montgomery had just released a new novel, *Mistress Pat*. And she had dedicated it "To Mr. and Mrs. Ernest Webb and Their Family."

*27 October 1935*
*Rather a cold day. Enid and Reuel & Walter out for the day.*
*Reuel & Enid went up to the baby's funeral. We were not wanted.*
*Baptist church at night. They had named the baby Miriam.*

It can be difficult to trace exactly when families become estranged, let alone what has caused the rift. In the 1920s, Myrtle's half-brother, Cecil Simpson, was a constant in the Webbs' lives, and Cecil's marriage to Leona increased, rather than lessened, how often the two families were together. But there was a falling out late in the spring of 1931. Perhaps it had something to do with Cecil's care of Ada. Perhaps it was a money matter; the Webbs had recently paid back some money that they had owed him. Perhaps it was a church matter; Myrtle pointedly told her diary that spring, "Cecil was to church."[19]

Whatever the cause, the households grew apart. Whereas Cecil had appeared 200 times in the diary up until then, now there was silence. Myrtle recorded the birth of his three sons in the early 1930s, but there is no indication that she ever met them. Although she maintained ties with her mother, their relationship seems to have suffered too. Myrtle wrote of Ada almost 200 times in the first seven years of the diary but only thirty-five in the next four. Now, Myrtle made no mention – or perhaps did not even know – of Cecil and Leona's new child until the girl had died. The Webbs tried to make contact, but "[w]e were not wanted."

The *Guardian* carried the Simpsons' tragic news in the worst possible way. The newspaper listed in its announcement of births,

SIMPSON – At Bayview, PEI, Oct. 8, 1935, to Mr. and Mrs. Cecil M. Simpson a daughter, Miriam Marguarita.

And then, just seven lines below, the announcement of deaths began,

SIMPSON – At Bayview, PEI, Oct. 26, 1935, Miriam Marguarita, infant daughter of Mr. and Mrs. Cecil M. Simpson, aged 18 days.[20]

*25 December 1935*
*15A. Excitement as usual. Dad and Pauline went to Manse to*
*hear the King in morning. Pauline & Edward went skating in*

*afternoon. Mother and Dad went for drive – over to John F's and then up to Austins and Mother stayed. They all came over in evening. Mr. Green sick with pneumonia.*

"Excitement as usual" on Christmas Day – which is to say, the ordinary excitement of holiday traditions. The only thing missing is reference to Santa being good to everyone, but perhaps that is because Anita, not her mother, wrote this entry. On Boxing Day, Myrtle travelled to North Carleton to visit Keith's family for a week. More or less healthy, and with her children grown up, Myrtle was getting freer to make her days her own.

It was another Christmas in which Aunt Maud sent the household a box of books – fifty on this occasion. This year more than any other shows the degree to which Maud's gift benefited the whole community. Edward, the teenage son of Myrtle's friend Ellice, came over twice for books. The Baptist Church minister, Rev. William Quigley, arrived first thing on New Year's Day and "took home a nice little collection of murder stories." The next day, Alec and May Macneill "got their books."[21]

## 1936

*10 March 1936*
*Mild and the ice all off of trees. Ernest at Cemetery all day, tired to-night. Hard digging so much frost in ground there. Not feeling extra good. Back badly twisted. Joseph Wetherbie here for night. Play practice and Egg Circle directors meeting. Herb Wyand has egg hauling for next year.*

The word had come the previous evening that a member of the Cavendish community had passed away, so Ernest was out the next morning digging the grave. This was the sixteenth time in the diary that he assisted with the task, thirteen of them in the months of January through April. Either a disproportionate number of Prince Edward Islanders died in winter or Ernest knew how hard the ground, and therefore the digging, would be at that time of year and that his help would always be welcome.[1]

On this occasion, it was eighty-six-year-old John F. Macneill who had died. Macneill was L.M. Montgomery's uncle and a man she had long detested. At the turn of the century, he is said to have been ready to remove her grandmother – his own mother – from her marital home, which by then belonged to him, so Maud had moved in to make such an eviction less likely. Years later, after she became a famous author, he tore down that home when he tired of literary pilgrims visiting it. Montgomery described him in her journal as "brutal, domineering, and insulting" to most children (including her), a man whose "traits of selfishness, bad temper and tyranny overrode everything else."[2]

And perhaps he was. But nothing in Myrtle Webb's diary gives such an impression. Instead, "John F" appears to have been a well-respected community elder whom the Webbs liked. In 1925, Cavendish gave him and his wife a surprise party on their golden anniversary; five years later, the community celebrated their fifty-fifth. Church meetings and parlour socials were hosted at the Macneills' home. Ernest helped the octogenarian couple with jobs such as cutting wood and picking potatoes. What is especially striking is the number of times one of the Webb parents visited the Macneills "with the kiddies" in the 1920s and that, as the children grew older, they continued to visit John F. in the 1930s, including after his wife's death.[3]

None of that precludes Macneill from being exactly as Montgomery described him. But so much of what we know about life in Cavendish in the early twentieth century comes from the author's voluminous journals. Lacking different points of view, readers may tend to take her opinions as facts.[4] But whereas Montgomery invented Avonlea, hers was just one interpretation of Cavendish.

*21 March 1936*
*48A. Nice morning but raining hard to-night. Ernest walked in to Allen Moffats for Queenie. Paid $135.00 for her. Edgar finished at the woods to-day. Finished piecing second Irish chain quilt. Blackbirds.*

One hundred and thirty-five dollars was a lot of money on Prince Edward Island in the 1930s – being equivalent to nine months of old-age pension in the system that the province had just adopted.[5] Queenie was, in fact, the most expensive purchase in the diary to date. But a good horse was worth a lot. Unlike cars, which were priced from about $1,000 new, a horse was an all-season, all-terrain vehicle. You could plow with it and take it to church.

*1 May 1936*
*Beautiful spring day – could almost see things growing. Started harrowing – got peas and gladiolii planted in garden. Finished quilt. Ham here for two meals – Peter Murray got some hay. Mr. Pat took Pauline & Neta down to YPS at Ben Woolner's. I was over to Austin's in evening. Planted glads.*

The Webbs were more financially secure than they had been a decade ago, and two of the children had moved away, but the vegetable garden was still important to them – particularly since the late-summer tourists ate some of its bounty. The family now had not just a garden to the east of the house but a field garden as well.[6]

At the beginning of March, the girls removed the straw that covered the garden in winter, the perennials peeking out underneath. In late April they sent off orders to Rennie Seed and Dominion Seed House, two well-known Ontario companies. They traditionally started work on the garden on the first day of May, if the season was far enough advanced, and this year it was. They planted two hotbeds on 2 May, as well as lettuce, chard, and onions. Beets, carrots, turnips, beans, tomatoes, cabbage, and of course, potatoes were all mentioned in the diary when picked that late summer and fall.[7]

It was eighteen-year-old Lorraine who wrote this entry and who planted much of the garden that year. A week earlier, Myrtle had written that the family had received word that Keith's wife, Margaret, late in a pregnancy, was "very very sick."[8] Mother Webb headed off to North Carleton to be of help to them.

*4 June 1936*
*New girl at Keiths. Mr Wright and Harry Muttart came up for Mother. Very wet afternoon. Dad finished sowing in morning. Got some things transplanted from hotbed. Ada Louise Webb*

Margaret had recovered, and Myrtle had returned to Cavendish in May, but it is Anita again writing here. Her mother had rushed back to North Carleton to meet Louise, her third grandchild in three years.

*15 June 1936*
*Everybody on the jump to-day. Clarence & Dad finished south*

*roof. Girls papered two ceilings and I did the cooking. Peter here putting out manure for turnips.*

It would have been more accurate to say that everybody was on the jump all month. The Webbs traditionally did whatever upkeep was needed to the house in June, after the spring planting in the fields and gardens, and before the summer tourist season. But in the 1930s, they started taking on more and more – in part because their tourist operation demanded it and in part because their now grown-up children could do more.

Even by these standards, 1936 was a busy year for fixups. More than half of Myrtle's entries that month reference a different project under way. Ernest put up a garden fence. He and neighbour Clarence Stewart shingled the roof. Myrtle, Anita, Lorraine, and Pauline, with occasional help from Ernest and Clarence, took on a host of jobs inside. They cleaned the house and cottages. They removed wallpaper and repapered walls and/or ceilings in the kitchen, the front room, four bedrooms, and the hall – that is, more than half the house. They scraped and painted the woodwork, scraped and waxed floors, and painted the floor of at least one bedroom, as well as the cottages. Anita dubbed the June spring cleaning "The biggest event of the year."[9]

It made perfect sense to invest all this time, sweat, and money since Green Gables was the Webbs' home. But more than that, it had become a principal foundation of their livelihood. They were keeping it up not only to accommodate the needs of actual lodgers but also to fulfill the imaginings of countless more would-be visitors. They were maintaining their authentic existence by tying their future to the re-creation of a fictional place. And they had every reason to believe that they would continue to live there for many years to come.

24 *June 1936*
*Lovely day. Dorothy Ward here for dinner, agent for the*
*National Magazine. Alvin came along to supper and took the*
*girls to Town. Raining. The National Park Commission here*
*with BW LePage in afternoon.*

There is nothing to suggest, in Myrtle's first reference in the diary to a national park, that she was at all concerned by the commissioners' visit. And why should she be? The two senior members of the National Parks Branch (later Parks Canada) – the deputy commissioner and soon to be commissioner, F.H.H. Williamson, and architect and landscape designer W.D. Cromarty – were scouting almost two dozen locations across the Island for a national park. It was hardly a surprise that the tourist hub of Cavendish and the North Shore had made it onto their list. Easing her mind further, the Webbs knew B.W. LePage, the Islander accompanying them. Besides being the president of the provincial government's Executive Council, he was the father of their good friend Reuel, who was married to Myrtle's stepsister Enid; LePage had visited their farm the previous year.[10]

What's more, although Myrtle herself had never visited a national park, she presumably knew what they were like – the *Charlottetown Guardian* having mentioned Banff, for example, about one hundred times in the first half of the decade. And there was nothing in their history to suggest that one could look at the landscape of the Webb farm, let alone the house itself, and see a national park. Beginning in the United States at Yosemite in 1872 and in Canada at Banff in 1885, national parks were sublime affairs, with mountains and vistas, wildlife and wilderness. There were parks that stretched this form – Acadia National Park in Maine, for example, having been established as something of an eastern version of a western park in the late 1920s – but the dominant landscape aesthetic still held.

However, the Depression had increased pressure on the Canadian government to distribute funding to every province, so the Parks Branch was under a mandate to truly nationalize the national park system. Williamson and Cromarty had come, at the PEI government's invitation, to find the best of the Island, regardless of whether it fit the traditional park mould – indeed, knowing it could not.[11] And they were impressed with the North Shore, particularly Cavendish. They believed that with its attractive and already-popular beach, Cavendish offered the greatest opportunity for park development.

Moreover, they had learned while there that it was the setting for *Anne of Green Gables*. The Lake of Shining Waters, Lover's Lane, and Dryad's Bubble, not to mention the house itself, all stood "in the area proposed to be included in the Park," they wrote in a report to their boss in late July. "These features have been preserved in their natural state and outside of the general interest of the house it is thought that the adjoining woodland and small trout stream merit inclusion."[12] The Webb home's association with *Anne of Green Gables*, an association that the family had helped to foster, commercialized, and benefited from, now made them vulnerable – but the Webbs did not know that yet.

So the fact that, as Anita put it in her diary, "The N.Park Comm gave us the once over" was at that moment of no greater import than a visit by Dorothy Ward of *National Magazine* or any other minor official or luminary.[13] Of far greater significance to the family was Lorraine's news of the previous day: she had finally landed a teaching position. She would be in charge of Cavendish School, just down the road, and making the princely sum of $158 for the fall term.[14] A busy spring-cleaning season was winding down, the tourist season was starting up, and another child was launching. The future looked bright.

*9 July 1936*
*Up to day and down stairs and out doors. Dad went to Town.*
*Girls busy. Bought 23 qts strawberries and stewed them.*

It is the brevity of berry season on Prince Edward Island that makes its arrival so special each year. That and the berries themselves. After much anticipation, they literally come to fruition, for use in pies, jams, jellies, and preserves. Myrtle continued to chronicle berry seasons in her diary, but the truth was that they were not quite so important to family life as in the past. Whereas berries had appeared forty times in the diary in 1924, they appeared just eight in 1940. The Webbs still farmed, but their dependence on food harvested on their own land was declining. They were relying more on the outside world. And when the outside world, in the form of tourism, kept them too busy to pick, they were not above buying berries.

By 1936, the Webbs were becoming old hands as tourism operators, and they were better prepared for it generally. They had two cottages to rent out, moving some of the activity away from their house. They hired "Annie Earl" – that is, neighbour Annie Simpson, wife of Earl – to help regularly with the laundry.[15] They could afford to buy extra supplies when needed, and they did. Although the diary became its traditional August blur, and there was still the occasional word of being "tired," there were also more visits to and from family and more chances for Myrtle to catch her breath – "a busy afternoon talking to strangers," she wrote one day.[16] Rather than being controlled by tourism, the Webbs were learning to control it.

Figure 30 | Photo by National Parks Branch site inspectors of Cavendish Road from the Webb farm, 1936. The accompanying caption reads, "View from road between 'Green Gables' and 'The Lake of Shining Waters' looking toward the sea – Most of this picture would be included in proposed National Park."

*21 September 1936*
*Fine day. Washed. Pauline went to Carleton with Wyands.*
*I cleaned the back porch this afternoon. Hon Mr Dunning,*
*Premier Campbell, BW Lepage & Peter Sinclair here this* AM.
*Committee meeting at night. Ice cream & Avalah.*

Rumours about a site for a national park had swirled around Prince Edward Island for some time, but this was the day that the Webbs learned for certain how much the government wanted Green Gables – and they learned it before a word was spoken. A visit by their member of Parliament, the federal minister of finance, Charles Dunning, along with their senator, Peter Sinclair, PEI premier Thane Campbell himself, and the head of his Cabinet, B.W. LePage, was an undeniable show of force.

Plans for the park were still somewhat nebulous, and it is unclear exactly what was said – or whether the politicians offered the Webbs any choice but to sell their farm. The Webbs were assured that they would be treated well. LePage later wrote that Dunning and Sinclair "practically assured" Ernest of employment in a new park that included Green Gables.[17]

The Webbs apparently believed when the visit was over that the matter was still under discussion. But later that very day, the provincial Cabinet formally accepted the National Parks Branch's recommendation for a North Shore park site that would include Cavendish.[18] Two days later, news of this plan broke on the front pages of local newspapers, and two days after that, Ernest went to Charlottetown to try to find out more.[19] There is nothing in the diary about the park for the following month.

In Ontario, L.M. Montgomery was distressed to hear from Marion that the Webb farm and others in Cavendish were to be bought up to make a park. "Where will the Webbs go? Another home I have loved blotted out ... I understand these farms were chosen because of *Anne of Green Gables*. It's a compliment I well could spare."[20]

"Green Gables"

In the Cavendish area proposed to be included in the National Park are the house and adjoining lands purported to be the original "Green Gables" of the well-known book, and moving picture "Ann of Green Gables".

Figure 31 | Photo and caption by National Parks Branch site inspectors of "Green Gables," 1936.

*8 October 1936*
*Nice day after the rain, very warm. Aunt Sadie and I went to shore and gathered Irish moss. Choir practice here at night.*

Meanwhile, life went on as usual. Visitors came and went. Pauline wallpapered the spare bedroom. Myrtle made and bottled plum jam, jelly, and chow (the relish more often known beyond the Island as chow chow). To the degree that the Webbs knew about the proposed park, they did not act as if it might soon disrupt their lives.

Myrtle's aunt Sadie, her mother's sister, was one of her closest relatives – appearing more often in the diary than Maud. She lived in Ontario but for years returned to the Island for the summer, before eventually moving back home to O'Leary for good.

This is the first reference in the diary to Irish moss, the seaweed that manufacturers used as an emulsifier to keep common mixed products

Figure 32 | Photo by National Parks Branch site inspectors of what the accompanying caption calls "'The Haunted Forest' mentioned in 'Ann of Green Gables,'" 1936.

such as paint or chocolate milk from separating back into their constituent elements. There had begun to be a small Irish moss commercial harvesting effort on Prince Edward Island in the 1920s and it is possible that Myrtle was gathering it for sale. Rural women were heavily involved in the Island's Irish moss industry when it took off in the 1940s; it was one of their few sources of income. But it is more likely that Myrtle was collecting it for home use. Guests were coming, and Irish moss was the prime ingredient in the dessert known elsewhere as *blancmange* and in the Maritimes as Irish moss pudding.[21]

*22 October 1936*
*Blowing a gale all day. Very busy, baking bread, pies, chicken, etc. for Chicken Supper in Hall. Big crowd. Maud Montgomery McDonald spoke. Made 43.05. Bayview Institute helped.*

It was another homecoming for L.M. Montgomery, this time speaking at the Cavendish Hall, where she had first spoken forty-seven years earlier.[22] She had spent all of October on the Island and been up around Cavendish since the tenth. Of her first night back at the Webb home, she told her journal, "It is good to be here. And yet it has been strangely lonesome. The last time I was here there were eight of us around the supper table. Tonight there were just three – Ernest, Myrtle, and myself! ... Keith is married and gone. Marion is married and gone. Anita is away on a temporary job of housekeeping in Albany. Pauline and Lorraine were in Ch'Town for the day. It is as if a hawk had swooped in since my last visit." But she was happy to learn the Webbs' very good news: they would not be leaving the farm. Ernest was to be a park warden of some sort and the family could stay on at Green Gables.[23]

Still, Maud bemoaned the changes that were coming. "Perhaps this dear old house will be torn down – it will certainly be remodelled." The fields, farmed for 150 years, "will never yield another crop." The old woods flanking Lover's Lane were an especially great loss; she wrote longest and most painfully about them. "My dear woods ... they will be mine no longer. They will be open to the public – desecrated by hordes of sight seers and by pleasure hunters ... I have loved them with everything there is of me to love. They can be mine no more."[24]

Maud's journal is a valuable record of this moment in Green Gables' history. But it also accentuates the absent voice of the family who actually owned and inhabited this house, these fields, these woods. Myrtle's diary is silent on what the family knew about their future and how they felt about it. It must have all seemed a strange purgatory – the idea that they could continue to stay where they were, maintain the property, and welcome summertime visitors but at the price of giving up farming, control, and ownership. Perhaps that explains Myrtle's silence: it was less troubling to imagine life unchanged.

> 4 November 1936
> Election day in U.S. and Roosevelt is returned with a very large majority. A good thing for Canadian trade. We had Mr Cautley, Mr Ross, McBeth and Prowse here for dinner. They are putting up their stakes prepatory to surveying. Raining hard to-night and all night. Francis Clark and Charlie Craswell married.

It would be another five months before the PEI government expropriated about one hundred properties for the national park, but the federal government was already literally putting down stakes. R.W. Cautley was the National Parks Branch's chief surveyor, and he and his team swarmed throughout the North Shore that November, identifying the exact land for the park.[25]

Ernest and Myrtle were given short-term duties in this operation – Ernest assisting the surveyors and Myrtle feeding them. That it was the Webbs who were hired was natural enough. They were locals already known to the Parks Branch, and their home was to have an intrinsic role in the future park – as were they. But whether the Webbs noticed it or not, their involvement would begin to set them apart from the community. Green Gables was becoming the beachhead for the national park's invasion.

> 11 December 1936
> Very mild and roads a perfect mess of mud. We three went to play practice at night. Only seven there. Lowell in to hear radio. Heard Prince Edward's farewell speech to the Empire. It was wonderful.

It was Lorraine, not Myrtle, who wrote this entry, reporting on the abdication of Prince Edward – "King Edward" in the entry just a day earlier – to marry the American divorcée Wallis Simpson. Myrtle had left for Norval a few days before to stay with Marion. She was to meet not just her granddaughter Pat for the first time but also a new grandson, Ian, who had been born in October.

Myrtle's visit stretched to three months that winter, an unprecedentedly long trip for her. This duration spoke to her ability to help Marion with the two children, to the fact that she no longer had small children of her own to take care of, and even to the fact that the planned park left everything else so uncertain. For the first time ever, there was little work for Myrtle at Green Gables.

> 23 December 1936
> Snowing and cold. Dad started for town early. We girls slept in until after nine. What would Dad say! Ham here doing barn work. Practice at Church at night. Elmer & Eric called. Arthur came up on the train along with Annie and Edward. Was home when we got home. Ham & I got tree.

With the cats away, the girls slept in. Even with their mother in Ontario, it was a wonderful Christmastime at Green Gables. There was skating on the pond during the day, and they listened to the radio at night. There were multiple plays and concerts to stage at the Cavendish Hall. There were "cards and parcels galore" and Maud's box of books too – "45 this year!" The big day itself was a beautiful cold morning. There was more skating in the afternoon, and a friend played guitar in the evening. And yes, "Santa was more than good to us."[26]

> 31 December 1936
> Silver thaw. Dad & I drove to Hunter's River, thence to town and oh what ice! Pavement just like glass, but fine for skating. Got my tooth out and partial plate in. Dad sold the farm. Came out on 3:20 train & I kept on to Carleton. Raining some. At Keiths for night.

"Dad sold the farm." Nineteen-year-old Lorraine could not have been more matter-of-fact, as if she and her father had gone into Charlottetown to run a couple of errands and real estate had just happened to be one of them.

Of course, it was and it was not that simple. The Webbs had known all autumn that their house and land were to become part of the proposed national park and that there was not much they could do about it. Canadian expropriation law of the era greatly favoured the state, with landowners given little say as to purchase price, let alone whether the purchase occurred.[27] The National Parks Branch had made the process much more palatable by stating that the Webbs could keep living at Green Gables for an undetermined future and that Ernest would be hired as a warden. These were not conditions for which the Webbs even had to ask but were facilitated by the provincial politicians on their behalf. That may seem surprising given that it was the PEI government doing the expropriating. But the province would turn the land over to the federal government immediately, so it was the Parks Branch that would face any costs or issues related to the Webbs' ongoing presence. The provincial government had no reason not to support the Webbs.

Price was another matter. It was the PEI government's responsibility to pay landowners and to transfer the land to Canada. The federal government would then reimburse Prince Edward Island but only for any *buildings* that the Parks Branch wished to retain. There turned out to be just two of those: Green Gables in the proposed park's west end and Dalvay-by-the-Sea, a stately summer home built in the 1890s by a president of Standard Oil, in the east end. In November 1936, Premier Thane Campbell wrote to the federal minister of the interior, T.A. Crerar, to say that Ernest Webb wanted $6,500 for his house and farm. This may have been a price that Webb named or that he and Campbell came up with together or that Campbell offered on his own. Campbell told Crerar that such a figure was likely the entire property's market value "under ordinary conditions," but given "the historic and sentimental associations of the house," $6,500 was a reasonable price for the buildings alone, so Canada should, when the sale went through, reimburse the PEI government the full $6,500. Having saved some money on Dalvay's sale – although still paying $15,000 for it, much more than it would pay for Green Gables – Crerar agreed.[28] When Ernest sold on New Year's Eve, he had no way of knowing that the $6,500 he received for the entire farm was the price the two governments had recently set for the house and barns alone.

Was $6,500 – about $140,000 today[29] – a fair price for Green Gables in 1936? Perhaps the best way to gauge that is to compare its sale to that of the almost one hundred properties that the province expropriated for the park in 1937. On the one hand, the Webbs received compensation greater than anyone whose land was expropriated, an amount double their property's assessed tax value. On the other hand, there were landowners who received an even greater premium above the assessed tax value in percentage and/or dollar terms.[30] And whereas the Webbs sold at the initial price, some of the expropriated owners, as will be seen, were ultimately offered higher settlements. But most importantly, unlike the great majority of those along the North Shore who would lose land to the park, the Webbs lost *all* their property. Of the sixty-three cases where more than 10 acres were acquired, only seven constituted the landowners' entire property. The Webb farm was also the second largest area purchased. Most landowners received a higher per-acre value for the part of their property that was taken, *and* they could develop the remainder of what would surely be more valuable land on the edge of a national park, whereas the Webbs had to be satisfied with a single cheque for their home.

Consider the Webbs' case compared to that of two farms right beside them, those owned by Ham Macneill and Jerry Simpson. The 140-acre Green Gables was assessed at $3,200 and sold for $6,500, or $46.50 per acre. Macneill's 45 acres was assessed at $1,400 and was ultimately expropriated for $2,500, or $55.50 per acre. Simpson's 180 acres was assessed at $4,500, but the park required only 17.1 acres, for which it paid him $1,000.35, or $58.50 per acre, and his remaining 160 acres were undoubtedly now worth much more.[31] What Premier Campbell had called the "historic and sentimental associations" of the Webb farm turned out not to be worth very much at all. Given the unique value of Green Gables, the Webbs' loss of their entire property, and the comparison to settlements made with other local landowners, a price tag closer to Dalvay's $15,000 would have been more reasonable. But that would still seem insufficient today.

All that said, the Webbs had reasons to be content. Before they got word of the national park, it was far from clear that any of the children would take over the farm. Now, the family had received a substantial amount of money for it, yet they could keep living there, and fifty-six-year-old Ernest would have his first ever salaried position overseeing it. And perhaps there was some consolation that, besides everything else, the family had no real choice.

But mixed feelings were natural. Anita wrote in her diary, "We've ended up the year by selling our farm to the Gov for N.P. Got 6500 for it but we feel rather sad."[32]

## 1937

*11 January 1937*
*10F. Clear and cold. Neta went to HR with Arthur and from there was going to town – then to Hampshire. Nothing much doing – family rather small. Ham here in afternoon. Had supper without a lamp for the first.*

With Keith in North Carleton and Myrtle with Marion in Ontario and only Ernest, Lorraine, Anita, and Pauline around, the winter of 1937 was a particularly quiet one on the Webb farm. Much time was spent listening to the family's new radio, their first. Its purchase was evidence of the Webbs' financial position, especially considering that Islanders' rate of radio ownership was still less than half the Canadian average.[1] They also got obsessed with a new board game that swept across North America that winter: Monopoly. Lorraine mentions the game eight times in the diary within a month and then never again.

Lorraine was doing diary double-duty: besides maintaining the family one, she had started keeping one of her own in the new year. In it, we learn that the "Arthur" wandering through the family diary in these years was a beau, Arthur Wright of North Carleton. "The boy," as she called him, headed off to Chicago for work in the spring, and Lorraine spent the rest of the year exchanging letters with him almost daily. She would go to the woods to read his letters, or to write him one, or just, as she would say, "for a chat with the boy."[2]

Meanwhile, Myrtle was in Norval enjoying a long stay over the winter with Marion and Murray Laird and helping them with toddler Pat and baby Ian. She and L.M. Montgomery visited each other, too, and on one occasion confessed their mutual concern about Pat, who appeared, in Maud's words, "not normal."[3] They feared Down syndrome. Montgomery, as she so often did, took others' troubles as her own. Already mourning the recent death of her favourite cat, she told her diary, "A few nights ago, I prayed, very humbly – that God would send me something to comfort me for the loss of Lucky. And *this* is His answer. I can never pray again."[4]

People with intellectual disabilities such as Down syndrome were not well treated in this era. They were stigmatized and usually institutionalized, and because their physical symptoms were not well treated either, they tended to die young. (Pat would, in fact, die at age forty.) Myrtle undoubtedly agonized over what such a diagnosis would mean for Pat's life and for Marion's life too. Later that spring, when Myrtle was back on the Island, the Lairds had the diagnosis confirmed. "Letter from Marion," Myrtle wrote. "Poor wee Pat."[5]

> *11 March 1937*
> *2 above. Cold and blowing hard and drifting but sunny. Heard Myron over radio. Choir practice at night. Very heavy ice in Strait and Car Ferry was four hours late so Mr Paterson didn't get home until after 11 PM with our horse.*

Myrtle arrived back from Ontario at the beginning of March to a house that was no longer hers. After a few days laid up with a bad back and a few more getting back into her old routine, she sat down on this uneventful winter day and wrote a letter to F.H.H. Williamson, the National Parks Branch administrator who had inspected and selected Green Gables the previous summer and was now the agency's chief. Myrtle spilled into the letter all of her family's uncertainties about the future. That she wrote the letter solely in her own name shows the degree to which she took responsibility for the family's tourist operation. Her letter survives in the national archives and online, with fragments missing from the right-hand side of the worn pages (as shown here with dashes).[6] Addressing the letter from "Green Gables" – quotation marks and all – Myrtle penned,

> Will you please pardon me for writing you at this time? I know you are busy, but there are so many things that we are anxious to find out about and you seem to be the proper person to come to for information at this time. In the first place, can you imagine the shock the Webb family received when the word came out in the press that the Cavendish Area had been your choice and the Green Gables property was to be included in the National Park – Prince Edward Island. Ever since LM Montgomery –
> of Green Gables we have done our best with very –
> to improve the place each year. In the last ten years –
> tourist problem has been our problem, too, for the –
> until the middle of October we never know who –
> see "Green Gables," ask questions, and roam through –
> and lanes. Our business has grown beyond our –

and for two years we have not been able to –
all that have written to us for summer or vacation –
I know we should have had running water in the house –
is an old house and we could not afford it ... I am getting letters asking for reservations of –
Can you please tell me what to tell these people? So far as I am concerned, I don't want to have to work quite as hard as I have the last three years. It has been one person's work many days in the summer time to interview the many people from all over Canada and the United States who come to see "Green Gables."

We understand that this property now belongs to the Federal Government and that we have the privilege of living here until there is some other place for us. Naturally we are wondering about our work. There are two rooms in the house that need papering, the living room, and the dining room. Shall we go ahead as we have other years and paper and paint this spring or will the Government be making such changes that we would be foolish to do this extra work?

Could you give us just a little idea of what we may expect in the way of changes ... Having no Parks in Eastern Canada until last year I feel –
so much to learn and am hoping to get information –
office soon. Thank you.

> Myrtle L. Webb
> Mrs. Ernest C. Webb

Williamson was understanding in his response but could offer no guidance, as the province had not yet handed the property over to the federal government. Best to write back in a couple of months and defer any action until then.[7]

*26 April 1937*
*Funeral in afternoon. Maria Matheson and Ham here for supper. WCTU at night, Mrs Wyand on war path.*

As uncertain as they were about what a future in the park would look like, at least the Webb family had been offered a price, accepted it, and been paid. They could begin to come to terms with things. The

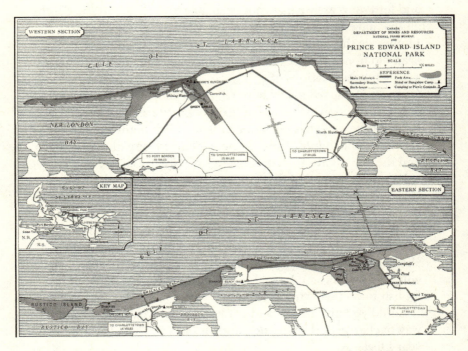

Figure 33 | Map of Prince Edward Island National Park, 1940. The Webb property was one of the few purchased in its entirety for the park.

day after this entry, they "cleaned attic and burned and burned." A few days later, they hosted fifty-eight at a Young People's Society banquet, knowing it was "The last probably."[8]

Although the national park site had been announced a full seven months earlier, it was only on 24 April that the PEI government actually expropriated the land and transferred it to federal ownership. It would be another six weeks before the landowners were notified and months more still before they were offered a price. Katherine Wyand apparently learned only that April day that the government wanted her 1.5 acres, including the seven Avonlea Lodge cottages that she had built by this point, plus a dining hall, kitchen, icehouse, and restaurant.[9] She had been friends with the Webbs for a long time, and they had helped one another while building up their tourist operations over the past decade. She had been up for supper as recently as a month earlier. But the park would put a strain on their friendship – as it did on the Webbs' relationships with other neighbours. They would blame Green Gables' existence for determining the park's location. And they would resent that the Webbs faced a different process, had been treated differently, had sold early, and yet were apparently staying on, with Ernest becoming the face of the new park.

> 5 May 1937
> *Lovely morning but clouded up and cooler in afternoon. Big day at Webbs, we bought our first car, a Chev. Girls went for mayflowers. Started harrowing. Very dry weather.*

First a radio, now a car: the Webbs were moving up in the world. But they were also still living as they always had, so on a spring day, they picked mayflowers and worked the land – land that they no longer owned.

After a few early attempts, Ernest and Myrtle apparently never did learn to drive the car, and Myrtle's subsequent diary references in which "Dad and I drove" meant, as it always had, that they had taken a horse and buggy. Twenty-six-year-old Anita became the family chauffeur. In her own diary, she documented what driver training looked like in the 1930s. On day one of them owning the car, the salesman drilled her with instructions. On day two, she drove around the yard for a while. On day three, "took Lem for a drive this a.m. and didn't kill anyone." By day four, she was an old hand.[10]

Even as Ernest was working the land, he was getting rid of much of the farm's livestock. Keith had taken a heifer, hens, and the incubator, a neighbour bought "the last of our young cattle," another bought thirty-six hens and two pigs, and another bought a cow.[11] That farm animals were not family was most evident in the case of Laddie. The horse had been a constant presence on the Webb farm since at least 1924, appearing in the diary's very first weeks. But the purchase of Queenie in 1936 and now the Chevrolet in 1937 made Laddie dispensable. In June, the Webbs sold him for $75.[12] Horsepower displaced horse power.

> 11 May 1937
> *Fine day. Mr Smart, Mr Cautley, and Mr Fenton here to dinner and Dad has the oversight of this end of Park. Nan took us to*

Figure 34 | Lorraine and Anita Webb, c. 1930s.

*the creek to-night and afterwards Dad and I drove as far as Alf Moores. Got radio battery so we will hear Coronation Ceremony to-morrow.*

The coronation of King George VI was big news – "and we heard it all as plain as could be," Anita told her diary the next day.[13] But the real excitement at Green Gables was, as Lorraine wrote in her diary, "Park men here and things settled at last." James Smart was the National Parks Branch's second-in-command (and by 1941 would be its chief), R.W. Cautley was its chief surveyor, and T.C. Fenton was an assistant engineer.[14] The three Ottawa men would oversee the park's development that year and were finally able to give the Webbs clarity about their future. (Just the previous week, Myrtle had written the Parks Branch to ask whether she could plant her gardens.)[15]

The next day, Smart put the offer to Ernest in a one-page letter. This appears to be the sole written statement defining the relationship between the Parks Branch and the Webbs going forward, and only the family has retained a copy; there is no sign of it in Parks Canada's archival record. Ernest was to be hired as a "temporary warden" and paid a wage of $75 per month during the park's development that summer and fall and $50 per month thereafter. In addition, Smart wrote, "[Y]ou will be allowed to occupy Green Gables rent free, and to provide yourself with dry wood from the Park lands."[16]

In the process of selling off the livestock, Ernest sought confirmation that he could go ahead and sell the barn and outbuildings too. From what the PEI government had told him, his understanding was that they were not part of the purchase. Surveyor Cautley told his Ottawa boss that Premier Thane Campbell denied there had been such an agreement but admitted that "something may have been said unofficially which gave Mr. Webb a wrong impression." Cautley noted that since Green Gables' value to the park "depends upon its setting for a farmhouse romance," he had informed Webb that the Parks Branch now owned the entire property and needed the barns. However, the Webbs could – should – move the two cottages and retain the proceeds. "Mr. Webb, who is a straightforward and reasonable person, accepted the above ruling unreservedly."[17]

Myrtle also learned, in early June, that she would not be permitted to keep boarders that summer. Parks Controller Williamson did not directly explain why but ended the letter, "I believe that you understand quite well the circumstances under which we have to issue the above instructions."[18] Given that Katherine Wyand was fast becoming a vocal opponent of the park's suspension of her tourist operation, Williamson likely felt there was no choice but to treat all such operations the same.

But it was also a matter of the Parks Branch still being unsure exactly what it wanted to do with Green Gables. In a note to the Privy Council that spring, the agency justified the house's purchase by saying that it was to serve as "a museum with restroom facilities."[19] Williamson thought it likely that once the golf course was complete, "the old house known as 'Green Gables' would be its clubhouse and the residence for the local park officer."[20] But Smart advised that the Parks Branch should move slowly in developing this new style of national park, with its different landscape and different settlement history in a different part of the country, "until we have more mature ideas" – maybe next spring.[21]

Such thinking extended the Webbs' uncertainty. Although their future was coming into some focus, they also realized that they had sold to the provincial government on little more than a gentleman's agreement and that this was not even the government with which they would now be dealing. What is striking is not only how little had been put in writing when they sold the farm but also, having seen the results of that, how little was put in writing thereafter. The Webbs would be living and working in a place that they did not own at the pleasure of the park.

6 June 1937
*Got home at 1 AM. Peggy is 30 years old to-day. A lovely day but wind cool. The country very beautiful and the apple bloom is very lovely this year. Baptist Church in afternoon. Dad and I went down to see Mrs Bonnell in evening.*

The family had been in Charlottetown the previous night to watch, as Myrtle put it, "the Coronation pictures and Spanky McFarlane" – that is, King George and George McFarland as Spanky from the film series *The Little Rascals*.[22] It was a quiet Sunday morning, so Myrtle, Ernest, and Anita decided to write a group letter to Marion ("Peggy") on her birthday. Ernest told her about selling the horses; two cows would be next to go. "I'll be lost," he wrote, "without the cows and horses, no pigs, and a dozen hens. We are realizing more everyday the change it's going to be for us." It would be the husk of a farm but with no farming. On a lighter note, Ernest reported that their new Newfoundland pup, Nero, was growing every day. "He will walk away with the table on his head some day he almost lifts it now when he stands up."[23]

Myrtle hinted at the ways that the park was distancing the Webbs from the community. "The Wyands are very independent this summer," she noted, and were not attending choir practice unless it suited them. And Ira McCoubrey, their next door neighbour, was pasturing fifteen cattle on the Webbs' fields! (Well, the park's.) "Its just like the gall of the McCoubreys." Myrtle wrapped up her part of the letter to Marion by noting that a letter from her to them had arrived yesterday. In a cryptic reference that was almost certainly about Pat being diagnosed with Down syndrome, she concluded, "I'm very sorry and very glad about some things. I was afraid of it when I was there. Love always, Mother."[24]

For her part, Anita updated her big sister about all the news of the community and shared the difficulties of driving the new car on the Island's greasy spring roads. Nevertheless, "The car is wonderful to have," she wrote. "It and Nero are about all we own now."[25]

> 30 July 1937
> Lovely day. Three people here looking around before I was up this morning. Pauline took the Carse family to Emerald this morning. Made goose berry jam. YPS at Gordon Lairds shore.

That summer was a mix of the new and the familiar for the Webbs. Some of their regular guests were back to see them – but now they were staying with Jerry Simpson or Katherine Wyand, who had taken reservations for, and then been granted, another year of business.[26] (Wyand printed new brochures that advertised her Avonlea Lodge as being in the "Centre of National Park.")[27] There were still plenty of mouths for Myrtle to feed, but now they were not tourists but Parks Branch staff and labourers or members of the commission appointed by the PEI government to set valuations on expropriated properties.[28]

Tourists swarmed all over Cavendish on word of the new Prince Edward Island National Park being established. On numerous days, there were 150 cars at a time parked down at the beach, more than ever before. Lorraine, in her diary, judged 16 August as seeing a "record number of tourists." Myrtle's diary that season is similarly awash in observations like "a lot of visitors," "quite a number of callers," and "talked to a large number of visitors."[29] Rather than boarding a relatively small number of people she got to know, Myrtle's days were spent greeting a growing mass of sightseers. How many times she must have explained that, no, this was not where L.M. Montgomery was born or grew up or wrote the book; that, no, this was not where Anne lived; and that, no, she was not Anne.

Tourists drove down lanes, picked cranberries, fished trout in the pond, and tore down fences all along the North Shore that summer. In effect, they did the Parks Branch's work for it, certifying the legitimacy of the park by trespassing on the property of the previous landowners, who were just starting to get letters of offer from the province. Ironically, some landowners were doing much the same thing: the Webbs' neighbours on both sides were now letting their cattle graze on the fields of Green Gables.[30] The Webb family was at the very centre of things in Cavendish that summer, but they must also have felt like bystanders.

> *25 August 1937*
> *Lovely day again. Very dry. Garden needs rain badly. Went to Rustico for mackerel but didn't get any. Lorraine & I went to shore in afternoon. Institute at Lowthers. Delegation from Cavendish went to town to-day to wait on the government about prices for their land.*

A Committee of Dispossessed Landowners from all over the park area – consisting, as the *Charlottetown Guardian* said, of "both sexes and shades of political opinion" – coalesced that August, almost a full year after the park had been announced. More than sixty landowners petitioned against the park's existence, the prices being offered for their properties, and above all the province's National Park Act, which had guided the expropriation and allowed no route for appeal.[31] The committee held public meetings along the North Shore to raise awareness and put pressure on the Campbell government. Katherine Wyand and Jerry Simpson were two of the most active members of the committee and were joined by many of the Webbs' closest friends and neighbours. Maud Montgomery soon received a "long meaty letter" from Myrtle. "There are bitter quarrels going on down there over the Park business," Maud told her journal, "I wish it had never been heard of, after all."[32]

> *28 September 1937*
> *Thrashed this forenoon. Had 13 men extra for dinner. Mr Hurst out from town treating poison ivy. Went to town in afternoon but missed seeing Lord Tweedsmuir. Had tea at Enids and came home in pouring rain. Mr Forsythe brought out the piano.*

As the Committee of Dispossessed Landowners rallied against the provincial government, the federal government's Parks Branch got started developing the park. Ernest and Myrtle Webb were integral to that. Ernest worked on building the park's perimeter fence that fall. That this was the first project that the Parks Branch undertook indicates that it recognized the importance of undoing a century-plus of prior land settlement and of establishing the new park's physical existence. For similar reasons, Ernest was tasked with nailing up notices that declared hunting in the park forbidden and then with patrolling the park grounds. (On the first day of duck season, Lorraine wrote in her diary, "Dad patrolling all day. Mother and I even had to milk.")[33] It is evident in the parks correspondence that because Ernest was easygoing and known to and respected by the local community, he was a useful ambassador in what were potentially difficult interactions with the dispossessed.[34] For her part, Myrtle fed the park's working men at least eighteen times that fall – and attempted to do so a nineteenth time: "Got a big dinner ready and not a man came to help eat it."[35]

The Webbs also had their own property matters to deal with. They completed the sale and removal of their two cottages. ("Got the big Cottage as far as the hollow. The flue fell off and someone might have been killed but wasn't," Myrtle wrote.)[36] And they readied themselves, as always, for the coming winter, by moving firewood and banking the house.[37] Green Gables was in the middle of Canada's newest national park, but it was still their home.

*27 November 1937*
*Cloudy & mild to-day. Mr Coles stumping in the new cemetery*
*plot. Dad and Anita went to Hunter River for a box of six*
*pheasants Ring-necked and we let them out back Lovers Lane.*
*Roads bad.*

Even while Ernest was warning hunters away from the new park, he was introducing a new game bird to it, presumably with the Parks Branch's approval. It was part of a program of the PEI government's Department of Agriculture in which Ontario swapped some of its pheasants for some of the Island's Hungarian partridges. The provincial minister hoped that it would foster "an added interest for tourists in our province and that such will be appreciated by our sportsmen at home."[38] That Green Gables was chosen as one of only ten sites for release of the pheasants suggests not only that it was a well-known Island location but also that, by virtue of now being part of the park, it was becoming associated with nature and conservation.

Alas, the only male among the six pheasants was killed and picked clean by a hawk or owl shortly thereafter; only its wings and claws remained.[39] But the Webbs were given a replacement male, and at least some of the pheasants lived around Green Gables in the years that followed. The ring-necked pheasant now breeds successfully on Prince Edward Island.

*24 December 1937*
*Snowed a little all day and blowing. Got house snugged up and made a big batch of doughnuts. Took the battery and anti-freeze out of car. The goose is ready for the oven. Good radio program to-night, listening to Vancouver.*

It had been a taxing year for the Webbs of Green Gables. They had needed to adjust to many changes imposed on them, while representing, in the eyes of many in the community, the imposers. But they also had a lot of reasons to be content. And for the most part, they were. Just a day earlier, thirty-nine Christmas cards had arrived, Maud's annual box of books had appeared at the train station, and thirty members of the Young People's Society had come to the house to decorate the Christmas tree.[40] The politics of the park were awkward but not debilitating. Myrtle had written Marion a few days earlier, and among her news, big and small, was that the Wyands had stopped going to the Baptist Church, with the consequence that "they are not adding to their popularity at all." Responding to news that Maud and another Islander now living in Ontario were well, Myrtle stated, "I know they will not believe quite all they hear from home about us."[41]

Christmas Day came sunny and snowy. They listened to the king's message on the radio and had friends and family over for lunch and supper. A letter came in the mail – on Christmas Day! – from Marion. That and 123 Christmas cards. Their world was big and small. On the first day of the new year, Anita wrote in her diary, "Hope '38 will bring as many joys as '37."[42]

## 1938

*15 January 1938*
*8 above this morning and 10 above to-night. Ernest out more to-day. Pretty sore, me. Got room fixed up in spare room with two beds. Gordon here this evening.*

For the first time in the diary, Myrtle and Ernest were out of commission at the same time, both of them with bad backs. Anita, twenty-six years of age and the oldest child at home, took up much of the slack, in terms of both housework and barn work. There was not much barn work to do anyway; by this point, the Webbs seem to have owned just a cow for milk and a horse for travel. It was Anita who sawed the wood that year. "Not very successful," she wrote after the first day, but she got it done. A week later, she mused in her diary, "Sometimes I wonder why I don't get married and let someone else do the slaving."[1] Ernest recovered, but Myrtle's poor health persisted throughout the winter, with quite a few days spent in bed. It was not a return to the early 1930s, but it was an unwelcome reminder of that protracted bout of illness. On 30 March, she wrote, "Had my first walk for a long long time."

*[Week of] 21 February 1938*
*Serious times in Europe this week. Hitlers speech made quite a sensation. Anthony Eden resigned as Foreign Sec'y.*

This was a rare occasion when Myrtle deemed the week's news so important that she scrawled a summary of it along the top of the diary's page. It is her first mention of Adolf Hitler or National Socialism or indeed any topic that might hint at the approach of a world war that was little more than eighteen months away.

What precipitated Myrtle's note was Hitler's three-hour speech to the Reichstag that was broadcast internationally and whose translation she may well have listened to. Hitler, besides being Germany's president and chancellor, had just named himself commander-in-chief of the armed forces. He was demanding the return of German colonies and vowed to protect Germans living in other nations. "Germans do not desire war, but they do not fear war," he announced.[2] Meanwhile, the British political and military position was in utter disarray. Foreign Secretary Anthony Eden resigned over Prime Minister Neville Chamberlain's appeasement policy toward Italy. A few weeks later, Myrtle reported the Anschluss, Germany's annexation of Austria: "Hitler in Austria to-day and the Germans have taken charge."³

> *2 April 1938*
> *Fine day, no frost last night. Men shoveled out hills to-day. Mrs Wyand has a real letter in Patriot to-day. <u>She will not budge</u>. Knitting a little suit for Ian.*

"The challenge which you have issued Democracy must be taken up," Katherine Wyand began, "even if it is taken by a woman." The Committee of Dispossessed Landowners had withered away after its initial burst of activity, so Wyand had renewed the battle against the park on her own. A scathing open letter that she wrote to the legislature appeared in both of Charlottetown's daily newspapers – a once-in-a-lifetime event, considering that the *Patriot* leaned reliably Conservative and the *Guardian* Liberal. In this and subsequent letters and articles, Wyand detailed the province's denial of property rights and the run-around that she had received from both levels of government. She embarrassed the governments by liberally quoting their letters to her and stated that an offer to run a park concession had been dangled before her, "but I decline to be a scullery-maid in any Government-sponsored kitchen."⁴

The squeaky Wyand gets the grease. The PEI government had initially offered Wyand $1,935 for her 1.5 acres – which she had bought for $450 in 1929–30 – but raised the price that spring to $3,000. What's more, she would be granted a twenty-one-year lease to 2 acres just south of that site, outside the park's borders, where she could move her cottages.⁵ And if she improved them to Parks Branch standards, she would be awarded its lucrative accommodation concession. Wyand accepted these terms.

Myrtle filled Marion in on these details in a letter in early June, when Wyand was getting set to move her cottages back from the shore. "She really has a better site than she had before ... She is trying to be nice after the way she has acted for the last year." Myrtle clearly still bore something of a grudge – against Katherine but perhaps also against the two levels of government, which had devoted more attention and resources to making Wyand happy than they had the Webbs. Alluding to Wyand's letter in the newspaper two months earlier, Myrtle noted that Katherine "will be a scullery maid in a Government Kitchen after all her boasting."⁶

*24 May 1938*
*Lovely day all day. Feeling better and got up in afternoon. Alvin and Jean arrived. Mr Smart, Mr Thompson and Mr Woods here for a few days.*

This understated entry anticipates arguably the most important event in the history of Green Gables, namely its metamorphosis from a long-cleared, working farm into a golf course, a change that has stamped this piece of land for close to a century now. And thanks to the national park system's principle of inviolability – that parks are to be preserved intact in their original form for future generations – the land will presumably remain a golf course for a long time to come.

Myrtle described the day in much greater detail in a letter to Marion. The Webbs were having a quiet Victoria Day morning, Myrtle in bed with a bad back, when word came from Dalvay that the Parks Branch's assistant controller, James Smart, and two other men were coming to Green Gables for lunch in an hour. A flustered Pauline pulled a meal together, and an aching Myrtle came down the stairs gingerly.

Smart, who had met the Webbs previously, introduced them to the two "recreational architects," Stanley Thompson and his apprentice, Norman Woods. Thompson was the leading golf course designer in Canada and had become the darling of the park system, having created deluxe courses at Jasper and Banff – the latter believed at the time to be the most expensive course ever built. Nicknamed "the Toronto terror," Thompson wowed the Webbs with his vision for the place that he was seeing in person for the first time. "Mr Thompson said the Island scenery was the most delightful he had ever seen and he has never found any place so ideal for a Golf course as this place here," Myrtle wrote. "He said there was a pull to have it at Dalvay but nothing doing, this was the place. We are quite excited about it dear."[7]

Thompson raved about the woods and the brook through the back of the property and about the view from the back field, looking toward the water. "There will be very little interference with the old walks," Myrtle assured her daughter. "They plan to make as few changes as possible but any they make will be to beautify it dear." Thompson and the others were off to work at the new Cape Breton Highlands National Park, but they would be back. "They were very nice men."[8]

Within a couple of months, Thompson was overseeing a crew of forty men on what would become the Green Gables Golf Course, more than the number working on the rest of the park combined.

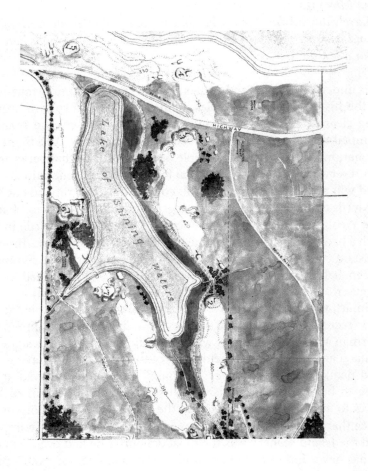

The cost of the course eventually ballooned to more than $300,000 – or almost four times what the province had spent in buying all the land for the park.[9]

*26 August 1938*
*Tractor rooted up our flower garden and piled things pretty high. Mr Thompson got us a supply of groceries and we are having a fair time with peaches and tomatoes galore. A very hectic day. Mr Smith here to dinner and the Cowan's friends and neighbours of*

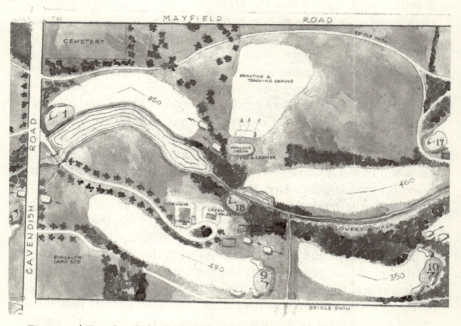

Figure 35 | Two details from Thompson, Jones, & Co's plan for
The Links at Green Gables, Prince Edward Island National Park, 1938. *At left:*
the course would run right to the shore, with two of the holes tucked against the
sand dunes. *At right:* Green Gables farmhouse would be surrounded by the golf
course and even serve as a backdrop to the eighteenth green.

> *Aunt Mauds here to supper with Mrs Campbell. Girls didn't go to
> group at night. Mrs Abb Hiscott very sick also Mrs Herb McEwen.
> Art Woolners new boy no1*

June had been quiet at Green Gables. With nothing to farm and told not to bother painting or papering this year, the Webbs had time on their hands. They risked planting a garden – "tho' it isn't one bit of use to plan," Myrtle wrote Marion, "and I do get bewildered. We may get it all planted and it may be all torn up before the summer is over." She spent some time in North Carleton visiting Keith's family. Word came from Ontario that Marion and Murray now had another child, Elaine.[10]

And after the calm came the storm – or more aptly an invasion, with the generals landing first. The federal minister of mines and resources, T.A. Crerar, and PEI premier Thane Campbell, along with their families, toured the new park on 12 July, beginning with the Webb home. The next day, government engineers and surveyors of what Myrtle revealingly called "the Golf Course Branch," as well as staff of Stanley Thompson's course design company and locally hired labourers, converged on Green Gables. Within days there were dozens of men pulling down fences, cutting down trees, and bulldozing sand dunes. "Marion's lane," which ran down through the woods in the southwest corner of the farm, was removed, although Lover's Lane remained intact. The men flattened hills and rounded levels. By early September, they were seeding the greens. In a matter of months, they had transformed a farm into a golf course.

There is little in Myrtle's diary to gauge exactly how she and the family felt about all the changes. She bristled at the loss of first their vegetable garden and then their flower garden. She mourned that "my big spruce is down to-night" and noted that Ernest was transplanting apple trees from the orchard before it was levelled.[11] But for the most part, the Webbs appear to have accepted the landscaping as just part and parcel of their new reality.[12] As so often occurs, L.M. Montgomery provides a useful second-hand view of events at Green Gables, even if it is a view refracted through her own prism. "I had a letter from Myrtle which I devoured hungrily," she informed her journal that September. "It told of all the changes being made in those old woods. Beautiful – but *new* beauty – not *our* beauty. Those cool green 'back pastures' where the sheep used to graze will soon be overrun by hordes of golfers."[13]

The "Mr Smith" Myrtle speaks of in her entry was Ernest Smith, the thirty-one-year-old Islander who was the new superintendent of Prince Edward Island National Park. Smith had been hired because the Parks Branch believed that for this new park to gain legitimacy it had to lose the trappings of long agricultural settlement and be rewilded – a task that Smith, as a trained forester, could oversee. The Webbs developed a close relationship with Smith, and in the years that followed, he became their trusted go-between in dealings with the Parks Branch. "Mr Smith" appears almost 150 times in the remainder of the diary – and on many occasions, with Myrtle feeding him a meal.[14]

28 September 1938
*A nice day. Anita went to Town to keep house for Mrs Bell. Lorraine taught to-day. Inspector there. Mr Thompson rather*

> on the blink and meals at all hours. Mr Woods has taken him to
> Town to-night. The war situation a little more hopeful to-night.
> Chamberlain, Deladier, Mussolini and Hitler to get together
> to-morrow for a four power conference.

In local news, Stanley Thompson had arrived back the day before, "a little the worse for wear," to oversee the wrapping-up of work for the season. Thompson was a heavy drinker and seems to have been in the middle of a bender.[15] He disappeared into Charlottetown for a time, and on return spent the next few days in bed, sick enough that his assistants grew seriously worried. He had started to recover by the first of the month – "but oh so thirsty," Myrtle notes.[16] Thompson is credited with designing the Green Gables Golf Course, but it was his assistant, Norman Woods, who supervised the day-to-day construction. When the course was completed that fall, it was to Woods that the workers gave a speech and gift.[17]

In international news, the British, French, Italian, and German leaders were meeting in Munich with the goal of preventing war. The next day, Myrtle, with the rest of the world, celebrated with "[a] sigh of relief and a prayer of thanksgiving to-night for the hope of peace instead of a world conflict as it would have been had Hitler marched on Checoslovakia."[18] Instead, Czechoslovakia was made to give up the Sudetenland peacefully – and a year later, the world was at war regardless. The Munich Agreement is remembered as the quintessential act of appeasement in the face of authoritarianism.

> 8 November 1938
> Foggy this morning. Painters came and got nearly all over the
> house to-day. Mr Smith here for dinner. Mr Murdie & McKay up
> and oh a confusing and busy day. Tired out tonight.

The Webbs had gotten used to life quieting down after the tourist season, but in 1938 it got much busier. With construction on the golf course wrapping up, the Parks Branch turned its attention that autumn to the Green Gables house. There was much to be done to beautify it – or as Smart said in a *Guardian* interview, to see it "restored to its original, farmhouse condition."[19]

This work involved, among other things, raising the house, putting sills under the kitchen, pouring a cement foundation, fixing the roof and reshingling it with more expensive cedar shingles, replacing some windows, installing shutters, replastering and painting throughout, installing plumbing and a septic tank and a bathroom, and painting the exterior white and the shutters, trim, and, yes, the gables green.[20] ("Looks nice with the green shutters," Lorraine noted.)[21]

It was possible to fit these renovations into a single sentence but not a single month. Multiple work crews upended Green Gables all that October and November. The Webbs had the advantage of knowing some of what was coming and that the end result would be a better, more modern home, but the work utterly governed their lives. Myrtle's diary occasionally speaks to this state of affairs – "very very busy. Shavings all over the house" and "a dozen and one interruptions through the day" – but there is never a sense of either excitement or frustration.[22] It was simply what it was, another imposed change in lives that had seen a few of them lately.

## 1939

*1 January 1939*
*A blustery cold day and spent quietly at home. Chicken dinner.*
*Nothing special.*

It was still home. The family lived in a newly renovated house in the middle of a golf course in the middle of a national park, but it was also the same home where they had lived for decades. Christmas had been much the same as always. There were the same old visits and visitors, the concert, the box of books from Maud.

And although the Webbs had sold Green Gables, they were still its homeowners in some ways. That winter, they still cut wood, which they sawed and split to heat the house. They continued to buy and haul coal from Rustico and Hunter River too. They cut ice from the pond for the summer.[1]

But most decisions about the property were no longer theirs. For a time in 1938, the Parks Branch had every intention of converting the house's main floor into a golf course clubhouse, and it was only Stanley Thompson who convinced the agency to use the barn instead.[2] When the barn lost part of its roof in a late-1938 windstorm, however, this plan was scrapped – as was the barn itself. In January, the park hired a local man to tear the barn down and set fire to its remnants.³ ("Last of the barn down," Lorraine wrote. "Looks queer.")⁴ The Parks Branch budgeted $12,000 for a brand-new clubhouse, but when told at a ministerial level that this was too extravagant, it got the cost down to $6,500 – the same price for which it had bought the entire Green Gables property two years earlier.⁵

Life was the same, and life was different. That January, Ernest informed Superintendent Smith that Cavendish's road overseer, Austin Laird, had run the winter road right over the new golf course because this was the path that it had taken for more than a century. Laird had told Webb that "neither Smith nor Crearer could stop him."⁶ Ernest was in a delicate position – still living his old life in many ways while, as park warden, informing neighbours of ways that they could no longer live theirs. Some tension did result. But it is a testament to Ernest's diplomacy and, more generally, to the respect for the Webbs in the community that the family's relations in Cavendish did not permanently suffer.

> *31 January 1939*
> *Quite a stormy day but we did our shopping and went to Capital at night. "True Confessions." Very cold day out here.*

"Not much to write about," Myrtle had reported two days earlier. There was not much work to do that winter, and for the first time in years, there was no word of a play. Myrtle and the girls were not even hooking or quilting, presumably because they would not be allowed to sell their work to summer tourists.

As a diversion, the Webbs went to the movies more often. Just the night before, in fact, they had seen the romance *The Three Comrades* and now were back in Charlottetown to see the Carol Lombard and Fred MacMurray screwball comedy *True Confession*. (No pithy reviews from Myrtle on these two. On other occasions, she called *Stanley and Livingstone* "great picture" and *Fast and Furious* – the 1939 one – "rather a poor picture.")⁷ Until 1937, it was rare for Myrtle to mention any of the family going to the movies twice in a single *year*. But now, with more time and spending money – and, importantly, a car to take them – they were in and out of Charlottetown much more often. The Webbs saw almost twice as many movies in 1937–39 as they had in all of 1924–36. Modernity – in the form of mass tourism, assembly-line automobiles, and bestselling novels – had brought the world to them, and it was also taking them to the world.

*3 March 1939*
*8A this morning. Glad Ernest was at Hunter River, will have a lovely day for travelling. Charlie went up to Joe Stewarts for grain. Charlie took Lorraine to Stanley to rink. Pauline coughing too much to go.*

Ernest was off to Ontario to visit Marion's family for two weeks. It was the fifty-eight-year-old farmer's first vacation off-Island.[8]

Whereas in 1937 and '38 the Webbs had just held on to see what next event the world would bring them, in 1939 they started regaining control of their lives. In early April, Anita received a letter from L.M. Montgomery. The author and her maid had fallen out, and Maud wondered whether Anita would be willing to move to Toronto and take over the job for a trial year. It would pay $25 per week.[9] Twenty-eight-year-old Anita had been languishing on the Island for years – all the more so after the new park limited what tourist work the Webbs could do at Green Gables. She had confessed to her diary the previous fall, "[H]ave decided I'll try hard to go to the USA."[10] But this opportunity was far better. It was both familiar and unfamiliar, family and not family. Anita accepted Maud's offer with pleasure. She would leave in June.

*18 May 1939*
*Poured all last night and very hard this afternoon. Bad road to go to election. Mr Smith here for dinner. We had to get Leonard Cullen to tow us up the hill. The last report is Liberals 26 – Con. 4.*

The Conservatives had tried half-heartedly to make the park expropriation process an issue in the provincial election, but it generated no interest; it was yesterday's news. Even in districts along the North Shore, the returns were practically unchanged from the 1935 election. For every landowner angry that their land had been seized, there were undoubtedly many more residents looking forward to what financial benefits the park would bring.

*8 June 1939*
*Everyone stepping lively to-day. The two greens near the house were torn up and re-built. Anita, Mrs Lowther, Ruth Woods, Bill Thompson, & myself went to town. Got two pairs shoes and corsets for me.*

It is a horror movie cliché: the mayhem is over, life is returning to normal, and the monster reappears one last time. Work on the transformation of Green Gables was winding down. Just the previous week, the laneway had been rerouted to provide a more romantic, winding entrance to the homestead. There were only a few more things to do that year: getting the plumbing working in the house, taking down the woodhouse, and moving the granary to the old orchard.[11] But then Stanley Thompson returned.

In a letter to Marion, Myrtle complained that the golf course designer ran roughshod over her home and hospitality for three days. Whereas until now there had been a buffer zone between work on the golf course and the house yard, this phase of landscaping lapped up against the shores of Green Gables itself. She wrote,

> He just had them run the tractor over two greens that were supposed to be finished, make a new bunker in the field behind the hen house, an extra tee down at Ham's, build up the bridge higher than the road and gravel it, take all the sods off all around this house for I don't know how many yards out, root out the healthy apple tree, move all our shrubs, run the tractor around the house a few times, fill in the old well, mark off a new drive way south of the garden willow tree and out into the field this way, and just a few other little odds and ends not worth mentioning.

When Thompson left for the final time, "[E]veryone fervently and reverently said, 'Thank God he's gone.'"[12]

*14 June 1939*
*A big day in PEI history. King George VI and Queen Elizabeth visited PEI for four hours. Rained most of day and made it very unpleasant but the look we got of their Majesties was worth the trip. The school children were there from all over the Island. Ruth Sheidow here to-night. Bad car accident at Halls hill.*

The week before, Myrtle had signed off her letter to Marion, "Love now always and we will remember you to the King."[13] The Webbs were among the 35,000 Islanders who gathered in Charlottetown to see the royals arrive in Charlottetown Harbour on the destroyer HMCS

*Skeena* as part of their cross-Canada tour, the first time a reigning monarch had set foot on Canadian soil.[14]

Three days later, Anita Webb was off on a tour of her own. She hitched a ride with golf course designer Norman Woods through New Brunswick, across New England, and on to Ontario. After two weeks at Norval visiting Marion's family, she arrived at L.M. Montgomery's Toronto home, "Journey's End," to start her new job and new life. "I think I'll be happy here," she told her diary.[15] She settled into life as Maud's maid, chauffeur, and companion.

*19 July 1939*
*A perfect day and the official opening of Golf Course. A big busy day. Mr Crerrar & Mr Howe played the first game. The* CBC *broadcasting trailer here all night. Fed about 70 people. Everyone satisfied and tired and glad its over.*

Five hundred people gathered around the first tee for a ceremony that was not, in fact, to open just the golf course but also Prince Edward Island National Park as a whole. The event was timed to be tucked into Confederation Week, the Island's celebration of the seventy-fifth anniversary of the Charlottetown Conference, which had led to Canadian Confederation. But Myrtle's mistake was understandable. Just as the golf course had dominated park development, it dominated the day. The highlight activity was a nine-hole "match of the century" between federal Minister of Transportation C.D. Howe and Minister of Mines and Resources T.A. Crerar. (Howe won.) Planes flew overhead, capturing footage of the game. The Canadian Broadcasting Corporation attempted to broadcast the ceremony live – and Ernest hurriedly telegrammed Anita in Toronto so that she and Maud would listen for it – but the network managed to create only a sound recording for later airing.[16]

The seventy people fed by Myrtle and the girls that day were not dignitaries but caddies and members of the Prince Edward Island Highlanders marching band.[17] Although the golf course surrounded the Green Gables house, it was Dalvay-by-the-Sea, almost an hour's drive away, that hosted the dignitaries for dinner. That was presumably intended to show off more of the park, but it also fit with the Parks Branch's bifurcated vision for it. Dalvay, reminiscent of a majestic park hotel, would appeal to "class," whereas Green Gables would welcome "mass." And today was about class.

There is no hint that the Webbs noticed how relatively uninvolved in the opening-day festivities they and the Green Gables house were – let alone that they would have minded. The seventy who were fed kept them busy enough. It was a little over three years since Parks Branch staff had first driven onto the property. "Glad its over" was a fitting farewell to the establishment and development phase of the park's creation, as much as to its opening day.

*23 July 1939*
*The busiest day yet. The Girl Guides here in afternoon. Over 200 registered. Everyone very tired to-night. Girls gave around 40 lunches.*

The opening opened the floodgates: visitors poured into the national park in the second half of the summer of 1939 in unprecedented numbers. Attendance had been an estimated 10,000 people in 1938, which was believed to be a significant increase from the previous year. In 1939, it was 35,000. Those who registered at Green Gables totalled 4,300, up from 1,600 the year before, but these numbers are misleadingly small because registration took place inside the house, and many tourists wandered around the grounds without ever signing in.[18]

Myrtle and the girls – Lorraine and Pauline, the only children still living at home by this point – ran the tearoom. They sold meals and snacks to tourists, and in return they paid the Parks Branch a rental fee of $15 per month and a share of the profits.[19] They also took golfers' green fees. It is striking just how few golfers there were in those early years, considering the fact that much more money had been spent on the course than on all other elements of the park combined. On one day that Myrtle classified as "busy," there were twenty-two golfers, and on another day, there were twenty-one. A "very busy" day saw thirty-six golfers.[20]

The tearoom concession was in Myrtle's name, and she often wrote of being busy and tired from the running of it, but she credited Pauline and Lorraine with doing much of the work. "Girls busy," "the girls had around 26 for afternoon tea and supper," and "girls had 30 for lunch" were typical diary entries that summer.[21] It was a markedly different business from the one that the Webbs had operated when they owned Green Gables. Rather than hosting

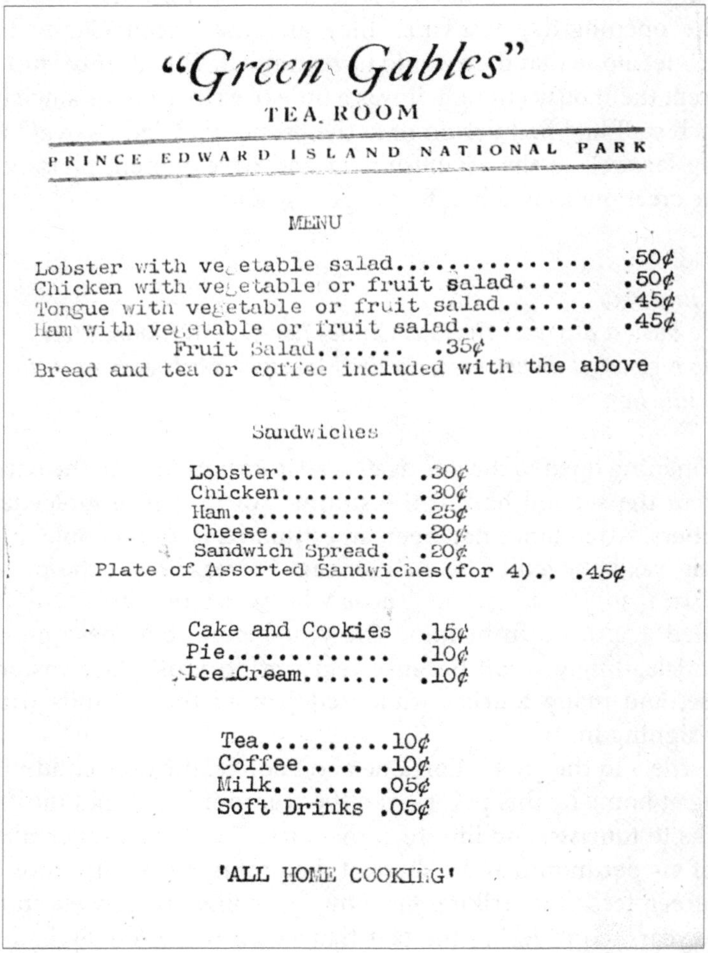

```
              "Green Gables"
                 TEA ROOM
    PRINCE EDWARD ISLAND NATIONAL PARK

                    MENU

    Lobster with vegetable salad..............  .50¢
    Chicken with vegetable or fruit salad......  .50¢
    Tongue with vegetable or fruit salad.......  .45¢
    Ham with vegetable or fruit salad..........  .45¢
              Fruit Salad........  .35¢
      Bread and tea or coffee included with the above


                  Sandwiches

              Lobster..........  .30¢
              Chicken..........  .30¢
              Ham..............  .25¢
              Cheese...........  .20¢
              Sandwich Spread.  .20¢
        Plate of Assorted Sandwiches(for 4)..  .45¢


              Cake and Cookies   .15¢
              Pie..............  .10¢
              Ice Cream........  .10¢


                 Tea..........10¢
                 Coffee......10¢
                 Milk........05¢
                 Soft Drinks .05¢


                'ALL HOME COOKING'
```

Figure 36 | Green Gables tearoom menu, undated.

boarders for days or weeks at a time, they were providing visitors with a quick service and hustling them out. Myrtle no longer talked in her diary about individual tourists. They were counted rather than named.

Myrtle experimented that summer with selling L.M. Montgomery's books, and it was a great success. She sold out of the original supply that she had on hand for the park's opening, wrote publisher

McClelland and Stewart for forty more immediately afterward, and ordered sixty-five more a month later. Montgomery always bemoaned the growing commercialization of Cavendish and how her literary career had contributed to it, but she never included the Webbs in this critique. Whether she admitted it or not, the Green Gables house had over the course of years become part of her brand – the house promoting the books as surely as the books promoted the house. By 1940, the books that Myrtle sold in the tearoom came signed by Montgomery in advance.[22]

*3 September 1939*
*Fine day, warm. Hitler determined to fight. So will England & France. Quite a number around but everyone very quiet and worried.*

People living through history do not necessarily speak of their times with the gravity that we might assume those days deserve. Their attention may be more focused on the mundane than on the momentous. In late August, when Myrtle wrote, "War clouds threatening Europe," it was the first time in four months that she had referred to political news whatsoever.[23] Although Britain declared war against Germany on 3 September, she never directly referenced this fact. Neither did she reference Canada's own declaration of war a week later. Instead, she wrote, "A lovely day and the O'Leary Webbs came down."[24]

There is a temptation to see this limited mention of the coming war as attributable to the Webbs' own situation. With four daughters, a son running his own farm, and the man of the house in his late fifties, there was no threat that any member of the family would be called up for military service overseas. But like all Canadians, the Webbs were worried for family, friends, neighbours, and countrymen who might be drafted into the fight. ("War news nerve racking," Anita wrote in her diary. "I have been thinking of all my boy friends.")[25] And they were as worried as anyone about war itself, let alone the possibility of a German victory.

The truth is that people living through history still go about their business, make supper, tend the fire. They still eye the weather too, so even a historically portentous day may also be a "Fine day." And even as they do identify the gravity of their time, they may believe – whether with reason or blind hope – that it will be short-lived and quickly reversible. Our ability to maintain normalcy may even surprise ourselves. Myrtle would recognize this fact later that September, telling her diary, "I made jam out of what I could salvage. Oh yes there is war in Europe."[26]

> *14 October 1939*
> *We had a grand stroll back through the trails, a perfect day. Weather has been grand all the week. Maud & I invited to Ern McNeill for supper and we had a very nice time. Ern brought us home. Premier Campbell & Mrs Campbell were here for a while in evening.*

A week into the war, L.M. Montgomery had arrived on Prince Edward Island. She travelled from Ontario by train with Marion's family, and Ernest and Myrtle met them on the New Brunswick side of the ferry. Maud was a wreck. She was worried about the war, about her sons, and about the possibility that her sons would be called to war. She was also dealing, as she had for years, with her husband's depression, which was bound up with a prescription drug dependency. On top of that, she had of late picked up a prescription drug dependency of her own.[27]

As she visited friends and family throughout Prince Edward Island, Maud did not see the Webbs much for the first part of her month-long stay, but she returned to Green Gables for her final week. Her time on the Island was reviving her. She held court for the premier and his wife one day and for the lieutenant governor and his wife another. She wandered through the fields-turned-fairways of Green Gables, which were, in effect, end products of her creativity and industry, and she was content. "Maud has been getting a lot of pictures of the place and loves every bit of it," Myrtle wrote. "She is feeling much better since she came."[28]

This is a rare instance when we learn of Maud through Myrtle rather than the other way around. In her despair, Maud had stopped writing in her journal that summer and so was uncharacteristically silent about this trip. It would be her last time on Prince Edward Island before her death.

*27 November 1939*
*Fine day and every one very busy getting ready for the shower for Mabel Simpson. Had around 170 people here. Cora Toombs helped the girls decorate.*

The declaration of war had the unexpected effect of making Green Gables more of a home again for the Webbs in the coming years. With the landscaping and remodelling of the park largely complete, the working men were around less often. Tourism's high season was relatively short, so the disturbance caused by tourists also had limits. The vast majority of expropriated local landowners had settled with the province, making their situations little different from that faced by the Webbs and allowing the family's relationship with neighbours to heal. The Parks Branch discovered that there was not as much local hustle (or capital) for tourism development as it had expected, so it could not afford to alienate the concessionaires that it did have, including the Webbs. And although the war did not stifle tourism as much as one might suppose, especially in its first years, it did batter the Parks Branch's budget, meaning that any more potential park development had to be deferred.

As a result, the Webbs had the freedom to re-establish themselves in their home and their community. Myrtle and Ernest were in the second half of their fifties, there was little farmwork to do, they had just a few farm animals – a horse, a cow, and the odd cat and dog – and only Lorraine, twenty-two, and Pauline, nineteen, were living at home.[29] Life within the national park was, if anything, suddenly quieter than during the years before it opened.

But not always. In mid-November, the girls learned that their friend Mabel, the daughter of Jerry and Anna Simpson, was to be married at the end of the month. So, on short notice – and with no indication that they had first asked the Parks Branch – they hosted a shower, with a huge crowd attending from near and far.[30] "The morning after the night before and a pretty dirty house to clean up," Myrtle wrote the next day.[31] Dirty but still home.

*25 December 1939*
*12°. A cold grey day, very chill wind. Charlie and Heber spent the day with us and we had a nice turkey for dinner with all the fixin's and plum pudding. The girls had a few in this evening for games.*

One could almost forget that Canada was at war that fall. The British called the first months of what would become the Second World War "the bore war" because so little was happening. In the run-up to this Christmas, there were fewer seasonal signposts than perhaps any previous one in Myrtle's diary. No word of books from Maud, of school or church concerts, of Christmas cards sent or received. But neither is there evidence that this was the case because of sadness or war worry. Life was maybe just a little slower, a little less newsworthy than it used to be.

Heber Jones had first appeared in the diary that past summer. Although he was not a golfer, the young Islander was hired to be the foreman groundskeeper on Stanley Thompson's golf course crew. He grew close to the Webbs that year, a friendship that only deepened when he became the Green Gables Golf Course's greenskeeper in 1940. From then on, he spent many an evening and night at the Webbs' home. In 1943, he and Pauline married.[32]

### 1940

*28 February 1940*
*A very nice day. Bobbie got along. Plenty of shoveling on the roads. Had a tramp on the snow shoes. CGIT at Arties. Washed.*

Of the seventy-two times that Myrtle speaks in her diary of going for a "tramp" or a "walk," almost one-third occurred between 1938 and 1940 alone. She was in a sweet spot in several senses: old enough to be free of the responsibilities of small children; young enough and, after some years of illness, healthy enough to be physically active; and fortunate enough to be living in the middle of a park.

Ernest was walking more too. Like Myrtle, he had less work to do and more time to do it. What's more, his job as warden entailed patrolling the west end of the park, and he regularly walked its range as far as New London Bay. The two of them also took the occasional walk together, as they always had. It was one of their few shared activities that Myrtle expressly mentions.[1]

*28 March 1940*
*A lovely day. Ernest went to Hunter River for coal, got home about 3.30. Knitting most of day. Lorraine went with Charlie to*

*choir practice at Bobs and Dad and I set up and listened to Foster Hewitt broadcast the hockey game from Detroit between Red Wings & Maple Leafs. Leafs won 3–1. Free for all 12 man fight.*

In 1940, a radio cost only slightly less than a cow.[2] But what had started as a luxury had become practically a necessity. It provided not only entertainment, as on this night, but also news of the wider world – news that was all the more urgent in wartime. In February, the radio informed the Webbs that the third contingent of Canadian troops had arrived in England and that Governor General Lord Tweedsmuir, aka novelist John Buchan, had suffered a stroke and died. On 26 March, the Webbs learned that William Lyon Mackenzie King's Liberals had been re-elected federally with a landslide victory, a show of Canadian solidarity for the war effort. "McKenzie King gave six days to the campaign and Manion" – Robert Manion, the Conservative leader calling for a wartime unity government – gave "six weeks of abuse and he got just what he deserved. Rather an exciting day for the Webb family."[3] It had been two Liberal governments, including King's, that had collaborated on the appropriation of Green Gables, but the Webbs clearly bore them no ill will because of it.[4]

The radio's value was most evident when it was on the fritz. Sunspot activity played havoc with radio reception across North America at the very end of March and into April. Storm-stayed for several days by a blast of severe winter weather and with their connections to the outside world broken, Myrtle wrote, "Telephone out, Radio dead. Pauline thinks we might as well be at the north pole."[5]

*22 May 1940*
*Still gray and cold. The electric light men here wiring the house and its a fine mess we are having. Mr Spence left a car with us this evening but we haven't bought it.*

The Webbs had bought their first automobile only three years ago, and they were not so well-off that they could afford to replace cars that frequently. But the Chevrolet had been constantly breaking down, so they replaced it with a Ford Mercury.[6]

Carpenters and plumbers had wrapped up most of the remaining work on Green Gables' interior over the fall and winter. There had long been a pump in the kitchen, but the family got indoor plumbing only in 1938. (This was not particularly late: although 90 per cent of urban Canadian homes had running water by 1941, only 12 per cent of farms did.)[7] However, the new plumbing system – an adjunct of the golf course's water system and installed without charge by Stanley Thompson's firm – now required a cascade of fixes, including a new hot water tank and then a new kitchen range to connect it to.[8] The kitchen had also received all new cupboards, and carpentry work was completed on a number of unspecified small projects. In early May, Myrtle noted, "The carpenters wont be here any more to meals and we are not sorry tho' they were nice men."

But in the very next sentence, she added, "Mr Smith and Mr Chappelle here about the wiring for electricity."[9] Green Gables was finally getting the lights. Surprisingly, Myrtle never celebrated the first flipping of the switch or commented on what electricity meant to the family. If nothing else, it opened up gift possibilities. In 1941, the girls gave their mother an electric iron for her birthday and their parents an electric toaster for their anniversary.[10]

*28 May 1940*
*Lorraine 23 today and she got her telegram from Ottawa to report as soon as possible. Another busy day. Pauline went to S. Side with Edward & Mary Willie & Reggie to see "Gone with the Wind."*

"The war situation has been terrible," Myrtle summarized.[11] German forces had launched a western offensive mid-month and already captured the Netherlands, Belgium, and much of France. Now, Allied troops were frantically escaping back to Britain from the French port town of Dunkirk.

Lorraine had been informed at the beginning of May that she was being called up into the civil service. The timing was ironic: having spent the previous year unable to find a job as a teacher, she had just learned that she had been given West Royalty School, on the outskirts of Charlottetown, for the fall. Showing a rare burst of emotion on the page, Myrtle wrote, "Lorraine getting her belongings packed up. Pretty hard to keep smiling with a lump of lead in your throat."[12] In the middle of a worsening war, the family at home would be down to just three. At the end of the month, Lorraine headed off to Ottawa. She spent the war as a code and cipher clerk in the naval service headquarters.

*19 June 1940*
*Still blowing and showery. Set out some plants this afternoon. Tired to-night. Got Green Gable dishes to-day.*

June used to be a frenzied month of remodelling the Webb home in anticipation of the tourist season. Now, what little of that there was, the family did not even do themselves: Myrtle picked out wallpaper and paint, and a man from the park did the work.[13] But there were still jobs for the Webbs to do. They planted a vegetable garden at their friend and neighbour Stirling Stewart's place, presumably because the Parks Branch did not allow them one at Green Gables. (If so, staff relented in future years. They likely realized that such a garden added rather than detracted from the rural idyll that this part of the park was looking to recreate.) As a result, Myrtle dedicated even more attention to maintaining a flower garden on what she called "our strip of ground around the house."[14]

In preparation for the tourist season, Myrtle doubled down on Green Gables merchandise to be sold in the tearoom. She had experimented with selling Montgomery's *Anne* books the previous summer, and it had been so successful that this year she stocked up with 125 copies straight out. She also purchased mass-produced Green Gables souvenir china for resale. These were not specially made for her or the national park; when she ran out of stock in early July, she simply went to Summerside and bought more. In 1941, she would add souvenir postcards to the inventory.[15] A decade earlier, it had made sense to sell one-of-a-kind crafts – hooked mats, painted shells – to boarders you spent time with and got to know. Now, the constant turnover of tourists made it not just possible but necessary to rely on mass-produced goods. Visitors could take home a souvenir of Green Gables as a reminder of a place that they had barely gotten time to know.

*14 July 1940*
*Another lovely day and such a crowd as we had around. Fed 68 and there wasn't much left in the house. Anita went to Baptist*

*Church at night and Pauline and Davis [?] went to Stanley. The Smileys here in evening.*

With Lorraine away in Ottawa, Anita had come home from Maud's for the summer to help Pauline and their mother in the tearoom. As in 1939, Myrtle credited the girls with doing most of the work. "The girls very busy. My back pretty sore but I helped some," she noted one typical day.[16] And it was a busy season. The war was not yet having an appreciable effect on tourism and attendance at Prince Edward Island National Park was unchanged from the previous year.[17]

It is worth stepping back and noting that Green Gables – home and property – was already well on its way to accomplishing exactly what the federal and provincial governments had hoped when they made it the cornerstone of the national park. The park was the Island's first genuine tourist attraction, and Green Gables was the jewel in its crown. More than that, it introduced to Islanders an example of an uncluttered, cultured, yet intrinsically homegrown "Island" tourism operation. On the last day of 1940, the new supervisor of the Prince Edward Island Travel Bureau, B. Graham Rogers, wrote a long article in the *Charlottetown Guardian* on "Our Tourist Industry." He singled out for praise just one destination and the three people most responsible for its running: "Our National Park is a wonderful asset and is growing in popularity steadily. Mr. Smith, the Superintendent, and Mr. and Mrs. Webb, at 'Anne of Green Gables' deserve a lot of credit."[18]

*18 September 1940*
*Didn't rain much this morning and we got the clothes dry and ironed. Feeling better. Made mustard pickles and cut up stuff for chow. Terrible air raids over London all night and day.*

Air raids and mustard pickles. Canadians' attention was divided in 1940, split between news from across the Atlantic and their as yet largely unaffected lives.

*12 October 1940*
*A lovely day. Pauline busy and I helped a little. We brought Mr Macdonald from Hunter River at night. He's quite a wreck, poor old man. Back still pretty sore.*

Ewen Macdonald and L.M. Montgomery's marriage had been fraught for a long time, but in 1940 they were both struggling desperately with prescription drug addictions. "Aunt Mauds nerves terrible," Myrtle wrote that May after receiving a letter from her daughters in Ontario. "He's a fine bundle of nerves," she wrote of Ewen in October.[19] Anita was glad to be living with them but felt helpless as she watched Maud's health deteriorate and her weight plummet.[20] In different circumstances, Maud and Ewen might have been able to keep each other afloat. Instead, the individual problems of one compounded those of the other, pulling them both down.

The Webbs did what they could to assist Ewen on his visit to the Island that fall. He may have stayed with them some, and they certainly drove him from place to place, including to see two doctors. His health improved, at least for a time, just as Maud's had a year earlier; one has to wonder if they had reduced access to drugs while on the Island. Myrtle's diary does not explicitly say when he left; he just stops being mentioned. Ewen lived in his wife's shadow and barely cast one of his own.

> *6 December 1940*
> *Margaret passed away this evening.*

The first two death notices in the next day's *Guardian* documented one of the worst weeks of the Webbs' lives:

MACNEILL – On Dec. 1., 1940, at her home in Knutsford, Mrs. Sadie JB MacNeill, age 75 years.

WEBB – At the Prince County Hospital on Friday, December 6, 1940, Mrs. Keith Webb, nee Margaret Lowther, aged 28 years.[21]

Earlier that fall, on word that Aunt Sadie was dying, Myrtle and Ernest had rushed up west to be with her.[22] She had held on two months longer.

And then Margaret, Keith's wife, had died. She had been pregnant, and Keith explained in a letter to Marion how she died. It was snowing on 28 November, making car travel impossible, but Keith and Margaret decided to go out anyway. They hitched up the horse and sleigh. "It was storming in good style and we only got part way and got stuck both had to get out to turn the sleigh but we got home O.K." Margaret presumably suffered internal injuries and became very sick that night. When the doctor eventually arrived – "so cold I had to take off his coats for him" – he told Keith that Margaret had to be taken to Prince County Hospital. Fifty-five local men shovelled a path through the snowdrifts to get her out. She improved for a time in the hospital, but on 3 December, the family learned that there was no hope. Ernest, on his sixtieth birthday, took the train to Summerside to be with Keith. A baby boy died one day and Margaret the next.[23]

Margaret's daughters, Ina and Louise, just five and four at the time, vividly remember their mother's funeral. She was laid out in the parlour of their North Carleton home, and their father swept them up, one in each arm, so they could kiss her and say goodbye. "It will be a queer Christmas here," Keith wrote Marion, "but for the kiddies sake we have to do the best we can."[24]

## 1941

*26 December 1940 to 1 January 1941*
*Felt alright in morning but something happened and Keith had to get Dr and Dad and I was in bed for several days. Got home on Dec 31st and still feeling anything but OK on Jan 1st 1941. Quite mild weather since Christmas. Poured rain on Dec 30th. Good car road on pavement.*

On word of Margaret's death, Myrtle had rushed down to be with Keith and to help take care of the children. (It had been Ernest who reported the death and maintained the diary in the weeks before Christmas.) The adults held it together until the holiday. "The children were happy and that was the main thing," Myrtle noted. "Keith went to pieces after Anne & Charles left."[1]

Then Myrtle did too. Writing to Marion in the new year, she said, "I felt so numb and useless. Just couldn't seem to forget until something must have snapped and forgetfulness." She felt terrible "to be such a flop and add to Keiths worries" but was still "feeling a bit wobbly on my pegs and its hard to think." She was glad to be back home. Anita headed to the Island from Ontario to take care of Keith's children for a time. "My heart aches for Maud but more for Anita. She's sure had it hard," Myrtle wrote, without explaining herself; perhaps she was referring to what Anita had been dealing with, helping take care of Maud and Ewen.[2] It was one of those times in a family's life when all were suffering, with no good news to be found anywhere.

> 19 February 1941
> Got some ironing done, not feeling very spry. Sadie has cold too.

The diary entries were as short as the days that winter, evidence of inactivity and weariness. This new Sadie was eighteen-year-old Sadie Hiscott from North Rustico, hired by Ernest to help out around the house while Pauline was in Ontario for a time.[3] Not that there was much to do. She was there to keep Myrtle company as much as anything.

> 18 March 1941
> Zero. Very cold all day and drifting. Party at Fred Clarkes at night. Heber and Sadie went. A big crowd there. George beat up Sadie.

"George beat up Sadie." This was most likely not Sadie Hiscott, who went with Heber to the party, four properties over from Green Gables. It was more likely Sadie Clark, wife of Fred's son George, given that a man could not beat up an eighteen-year-old neighbour girl with as much impunity as he could his wife. The Charlottetown Police, for example, differentiated between "Assault on female" and "Assault on female (wife beating)," and there is some evidence that the courts handed down stiffer sentences for the former than for the latter.[4]

If this was in fact Sadie and George Clark, they were Myrtle and Ernest's friends, both before and after that night. The couples would continue to visit one another in the years that followed. When Myrtle broke her ankle in 1943, George was one of the neighbours who rushed to help. At Ernest's funeral, George would even sing a solo, "Beautiful Isle of Somewhere."[5]

Regardless of which George and Sadie are being discussed, did he beat her up at the party itself? If so, how did the bystanders react? And what was Myrtle's intent in documenting the assault? Was it just a statement of fact, without much judgment? Or was she shocked and disgusted but knew that, constrained by custom, there was little she could do – except leave a record, if only for herself, of George's action? And a record of everyone, including herself, who had let this happen without apparent repercussions?

> *12 April 1941*
> *Another lovely day and four girls came back and finished quilting their autograph quilt. Temp up to 40 and not much frost to-night.*

The Webbs slowly arose from that winter's hibernation and grief. In early April, Myrtle had her first walk since November. Ernest went around collecting for the Canadian War Services, which provided goods for soldiers overseas. (It had been launched on the Island with Royal Air Force planes "bombing" Summerside and Charlottetown with pamphlets.) And after being away for six months, Ernest and Myrtle returned to church.[6]

They were drawn out in part because the world kept coming to them. Even with all the Webb girls grown and only Pauline at home, it was at Green Gables that the Cavendish branch of the Canadian Girls in Training made their quilts. Myrtle was likely teaching them, and perhaps the house's significant size – and relative emptiness now – made it the perfect place to leave out large quilting frames. But one can easily imagine that the girls also enjoyed the romance of spending the day quilting in a house that they knew from literature.

> *16 April 1941*
> *A perfect day. West wind. Summerside Airport officially opened and a lot of planes flying to-day. Washed and I did part of ironing.*

The airport's opening can be said to have been the beginning of the Webbs' wartime. Before that, the war was largely heard about on the radio or read about in the newspaper. Now it felt close to home. At the outset of the war, Canada had negotiated that its major initial contribution to the effort would be to play a principal role in the British Commonwealth Air Training Plan for military aircrews. Canada's size, plus the fact that it was within range of the war in Europe and Asia but too distant to be in danger of an air attack, made it the perfect host for such work.[7]

The Air Training Plan's schools were established all across Canada, but Prince Edward Island was disproportionately favoured. The minister of national defence was J.L. Ralston, a Nova Scotian who had recently been parachuted – figuratively – into a riding on the Island's west end. He ensured that his constituency was well treated. The province received training schools in Summerside and Mount Pleasant and an emergency landing strip in Wellington, not to mention a top-secret radar base in Tignish, all in addition to its Royal Canadian Air Force (RCAF) base in Charlottetown. On this day, Ralston himself presented wings to the first Summerside graduates, calling it the school's "first installment of bad news for Hitler."[8]

The training schools meant that in the years that followed there would be thousands of young airmen from Britain, Canada, and the rest of the Commonwealth on Prince Edward Island. When not in training, they would explore the North Shore and welcome a refuge where they might golf, swim, walk in nature, or just have a cup of tea.[9]

*1 June 1941*
*The worst tragedy Cavendish has known. Two Montreal RCAF boys and Harvard training plane crashed at the beach and burst into flames. I saw it from Old Orchard and we had a hard time getting central and S.Side. About all in at night. Gave supper to five and waited up until the rest of family got home from O'Leary. They took Keiths along with them. Aunt Lizzie has had two strokes and is very poorly.*

It was a cool Sunday afternoon on Cavendish Beach, with a few bathers trying to will the summer into existence. A small yellow prop plane out of Summerside came in low over the water, circled several times, and smashed into a field behind the dunes. One pilot was thrown from the wreckage, and the other did not escape as the plane caught fire. The dead were Bonar Robertson, twenty-three years old, and Glen Fletcher, twenty, of Mount Royal, Quebec. The *Charlottetown Guardian* expressed shock that "the quiet picturesque land of 'Green Gables' should have been the scene of Sunday's grim tragedy ... Not even a quiet corner in rural Prince Edward Island can escape the stern realities of war."[10]

*22 July 1941*
*Pretty tired but busy all day. Fed 49. Anita went to Town in*

> *morning. Premier Campbell phoned asking us to give supper to Col. Ralston and party. The last straw. All in.*

Prince Edward Island tourism still seemed war-proof in 1941. The federal and provincial governments, which had discovered the economic value of the industry in the previous decade, were continuing to promote it heavily – especially to Americans, who were not yet in the fray and found Canada a safe destination. A new, twice-daily bus service between Charlottetown and Summerside was launched for the season, with stops in Dalvay, Stanhope, Brackley, and Cavendish, making the national park considerably more accessible.[11] Although that summer was a tremendously rainy one, the number of visitors to the park increased to 40,000 from the previous year's 35,000, meaning that in just its fifth year, it became the fifth most attended national park in Canada.[12]

The park's popularity was rooted in the fact that it was a picturesque blend of the sea and the pastoral and of the new and the old-fashioned. Assessing the site that summer, the Parks Branch's new director, James Smart, noted that the Green Gables house was looking particularly attractive. "The caretaker and his family are taking very good care of the property. Mr. Webb had done a lot of planting of flowers and shrubbery at his own expense around the building."[13] Smart felt sufficiently comfortable with the Webbs' work – and sufficiently concerned about the park's lack of accommodations – that Myrtle was asked that spring if, as well as operating the tearoom, she would run the "Bonnell cottage" across from the Green Gables farm, which the park had bought. Myrtle declined, citing recent poor health for why she did not want to assume more responsibilities.[14]

That was a wise choice because it turned out to be a hectic summer. Anita, Pauline, and Myrtle regularly fed fifty people each day, many more tourists were wandering around, and the golf course was enjoying its busiest year yet.[15] More bothersome, politicians and civil servants had begun using Green Gables as a place to host luminaries on little or no notice. One day, it was Stanley Thompson with a group, and another day it was the lieutenant governor and the premier with the South African representative in Canada. Little wonder that the premier's last-minute call to feed the defence minister's party was Myrtle's "last straw."[16] Except, of course, it wasn't. She hosted them, just as she did everything else that was asked of her.

*28 July 1941*
*Finer to day but still cold. Temp 50 to-night and such a roar on the sea. Mrs Rainsford Keith of Havelock and Virginia were here this afternoon and until the bus came at 9 PM.*

It was not just airmen who became wartime tourists at Green Gables but also their wives and families, on the Island to see their loved ones. Twenty-one-year-old Rainsford Keith had been a bank clerk before enlisting with the RCAF in 1940. He trained first in Toronto and then in Summerside, receiving his pilot's badge just days after this diary entry and was sent overseas. One night in February 1942, he was flying a Hurricane south of Salisbury, England, when he lost his way, ran low on fuel, and attempted unsuccessfully to land. "He appeared to be very excited," his service file states blandly. A stone memorial with a plaque commemorates the crash site.[17]

There is a change in Myrtle's diary during the war. Beginning around 1941, she takes care to provide the names of military personnel she meets – more care than she has ever taken for ordinary visitors to Green Gables. She holds a little tighter to their memory, presumably not in case they return but in case they don't.

Rainsford Keith, however, is a different matter because there is no indication that she ever met him. But she did know "Mrs Rainsford Keith" – who was his mother, not his wife, as the pilot was unmarried. Myrtle and her mother had lived with the family of Rainsford's grandparents for a decade in Havelock, New Brunswick, at the end of the previous century before coming to Prince Edward Island. The Keiths were family of a sort – she had been given a middle name in honour of them, and she had named her son for them – even though Myrtle had never previously spoken of them in the diary.[18]

*10 August 1941*
*A terrible storm and Dads trousers are mostly in Ch.Town. 6R Air Force here Don Ken Dick Lem, Les and Maurice and the Allens here in the evening.*

For a time, a group of young members of Britain's Royal Air Force made Green Gables their second home while training on the Island. It appears to have happened just by one or two getting to know the

Figure 37 | Pauline and Anita Webb with servicemen identified only as Larry, Joe, and Ted, c. 1942.

Webbs and then returning with friends. Myrtle chronicled their many appearances. "Ken Brookmen, Les, Lorne and Maurice" stayed at Green Gables for a weekend. The Webbs were "guests of the Air Force" for dinner and a show in Charlottetown. Don, Maurice, and Les came for a long weekend, and they all had a campfire at the shore. "Two new boys came out with Dickman-Wilkes Dick Hovers and Gordon Hatherly." The Webb girls took Maurice and Les to Summerside. "Air Force everywhere" around Green Gables. Maurice, Les, and Len came for a picnic supper. The girls made Maurice a birthday cake. Five Royal Air Force boys came one afternoon, played crokinole for hours, and had an evening corn boil. "They are nice boys."[19]

Of course, the airmen for whom Myrtle provides only a first name cannot be traced. But some of the others can be. "Ken Brookmen" was likely Kenneth Brookman, a twenty-four-year-old from Leicestershire, England; he would die two years later in India

Figure 38 | Pauline, Lorraine, and Myrtle Webb with unidentified servicemen, Green Gables, c. 1942.

when his plane crashed during a dust storm.[20] Dick Hovers may have been Richard Collinson Hovers, a twenty-one-year-old from Warwickshire, England, who a year later was flying a bomber that never returned to its base in Gibraltar; his body was never found.[21] Gordon Hatherly was almost certainly a twenty-one-year-old from Middlesex, England, who went on to fly anti-submarine missions out of Reykjavik; he received a Distinguished Flying Cross and lived almost into the next century.[22]

Maurice Bird, a twenty-five-year-old from Bournemouth, England, was the most regular visitor to Green Gables in this period and the one who grew closest to the Webbs. Unlike most of the others, he kept coming back after being stationed elsewhere. That October, he and Les flew from their base in Debert, Nova Scotia, to Charlottetown and grabbed a taxi out to Cavendish just for the day. In November, Bird returned to Green Gables and stayed overnight. Then, in December, his plane was lost without a trace during night flying. Wreckage washed up along the Minas Basin, but no body was recovered. The Webbs learned of Maurice Bird's fate, unlike that of most of the others. They received word from a fellow flier that Bird's plane had gone missing. And, in March 1942, they received a letter from Bird's girlfriend.[23]

These few details are all that we have. We never learn what the Webb home meant to the young British airmen, what the Webbs appreciated about their visits, what they talked about, what Bird told his girlfriend about the Webbs, or what she wrote them. We must imagine these details for ourselves.

*16 November 1941*
*Sunday. Very mild, light rain* AM. *Still alone all day and night. Great life if you like it.*

This was Ernest writing. He was holding down the fort all October and November while Myrtle was in Norval visiting Marion's family. Lorraine was working as a cipher clerk in Ottawa. Anita was helping Keith with his kids in North Carleton. Only Pauline was around – until she left for Ontario too, perhaps to assist Aunt Maud in Anita's absence.[24] There was not much for Ernest to write about. So he didn't.

*30 November 1941*
*Fine day but snow had drifted around some. Heber took me up for Mother. Got stuck in Cecils Lane but got Mother home* OK.

Myrtle was back home from Ontario for just two days when she went up to her half-brother's place in Bayview and took her mother, Ada, home to live with her. The seventy-nine-year-old was beginning to fail, and the half-siblings presumably agreed that she could get more constant attention at the Webbs'. But this arrangement did not signal a rapprochement between Cecil and Myrtle; their decade-long estrangement persisted. Ada lived at Green Gables for the next ten months.

Bad war news came a week later. Japan had bombed Pearl Harbor and Manila and had declared war on the Allied nations, including Canada. The next day, Myrtle wrote, "United States declared war on Japan we didn't do much but listen to the radio."[25] Then they heard that Japanese forces had sunk Great Britain's two largest warships,

HMS *Repulse* and HMS *Prince of Wales*, with great loss of life. It felt like the lowest point of the war. And it was. The entrance of the United States into the war would help to tip the balance back.

> *29 December 1941*
> *Just busy last week and both of us very lonely but we wouldn't admit it. Christmas was a mild rainy day. Mother seemed so weak. We did not decorate. The Christmas cactus was beautiful. Got all my gifts away by the 26th. Ernest went to Town the 24th and Heber didn't come out. The weather has kept very mild but cloudy all the week. Annie & Alfred Moore and Hester & Fred Clarke were our only visitors. The chick-a-dees are eating out of my hand to-day. Thought Mother would get up but she doesn't feel able and looks bad. The fall of Hong Kong and Winston Churchills arrival In the United States have been the big events as well as Germans retreating all along Russian front.*

The first Christmas without children. Even Keith and Anita, still on the Island, did not visit over the holidays. Keith and Ernest arranged to meet halfway between Cavendish and North Carleton, and they exchanged presents there.

It was not just the children whose absence was felt. Few friends visited. And there is no word of the cards and gifts that in past years had reached them from around the world. The war undoubtedly dampened people's inclination and ability to send mail. But their solitude also speaks to how the Webbs' lives had changed now that they were no longer taking in boarders: it was more difficult to form the same friendships with tourists they met only fleetingly.

## 1942

> *8 March 1942*
> *s. Lovely day but cool wind. Good walking on the crust. A long lonely day.*

The quiet spilled into the winter of 1942. Ernest puttered around at his winter tasks, which still included cutting ice from the pond and splitting and piling wood. Myrtle fell downstairs headfirst – "Might have broken my neck" – and was lucky to escape with some soreness. Ada was not in pain but was weak and tired, and she lamented the infrequency of visitors. The family had one of the children home, at least for a while: Anita arrived from Keith's place in North Carleton at the end of January, before heading back to Aunt Maud's home in Ontario just a few days before this entry.[1]

In Myrtle's handwriting, a *v* is a quick downstroke and upstroke, with the exit occurring at the top toward the next letter. In an *n*, by contrast, after the downstroke and upstroke, the pencil plunges downward once more and heads to the next letter from there. So as much as one might wish to read that Myrtle Webb's 8 March 1942 was "A long lovely day," it seems to have been "lonely."

> 24 and 25 April 1942
> *Aunt Maud, L.M. Montgomery Macdonald died in Toronto this afternoon.*
>   72A. *Not feeling very good and the news of Mauds death came as a shock. A wire from Stuart help us and Ernest had a busy day as well as Pauline & myself. Mother too was very busy all day making all the funeral plans. Anna over in evening. Ernest phoned Mr Stirling, Keith, Mrs Campbell & ChTown from Art Simpsons.*

It was Anita who found Aunt Maud's body in the bedroom of her Toronto home and contacted the doctor. Ewen was in the house at the time, but according to Maud's biographer, he was so ill that he barely understood what was happening. Later, Anita would tell people that Montgomery had died of suicide, but whether this was her own interpretation or that of the doctors on the scene is unknown.[2]

Maud's death displaced everything else in the Webbs' life for the next week. The family made many of the local arrangements on the Macdonalds' behalf, including asking Rev. John Stirling, who had performed Maud's wedding in 1911, to now perform her funeral. They got the house in order, Ernest and Pauline went to Hunter River to meet the train carrying Maud's body, and then they escorted the hearse that delivered her to Green Gables. Myrtle wrote, "Maud was brought home."[3]

Maybe Myrtle meant brought to her own home or maybe to Maud's home community of Cavendish, but it is hard to imagine that she meant Maud's home of Green Gables. It had never been that. Yet the fact that the wake was held in the Webbs' dining room, not in the home of Maud's Park Corner relatives or in the Cavendish church where the funeral was to take place, speaks to the degree to which, over the course of years, Maud had taken possession of Green Gables. The *Charlottetown Guardian* noted that her remains were at rest in "the house made known by her throughout the world in the book 'Anne of Green Gables.'"[4] Despite being another family's home – not to mention part of a national park – Green Gables was also indisputably and inescapably Lucy Maud Montgomery's.[5]

Hundreds from across the Island attended the funeral at Cavendish United Church and the burial in the Cavendish Cemetery. Although local men served as pallbearers, neither Ernest nor Keith were among them; the Macdonalds may have felt that the family was doing enough already. The following day, the Webbs saw Maud's two boys off on the train, and that was it. Everyone was exhausted. "Pauline washed up the bedding that had been used and I did the ironing in the evening" was Myrtle's entire diary entry for the next day.[6]

*6 May 1942*
*My first trip to Town this year. Took Fred Clark Annie Moore and Bessie. Got a gorgeous calceolaria at Taits. Got the paper for hall and kitchen etc. Dads hand went bad, numb.*

There would be fewer car trips for Myrtle in 1942 both because she was caring for her mother and because, as part of the war effort, the Canadian government had instituted gas rationing on 1 April. (Myrtle jotted down the numbers of the Webbs' ration books in the inside cover of her diary: Ernest's number was CN41037 and hers CN41038.) Rationing would impact attendance at Prince Edward Island National Park too, particularly at the Cavendish end, which would draw fewer visitors from Charlottetown that year. In accordance with wartime belt-tightening, the Parks Branch also reduced maintenance in the park and decided to open just nine holes of the golf course.[7] All of these changes meant that Green Gables would be a more typical home that summer than it had been at any time since the park's creation. The Webbs painted and papered a couple of rooms on their own. (Well, Pauline did.) They picked more berries than they had in recent years. They planted a substantial vegetable garden – a Victory Garden – near the house, and it grew well.

Ernest's health in this era is a bit of a mystery. Myrtle certainly never writes about her husband having chronic complaints, in contrast to how she, in different periods, writes about her own. He was still working around the property and still warden for the western end of the park. Yet in January, Ernest stayed overnight at Prince County Hospital for what seems to have been a scheduled appointment, and the Summerside surgeon Dr Claude Simpson "found him much better," in Myrtle's words. The numbness in Ernest's hands went away after a few days in May, but in June he spent the best part of a week in hospital and rested for two weeks on his return. In July, "Dr. Claude" pronounced him the best he had been for a year.[8] Ernest went back to being a constant, reliable presence in Myrtle's diary and in her life.

10 July 1942
*Another perfect day. A grand rain this morning. No one to register to-day. The war pretty bad right now. Milton Green got a fish hook in his finger. Rueben Macdonald, Editor of the Patriot died.*

It was highly unusual for *no one* to register at Green Gables on a day in July, but it speaks to the home-front quiet of this wartime summer. Anita came home from Ontario to help Pauline run the tearoom, Myrtle and Ernest puttered around (when up to it), and Ada was bedridden. The season picked up in August, and by the end of the year, attendance at Prince Edward Island National Park had reached a respectable 25,000. This figure was a 37 per cent drop from a year earlier, but across Canada as a whole, park visitation was down 55 per cent.[9]

For Myrtle, the highlight of the summer was a two-week visit from Marion and her daughter Elaine. Myrtle clearly worried about how her oldest daughter's present and future life would be affected by her daughter Pat's Down syndrome. So she was pleased to have Marion home, relaxed and happy. She wrote in her diary about everything they did and everyone they visited. The day before Marion headed back to Ontario, she received word from her husband that (in Myrtle's words) "he had taken Pat to Orillia to the school or Hospital there." Whether Marion had known Murray was going to institutionalize the six-year-old Pat during her vacation is not known. Neither is her reaction to the news. A week later, Myrtle received a letter from Marion. "She arrived home safe and sound," Myrtle wrote, "and will have a chance to live now."[10] Pat's name does not appear again in Myrtle's diary.

> *1 August 1942*
> *Cloudy and raining this afternoon. Clair Hope and Otto Groskorth came in after dinner. We went to Town at night, the first Saturday night this summer. Dad & I went to a show and the girls went to the Prince Edward. Elaine stayed with Mother.*

Shortly after enlisting in the Royal Canadian Air Force, Clarence – Clair – Hope was at a party at L.M. Montgomery's Toronto home. A devoted reader of *Anne of Green Gables*, he struck up a conversation with the author's "niece" – Anita Webb – who invited him to Green Gables if his war travels ever took him to Prince Edward Island. When he was stationed at Dartmouth, Nova Scotia, later that year, he decided to take her up on the offer. He hitch-hiked to the Island and visited Anita and the Webbs for the weekend, staying in the east gable bedroom now known as "Anne's room." "Many times since then," he wrote later in life, "I have hastily explained that Anne was not there."[11]

Hope returned to Green Gables several times, but his written reminiscences of these visits never include Otto Groskorth, a half-German and half-Canadian airman also stationed at the Dartmouth base. Whatever brought Groskorth to Cavendish – besides Hope – the time spent there obviously meant something to him too. While he was there, he bought a copy of *Anne of Green Gables*, in which he wrote a note to his parents asking that they be sure to keep it for him; he wanted to read it on his return from war.[12]

> *12 September 1942*
> *A lovely day and everyone busy. Started knitting a little red suit for a 2 yr old boy. Cecil came for Mother in the evening and got her home. A big relief to me.*

Myrtle had taken in her mother with a good heart, but by the summer, she was finding it difficult. "Mother in not very sweet humor and my nerves pretty much on edge," Myrtle wrote one day. "My nerves a wreck," she noted on another occasion. Her half-brother, Cecil, must have gotten wind of it because he came to Green Gables and informed Myrtle that he would be taking Ada back. It was a relief to Myrtle – but this did not mean that she had to accept that Cecil was a better caregiver than she was. When next she visited her mother at Cecil's place, she reported to her diary, "She was sitting up all the afternoon. Talk about flies."[13]

> *5 November 1942*
> *A lovely fine day and not very cold. Had two* RCAF *boys come in just as I had finished washing the dinner dishes. Gave them dinner. Almost finished another dress. War news better. Wm Robinson died in Hospital.*

Myrtle and the girls had closed the tearoom on Labour Day, ending their commitment to the park for another year. Anita and Pauline left soon after for work in Ontario – stopping on the way to see Lorraine, who had transferred to Rimouski, Quebec. With Ada and now the remaining girls gone, the Webb home was the emptiest it had been for decades.

Or it would have been, if not for the war. Even with the tearoom and golf course closed, a steady stream of off-duty fliers visited Green Gables. Myrtle and Ernest's thirty-seventh wedding anniversary was interrupted by the arrival first of four airmen from the RCAF, who stayed for lunch, and then by the arrival of two from Britain's Royal Air Force, who stayed for tea. One day, three members of the RCAF Women's Division stopped by, and on another, three Royal Air Force airmen out on the golf course got caught in the rain; Myrtle fed them tea and cookies. "Homesick nice English lads," Myrtle wrote of yet another group.[14]

They undoubtedly chatted about the war. After the summer's disastrous Canadian-led raid on Dieppe, news turned markedly better for the Allies that fall. The Russians held Stalingrad from the Germans at great cost, the Americans and British landed in occupied North Africa, and the Japanese sustained heavy losses at Guadalcanal. For the first time, Myrtle was able to report, "War news grand."[15]

> *25 December 1942*
> *A lovely day and we opened our gifts from the family. Ernest got three new books and some nice gifts that he needed. I got a book*

*from Marion & Murray. Sugar bowl & 1 lb sugar from Anita and a pair of gloves from the girls. Lorraine gave me a slip and perfume and snap Album. Keith a picture "Mother" and stockings. Stationary from Enid and Readers Digest from Elaine. After a nice chicken dinner we had a sleigh ride, called at Miltons Lornes and Alecs.*

The kids were still away, the world still at war, yet this Christmas, the holidays felt so much brighter to Myrtle than they had during the low point of Christmas 1941. Myrtle herself noted one reason for the change, stating on New Year's Day, "War news better than at this time last year."[16] But beyond that, her minimalist diary is not a fine instrument for explaining the contrast. Perhaps it was that she and Ernest were reasonably healthy at the moment, that she did not have to care daily for Ada, and that she was not worrying about Maud or Marion. Or perhaps she was just finding joy in small pleasures – such as a pound of rationed sugar, as precious a gift in wartime as the bowl to put it in.

# 1943

*5 February 1943*
*Mild. Mother fell on cellar steps and broke ankle. Anna, Mabel Stewart, George & Reg came to my assistance. Phoned Dad. He came home in evening. Some day.*

This was Lorraine's writing. Luckily, she had arrived back on the Island two weeks earlier. (Her mother had written, "We are quite happy with one of our family home for a while.")[1] Myrtle was eventually taken to the Charlottetown Hospital and ended up being admitted for an entire month. Lorraine took over all the household tasks, including the diary.

Myrtle recuperated slowly. She did not lose the cast until late March, could not put a shoe on her foot until late May, did not have the last bandage removed until almost July.[2] But somehow, it did not get her down as past convalescences had. Lorraine's early diagnosis described her mother's entire recovery: "Mother in great cheer but ankle awfully sore."[3]

*17 May 1943*
*Rained but we washed and got most of clothes dry in afternoon.*
*Report of Submarines in Straits.*

News of submarines was in the air. That very day, the mayor of Charlottetown, Roy Holman, had proclaimed it "Allied Nations Navy Week" in part because the new HMCS *Charlottetown* was about to be launched. The frigate was to protect the home front and shipping from German U-boats, and Holman thanked "the gallant boys of the Navy ... for chasing and harrying the infamous and deadly wolf packs of Hitlerite submarines forever from the face of the Seven Seas."[4]

This entry was Myrtle Webb's second reference to U-boats in the Gulf of St Lawrence that month. Where she got her information is unknown: newspapers and radio were understandably wary of reporting sightings, for fear of inciting panic.[5] German submarines were actually far less active in Canadian waters in 1943 than in '42 or '44. But Myrtle's earlier reference had in fact closely coincided with what, after the war, was discovered to have been a daring German mission to have the *U-262* surface off the Island's North Cape and to pick up escaped soldiers from a prisoner-of-war camp in Fredericton, New Brunswick. The prison break failed, but the U-boat did arrive and await escapees.[6] It is impossible to know whether Myrtle's entries refer to sightings that were accurate. But it was only natural that Maritimers, out of harm's way for the most part, looked out over the waters and thought that they spied the war just below the surface.

*10 July 1943*
*Fine then clouded over then cleared up lovely and Pauline and Heber were married at 1 PM on the lawn. Both looked very nice. Enid and Reuel came out early. They helped a whole lot with final fixin's and everything went very well. The Webb family from Carleton got up in good time. Rev DK Ross married them. Ina and Louise stayed up.*

Even before his marriage to Pauline, Heber Jones had become part of the family. He had worked at the national park since 1939, often helping Ernest with projects and often staying for mealtime. Myrtle had spoken of him in the diary 170 times already – rarely mentioning Pauline

Figure 39 | Green Gables Golf Course, 1942.

Figure 40 | Wedding of Pauline Webb and Heber Jones, Green Gables, 1943.

in the same sentence. The first indication that they were a couple, let alone planning to marry, was just a few days earlier, when eighty-five people had attended a shower for Pauline at Green Gables.[7]

That summer was, like the one before it, more of a private, family summer than the Webbs had experienced of late. The Parks Branch decided to keep the golf course closed for the season because it had lost so much money the year before. Although the agency relented in the second half of the summer – opening nine holes expressly to accommodate the 6,000 airmen and other members of the forces on Prince Edward Island – the course never got busy. With the course's revenue for the season barely $300, the greens were always in the red.[8]

Figure 41 | The Webb family, Green Gables, c. 1943. *Back row:* Anita, Lorraine, Keith, and Pauline. *Front row:* Louise, Myrtle, Ernest, and Ina.

The Webbs were able to plant a garden and to do their own papering and painting projects around the house – and they even seem to have kept a few boarders for the first time since the park came in.[9]

At various times, particularly in August, there were, as Myrtle would say, "a good many around." These visitors included Islanders making the most of a sunny day, Maritimers enjoying nearby places during the war, and servicemen from the Summerside airbase being dropped off fifty at a time by the summer bus service. It was busy, but it was manageable, and Myrtle's diary does not evince the sense of her being hurried and harried as it once did.[10]

*[1–]22 September 1943*
*September a lovely month. Had two bad storms but for the most part wonderful harvest weather. Keith sold out on the 9th all but farm and got the mortgage from Mrs Lowther and is finished with her for all time we hope. Ina & Louise came up Sept 9th. Keith and Anita left for Toronto this morning so we are alone again.*

Figure 42 | Louise and Ina Webb on Green Gables Golf Course, c. 1943.

"Keith has decided to make a change," Myrtle had written in mid-August, "and we may have the children for the winter."[11] Since the death of his wife, Margaret, he had been running himself ragged keeping up the North Carleton farm as well as raising Ina and Louise, and he had concluded that he should start over in Ontario. He would go on ahead while his parents took care of the girls.[12]

The decision led to a permanent falling out with Margaret's mother and Myrtle's long-time friend, Ellice Lowther. The quarrel was over Keith selling what had once been Ellice's family farm; that he planned to move her granddaughters far away undoubtedly didn't help matters. Although Myrtle and Ellice had been important to one another for at least forty years, Myrtle spoke only of "Mrs. Lowther" a few times in the diary thereafter. It would take Lowther's death in 1949 for Myrtle to refer to her again as "Ellice."[13]

Now, Ernest and Myrtle – sixty-two and sixty – were parenting small children again. For their part, Ina and Louise – eight and seven – took it all in stride. They were already close to their grandparents and had often visited them at Green Gables. What's more, their recent position had not been ideal. "We had been living in a dead-end road in North Carleton," Ina recalls, "No electricity, no car." It was a four-kilometre walk to school each day. And they had a father who knew only how to work. They remember him standing them on chairs by the sink, showing one how to wash the dishes and the other to dry, before he headed out to the barn.

Now, they had two grandparents with time to dote on them. They also had aunts. "We were blessed with very wonderful aunts," Louise says. Green Gables was a better home and, in some ways, a better situation.[14]

*30 October 1943*
*Mr Coffin took me to Hunter River this morning about my bond in the 5th Victory Loan. Got a box of cookies. Cleaned the house in afternoon and made a cake. Girls good and very busy. Hockey games started at Maple Leaf Gardens to-night. Maria Matheson has had a stroke. Dad has a good many outside windows on.*

With children in the house, life at Green Gables picked up again. Ina and Louise were happy to be attending Cavendish School; rather than a long trudge, it was just a short walk through the Haunted Woods and over a stile that Ernest had made especially for them. Louise recalls getting into trouble with the teacher one day for taking the Webbs' bulldog, Nickey, to school to show off to her new friends.[15]

*14–18 December 1943*
*Got telegram from Chester. Chester and Stuart arrived Friday night at Hunter River with their Fathers body. Jim Andrews brought the body over Sat morning the 18th. Had Annie Earl for two days. Funeral here Saturday afternoon the 18th. Desperately cold all week. Mr Coffin helped Dad in the trips to Hunter River. Rev Buntain of Clifton was the officiating clergyman, Mr Coffin assisting. Jim Campbell came.*

Eighteen months after L.M. Montgomery's death, her husband, Ewen, followed her. He had been living in an assisted-care facility in Toronto. Like Maud, he was brought home by train to Prince Edward Island and given a wake at Green Gables – "the old farm house which figured prominently in the Anne stories," as the *Charlottetown*

*Guardian* put it. Unlike Maud's funeral, his was held there too, for it was a smaller affair than hers had been. He was buried in the Cavendish Cemetery beside his wife.[16]

Ina and Louise have a vivid memory from that time. Ewen was being waked in the sitting room, which is in the southwest corner of Green Gables. Before the ceremony, the girls crept upstairs to what is now "Marilla's room," directly above, and peeked down on him through the hole for the stovepipe. There, in the casket, sitting on Ewen's chest, was a cat, unsuccessfully seeking warmth. The girls were mortified and ran off to tell their grandmother. But Myrtle was busy getting things ready and told them to shoo it away themselves. Louise, the youngest, got the job.[17]

## 1944

> *8 January 1944*
> *Busy all day. Eric & Alvin came up to coast and stayed the evening. Ina and Louise just about reached the limits. Lorne & Mary here until 11 PM. Tired? Oh no.*

Myrtle and Ernest were kept busy keeping their granddaughters busy that winter. Fortunately, Keith had sent the girls skis for Christmas. Ernest took the horse and sleigh to Hunter River two days before Christmas to pick up the skis and "froze his nose," according to the diary.[1] When Louise saw the gift, she realized that there was no Santa Claus, as the card was in her father's handwriting.[2] Ina and Louise spent the winter skiing and sleighing and being taught by Myrtle how to knit and quilt.

Beyond taking care of the grandchildren, there was not much that needed doing. Myrtle washed the clothes, and Ernest hung them to dry in the golf course clubhouse. They received letters from each of the kids every week, and Myrtle wrote back in return. They resurrected Sunday night singsongs in the kitchen, presumably for the grandkids. But otherwise, life was slow. "Washed and ironed so have nothing to do for a week," Myrtle wrote one day in early April.[3]

The only exciting news was that Lorraine's job in Ottawa was wrapping up and that she was moving home. Louise recalls her eight-year-old self sitting and knitting on the couch under the stairs in the kitchen, constantly looking down the lane, restlessly waiting for her aunt to arrive. She kept dropping stitches, to her grandmother's growing exasperation, until Lorraine drove in.[4]

> *19 May to 6 June 1944*
> *Fine to-day. Lorraine cleaning the S.East room and her own. Pretty busy from this time on until I started my trip to Ontario with the two girls, Ina and Louise on the 30th. Went to Pickering for a week. Rome was captured on June 4th and the invasion started on June 6th.*

Perhaps, by 1944, Myrtle was scared to jinx things by reporting war news. Perhaps the war was most on her mind when young airmen visited Green Gables, tourist season having become war season. Or perhaps she was just weary of such news. Whatever the reason, this entry that reports the Allied capture of Rome and the D-Day invasion of Normandy was her first mention of war so far that year.[5]

In January, the Webbs had received a letter from Keith, who was in Pickering, Ontario, managing a farm owned by E.L. Ruddy, recently retired as the leading advertising man in Canada.[6] Keith announced that he was soon to be married – and asked his parents to tell his girls. His new bride was Ethel Swindlehurst, who worked for Marion helping to care for a household that included Marion's deaf mother-in-law and, for a time, her daughter, Pat. "Dad found someone who would be good with the girls and married her," Louise says now.[7] She and her sister would come to like Ethel, but at the time, they had never met her – indeed, never heard of her. So at the end of May, Myrtle accompanied the girls on the train to Ontario, where they would start their new life and meet their new mother.

> *27 June 1944*
> *A lovely day. Girls washed. I did a little bit of everything. Lorraine made 3 pints of wild strawberry jam. We went to Rustico for fish, got an 8 lb fish for 40c went in to Alfreds on the way home and fixed Annie up for the night. Rubbed her and bathed her.*

With its focus on food, and with no word of war or the park, one might mistake this as an entry from ten or twenty years earlier. But, of course, food had also changed at Green Gables. Even if Myrtle and Ernest were young enough or if the children were around enough or if the need was great enough to forage for food, the Webbs were not allowed to gather food from within the park's boundaries. In 1924, Myrtle had written of gathering smelts, perch, trout, gaspereau, clams, strawberries, raspberries, blueberries, cranberries, and apples from their immediate surroundings. But this year, she mentions only these wild strawberries (which they may well have bought) and one feed of clams (which, beyond the tide's high-water mark, were not residents of the park). The Webbs owed their way of life now more to the imaginary world of Anne, and to everything that it had wrought, than to their real-world surroundings.

> *9 August 1944*
> *Lorraine and Harold Vessey married. We had a nice wedding in the church at 6 PM. A perfect day all day. All the invited guests here except Heber and he went to Kentville this week to an Odd Fellow convention and couldn't get back in time. Terry a darling and loved by all. Lorraine & Harold going to Keiths and Marions and Niagara. We have had a very little rain lately and fields are getting very dry and hard.*

A month earlier, Pauline had given birth to her first child, Terry, who was a darling. How do we know? Because Myrtle said so. Often. "Little Terry a darling." "Terry a darling, is growing and so happy." "Terry is a darling." "Terry is a darling." "Terry is a darling and has grown so."[8] It was not very descriptive writing, except by its insistence.

Lorraine's new husband was, by comparison, a dark horse in the diary. Myrtle had referred to Harold Vessey of York only once previously, when he had come with his mother to dinner at Green Gables a year earlier; she had never written his name and Lorraine's together. When the Webb children were younger and at home, the diary had inadvertently traced their blossoming courtships, but now, with them living away, it could report only the results. Lorraine's previous boyfriend, Arthur Wright – "the boy" – had been cool to her when he had come home from Chicago at Christmastime in 1938. "Grand to have Art here," Lorraine told her diary, "but oh, things are different." She did not know why, and it took her two years to find out. When she was living in Ottawa late in 1940, he visited, "and we found out what was what at last." She moved on.

Two months after Arthur's visit, she told of seeing another Islander in Ottawa: Harold Vessey.[9]

(And still Lorraine and Arthur's story was not yet over. After almost thirty years of marriage to Harold, Lorraine became a widow. A decade later, when she was in her mid-sixties, she again met Arthur, now a widower. And she married him.)

Lorraine and Harold had planned to marry on the front lawn of Green Gables, but they were bumped that day by a golf tournament.[10] This is surprising given how quiet the golf course was in 1944: the Parks Branch continued to run it on a low wartime ebb and so kept just nine holes open. In fact, the Webbs may not have opened the tearoom that summer at all; Parks Branch correspondence suggests as much, and Myrtle's diary makes no mention of feeding or registering people or selling books.[11]

The day after this entry, Myrtle went up to Bayview to visit her eighty-two-year-old mother and found her failing and eating little. Ada lasted only a couple of more weeks. Myrtle was with her at the end: "It was pretty terrible. We did what we could and came home around 10 PM."[12] Ada was buried in the Cavendish Cemetery, forty-eight years after bringing Myrtle back to the community.

A birth, a wedding, and a funeral. After so many summers defined by tourism and farming, these events were what defined the Webbs' summer of 1944. Myrtle and Ernest were fortunate to have the freedom and time to be present for these family milestones. But it also signalled that, between the war and their own advancing age, they were not so intrinsic to the park's running as they had once been.

> *17–18 September 1944*
> *We got away on our trip at about 2:30. Didn't have long to wait at the boat and got to Moncton and settled in a not too warm cabin by dark. Called Mrs Rain Keith on 'phone and we had dinner there on Monday and spent a few hours looking around. Saw Gertrude Corey Perry and Soph McKnight. Saw the place after being away forty-two years.*

Havelock, New Brunswick, was only a short ferry ride and a couple of hundred kilometres from Cavendish. But this trip was Myrtle's first since the beginning of the century to the place where she and Ada had once lived. It may well have been precipitated by Beatrice Keith's visit to Green Gables in 1941, when her son was training in Summerside. In Havelock, Myrtle visited old haunts, caught up with the Keiths and old childhood friends, and undoubtedly thought of her late mother. "A wonderful trip," she declared on her return.[13]

*28 September 1944*
*Pouring rain and Ernest fell when bring in the ice, slipped on the slope by Club House and tore the ligament of his left arm. Mr Coffin took him to S.Side to see Dr Claude. Just poured rain all day. Grant away all day.*

Ernest's accident accentuated the degree to which, at this stage of life, he and Myrtle were increasingly relying on others rather than the other way around. Rev. Eric Coffin, inducted as minister of the Cavendish church a year earlier, had become their regular chauffeur when they needed to get to Charlottetown or Summerside. Superintendent Ernest Smith still came to Green Gables regularly for meals but also came with food and gave them drives as well. Likewise, "Grant" – the warden of the park's east end, Grant MacCallum – had become a close friend of the Webbs in the past few years, helping them whenever he could.[14] Other park staff helped Ernest with work on the house, putting in some hay, and getting the wood home and in. Not only were the Webbs now doing less for the park, but they were also growing somewhat reliant on its staff.

*23–25 November 1944*
*Howard Hurst & Fred Hussey P/O came in the evening for a four days stay for Howard, two for Fred. Weather not very good on the 24 & 25 but the boys played golf on the 25th in the rain and wind. Jack & Mary down this evening & Jack & Dad took Fred to Hunter River at 10 PM.*

Earlier that fall, Anita had been offered a job as a cook at Knox College in Toronto at $50 per month, so once more she had left, and once more Ernest and Myrtle were without any of their children at home. With the house so big and them alone there, they occasionally took in visitors in 1944. Sometimes, as on this occasion, it was servicemen they had gotten to know. Other times, it was just someone who had contacted them asking about Green Gables' availability. "Col Dodge and wife" had stayed for ten days in September, and even when they left, all that Myrtle knew of these "very quiet nice people" was "think maybe they were bride and groom."[15]

Howard Hurst was most likely a twenty-two-year-old from Sarnia, Ontario, the son of a veteran of the First World War, who had enlisted in the Royal Canadian Air Force in 1942; if so, he lived for another six decades.[16] Fred Hussey may have been the same airman who took an RCAF meteorological observer's course in Toronto earlier that year; if so, what became of him is unknown.[17] All we know for sure is that these two chose, as a brief respite from the war, to golf at Green Gables on a wet, windy, and near-freezing day in November.[18]

*31 December 1944*
*s. A fine day but roads heavy. Got a few letters written in evening. Its been a long hard year for many many people the world over.*

Although Allied forces had made great advances in 1944, it had indeed been a hard year the world over. But Myrtle may also have been thinking closer to home. On 19 December, she and Ernest had received a letter from Marion and Murray telling them that their eight-year-old, Ian, had died a week earlier. "A terrible shock to us," Myrtle told her diary, "as there just wasn't any particulars." The next day, Rev. Coffin received a letter with more details: Ian had died of pneumonia after only a night's illness. On Christmas Eve, Murray sent the Webbs a cheque for tickets to come to Toronto, but as Myrtle wrote, "[H]ow can we leave here" – they were immobilized with grief. Although friends invited them out for Christmas Day, Myrtle and Ernest chose to stay home alone.[19]

# 1945

*12 March 1945*
*12A. A frosty morning and chill wind all day. Ice in the Gulf solid. War news good these days for us but not so good for Hitler. Ernest went up to the Hall to help them fix up for a concert on the 15th.*

Myrtle and Ernest mostly just kept the fires on that winter and mourned the death of their grandson. Life brightened up only when one of the kids visited. Pauline, Heber, and Terry – the darling – came for a day in early January, and "'twas mighty good to have 'em." Keith and his new wife, Ethel, arrived from Ontario in February; they snowshoed and just stayed around Green Gables for a week. Again, "Pretty good to have them."[1]

Time helped the Webbs to weather the loss of Ian, and by March there were signs that they could imagine a brighter future. In Europe, German forces were collapsing between Allied forces to the west and Russians to the east. And in Cavendish, Myrtle took note of the first arrival of birds to a degree that she never had before – spring sparrows one day, robins the next, blackbirds another.[2]

> 8 May 1945
> *The war in Germany is over and has been celebrated all across Canada. Halifax had a real riot and millions of dollars worth of damage done in the city by a drunken mob of hysterical people. Mr & Mrs Ben Woolner here in the afternoon. I put out a wash in the morning, and Howard Hurst arrived around 5:15 PM. Pretty near all in to-night. My feet terribly sore.*

One might think that the run-up to victory in Europe would have been a period of mounting elation for the Webbs, as they awaited confirmation of the good news. But April and early May had been tense, for reasons both political and personal. First, there was the stunning news mid-month of US president Franklin D. Roosevelt's passing; Myrtle devoted a full three days of the diary to his death and burial. "A shock to the States and the Allied World ... He gave his life for his country and his friends." Then at the end of the month, she and Ernest got word that Marion had been very sick all month – "but they didn't tell us" – and was in Toronto General Hospital. "Both of us wrecks." Their oldest child started to improve only in early May.[3]

By comparison, the war news in this period was good – almost too good to be true. Myrtle refused to build up hope. "A rumor started that Germany had quit fighting but there is no truth in it, not yet," she wrote in late April. Then she noted, "Hitler reported to have died on May 2nd but no one is sure of that." (He had, indeed, committed suicide on 30 April.) To be on the safe side, even when word came on 7 May that the war with Germany was over, she stated that this news was "not official." Only on 8 May – Victory in Europe (VE) Day – did she submit to relief. The Webbs must have been particularly happy to have their young RCAF friend Howard Hurst there to celebrate the occasion with them. But the next day, back to her cautious self, Myrtle reminded her diary, "For Britain and Canada there is still the war in the Pacific to finish with the Americans."[4]

*11 June 1945*
*Monday washed and Anita ironed and she & Dad painted the kitchen and we went to Mayfield to vote for McKenzie King. Austin Laird refused Nan a vote but McKenzie King is in anyway. We went to Town.*

Life was returning to normal at Green Gables. The Webbs were doing their regular June spring cleaning and fixing up the house. They were voting Liberal, helping William Lyon Mackenzie King to win his sixth federal election. And Anita was back home from Ontario for another summer – even if she had stayed away so long that her Island residency was contested at the polling booth.

*4 July 1945*
*A perfect day. Anita took car to S.Side and Una came up with me for the day. We all went to Rustico to see the play "Peg." Twas good. Not much happened the rest of week. Anita keeps the table in straw-berries. Letters from Lorraine telling us that alls well and Donna is very lovely.*

The Second World War would not be over until September, but you would never know it from the diary. After VE Day, there is no reference to the war again – no nuclear bombing of Hiroshima and Nagasaki, no Victory over Japan (VJ) Day, no formal surrender.[5] The brisk tourist trade that summer suggests that Myrtle was far from the only person intent on moving past the war. Prince Edward Island National Park had a record season, its 48,000 visitors almost doubling the numbers from just two years earlier. The park was now the fourth most popular in Canada.[6]

As this entry suggests, the busyness of the park did not translate into busyness for the Webbs – or at least the diary offers no indication of that. Myrtle does not write about any park-related work that she or Ernest did that summer. Instead, she focuses on family events, such as the birth of Lorraine's baby girl, Donna Marilyn Vessey, and a visit from Pauline's family. Myrtle did operate the tearoom, but we know that not from the diary but from a visitor to the Green Gables clubhouse: Wanda Wyatt of Summerside wrote in her own diary that when her group stopped in at the clubhouse grounds after a dip at the beach, "Mrs. Webb gave us a table and chairs under the trees and we certainly enjoyed our meal."[7] Myrtle had reached a place in her life when she no longer let tourists, the park, or the pressure of making Green Gables Green Gables overwhelm her.

> *20 September 1945*
> *Our fortieth anniversary. We took the Bus to S. Side and looked around the stores. Got home around 5 PM and Ralph Burdette took us to Town to a show "I'll be Seeing You." A very nice day all round.*

Ernest is often an invisible man in the diary: you know he is there but he isn't mentioned. In fact, Myrtle had not written his name since April – although, to be fair, she had spoken of "Dad" a couple of times. Even on this important occasion, his name goes unstated.

But Ernest's inconspicuousness in Myrtle's diary was of course a product of his ubiquity in her life itself. Even more than when they had farmed, they were always together now. In these later years, she more often speaks of him working around the house, setting the bread, or doing the dishes. (Earlier that year, when she had been sick for a week, she had saluted "Ernest chief cook and bottle washer.")[8] Forty years on, they were more inseparable than ever. "Our" said it all.

> *3 October 1945*
> *Finer in the morning and I did a big washing. Pauline left Terry here and went to the sale at Mt Pleasant with Heber. They got home at 7:30 and Terry was a darling good little boy. Went to the 25 Anniversary supper in the Womens Institute in the Hall at night. 90 sat down at one time. Mary Stewart put on the supper.*

Twenty-five years earlier, when forming a local branch of the Women's Institute, the women of Cavendish had dubbed the branch "Avonlea," in homage to the works of L.M. Montgomery. It was perhaps the last

Figure 43 | Myrtle and Ernest Webb, with dog Nickey, 1940s.

time that the community had been in full control of the association between the author's fictional world and their real one. Since then, the broader world had imposed its own connections.

In one sense, twenty-five years was a long time – enough time to see Cavendish become a major Canadian literary site and tourism destination, to see much of it absorbed into a national park, and to see signs of it transitioning from a subsistence economy to a service economy.[9] But in another sense, twenty-five years was a heartbeat compared to what the future promised. Green Gables and all the land taken over for the national park were now subject to the park system's principle of inviolability and were to be maintained in their present form, free from development or encroachment, for as long as there is a Canada. The landscaping and construction of the park's first years offered an illusion of change, but now the park was to be locked in as it was.

At the same time, the principle of inviolability offered only an illusion of constancy. What had been the Webb farm, for example, was now to be "natural," so every day of every season, nature would be working to reclaim it. But the place was also "cultural" and thus would always have to adapt to changing cultural forces – public tastes, tourism trends, government priorities, and so on – which meant that although the Parks Branch as an agency espoused permanence, its staff members were by necessity constantly making adjustments or even backtracking on decisions previously made.

*19 November 1945*
*Mr Smith came up to-day and told Dad that his job ended on Dec 2nd, also that he had 18 days holidays coming.*

The Webbs were floored by the news. This entry is followed by a three-week silence that Myrtle broke by stating, "Haven't felt much like writing in Diary." She later described this period as a nightmare, in which she and Ernest would wake in the middle of the night and be unable to sleep for hours.[10]

The rationale for the park's notification was simple enough: Ernest Webb would turn sixty-five on 3 December, and Superintendent Ernest Smith was giving him two weeks' notice that he was being retired. But the questions that the retirement raised were not so straightforward. Were the Webbs to keep running the tearoom? Were they to keep maintaining the house in which they lived? Were they even allowed to keep living at Green Gables? On 10 December, the Webbs were given their answer. "Mr. Smith up at noon to tell us that we won't get any more cheques from Ottawa. So it means find another home somewhere."[11]

How did this turn of events catch the Webbs so completely unaware? They knew that Ernest was reaching retirement age.[12] In Myrtle's diary, in her correspondence, even in the memories that the family has passed down, there is no explicit evidence that the Webbs believed, when selling their farm in 1936, that they were promised lifetime tenancy. But they clearly did believe that they had been given assurances – whether from provincial or federal politicians or the Parks Branch itself – that their interests would be taken care of. But these assurances were not on paper. Nor were any of the 1945 communications. The agency relied on Superintendent Smith's personal friendship with the Webbs and had him speak with them directly. As in 1936, the government that dealt with the Webbs preferred not to put its arrangements in writing.

From the Parks Branch's perspective, this was an ideal time to ease the Webbs out. Ernest, after all, *was* of retirement age, and he had suffered a minor workplace injury a year earlier and was showing signs of slowing down generally. The war, by reducing activity in the park, had reduced Ernest and Myrtle's value to the park. What's more, having the Webbs gone would allow the Parks Branch to repurpose Green Gables. Just a month later, in January 1946, the agency's publicity and information director, Robert J.C. Stead, outlined to the head of the Prince Edward Island Travel Bureau, B. Graham Rogers, what was in store for Green Gables. The Cavendish end of the park would have a new warden – "Naturally, he will have to be a returned soldier" – but he would not live at Green Gables. "Our plan is to establish this as a tourist attraction and furnish it ... and carry on a tea-room concession in the building." Since the house would be "open for public inspection," it could no longer serve as a home.[13] This moment in the lull between war and peace was the perfect opportunity for the Parks Branch to reinvent Green Gables as a site devoted entirely to L.M. Montgomery and her fictional world, sweeping aside the vestiges of its real-world past.

> *14–17 December 1945*
> *Got Pauline's letter and started packing this afternoon and with*
> *the help of good neighbours got packed and away by the 18th. The*
> *Community gave us a very nice evening at George McCoubreys*
> *on the 17th and we went back to the old home for our last night*
> *there both very tired.*

The Webbs started moving out only four days after confirming with Superintendent Smith that they would have to. Myrtle called it "one mad rush" before the snow came and blocked the lane.[14] With the help of a few neighbours, they pulled family things out of the attic and had a fire. While a light dusting of snow fell, they sold the coal and coke out of the basement, leaving a light film of black on white everywhere. Heber and Pauline came out from Charlottetown and helped to pack up much of the furniture and books. A chest of bedspreads, quilts, and tablecloths was set aside for Anita. Their friend Rev. Coffin took the piano and the Christmas cactus. "All my geraniums were taken out of the pots and thrown out." Even the dogs had to go. One neighbour took Happy, and another welcomed Nickey. "It seemed more than I could stand when Fenner put the chain on [Nickey]," Myrtle wrote, but she assured Anita that the bulldog would be well taken care of.

The community event at the McCoubreys' meant a lot to them. "The country side in general is up in arms," Myrtle told the kids, and a neighbour had written to the local member of Parliament "about the way we have been used." But Ernest and Myrtle Webb in the 1940s were not Katherine Wyand in the 1930s. They were not the sort to put up a fight. "Its no use," Myrtle wrote, "and we will certainly not give Mr. Smart a chance to fire us again." They came home from the McCoubreys' with a nice note, which was accompanied by a collection of $72 from the neighbours, and spent their final night at Green Gables.

The Webbs took refuge at Pauline and Heber's house in Charlottetown, not knowing for how long or what was to come next. They brought their jam, potatoes, carrots, and beets with them, plus a few houseplants – including Aunt Maud's ferns. Myrtle was terribly worried about Ernest. "Dad seems to have aged so in the last month." He had run himself ragged in the move and now did not know what to do with himself. But Myrtle admitted that she was worried for herself too: "You can[not] have any idea how things have hurt. I don't want to make any mistakes in our next move wherever it might be."

Their old home was a mess when the Webbs drove away from it a week before Christmas 1945, but Superintendent Smith assured them that its condition was fine, as no one would be living there.[15] There is no evidence that Myrtle and Ernest Webb ever visited Green Gables again.

# Conclusion

Green Gables stood empty after the Webbs left. All that remained were a few items donated to the house since the national park had come in, such as L.M. Montgomery's first typewriter and a wreath of silk thread flowers made by Katherine Smart, wife of the National Parks Branch's controller, James Smart.[1] In January 1946, the agency laid out its postwar plans for the park, assuring Islanders that its intention was to recreate the Green Gables site, as it said, "in happy perpetuation of the famous legend."[2] But if the Parks Branch had access to an Architectural and Landscaping Division, it had less direct expertise in – and still fewer funds for – interior design, so no progress was made in furnishing it.

To ensure that tourists and golfers could have a bite to eat, the tearoom was reopened in the house for the 1947 tourist season, the concession given without competition to local hotelier A.B. LePage – nephew of B.W. LePage, the lieutenant governor who had been active in convincing the Webbs to sell. In 1948, A.B. LePage was also granted a concession to rent rooms out to guests.[3] But the situation was clearly unsatisfactory. Both *Anne* devotees and ordinary tourists who visited the site were puzzled as to why they were wandering through a largely empty house that showed evidence of being used as a restaurant and hotel but was otherwise devoid of furniture, staff, and signage.[4]

It was local women who spearheaded a drive to commemorate L.M. Montgomery and *Anne* at Green Gables. The Women's Institutes of Prince Edward Island, the Avonlea branch in particular, launched a public effort to have the house become a provincial museum, with a collection of Montgomery's works and with rooms decorated in

Figure 44 | L.M. Montgomery memorial ceremony, Green Gables, likely 1948.

line with the *Anne* books.[5] Katherine Wyand became a leading voice in this effort, in part because she already knew and was known to staff at the Parks Branch. The agency had no interest in maintaining a provincial museum within a national park, but the pressure of the Women's Institutes convinced the Parks Branch that the site had to be memorialized in some fashion.

As a result, in September 1948, a crowd of 1,500 gathered behind the Green Gables house for the unveiling of a Historic Sites and Monuments Board monument commemorating the life and career of L.M. Montgomery. It was a highly unusual designation, since the board typically commemorates physical *sites* and was expressly not doing so in this case because it did not deem Green Gables a historic site.[6] (L.M. Montgomery's Cavendish National Historic Site, which includes Green Gables Heritage Place, was designated in 2003.)[7] Island women had led the drive, but the four speakers for the ceremony were Premier J. Walter Jones, former premier Thane Campbell, Lieutenant Governor J.A. Bernard, and board member D.C. Harvey – not a woman among them.

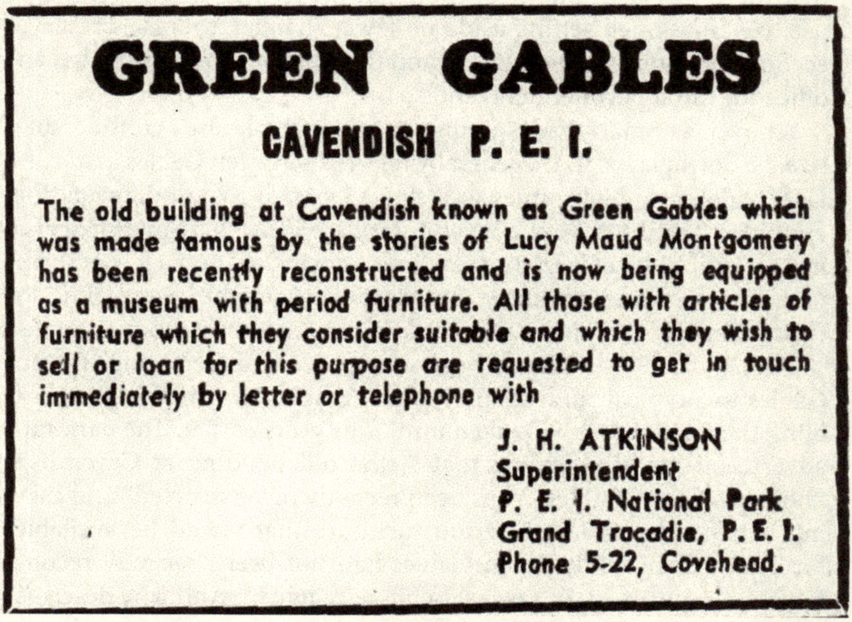

> # GREEN GABLES
> ## CAVENDISH P. E. I.
>
> The old building at Cavendish known as Green Gables which was made famous by the stories of Lucy Maud Montgomery has been recently reconstructed and is now being equipped as a museum with period furniture. All those with articles of furniture which they consider suitable and which they wish to sell or loan for this purpose are requested to get in touch immediately by letter or telephone with
>
> J. H. ATKINSON
> Superintendent
> P. E. I. National Park
> Grand Tracadie, P. E. I.
> Phone 5-22, Covehead.

Figure 45 | Advertisement for Prince Edward Island National Park seeking furniture for Green Gables, 1949.

Nor any Webbs. The family had been instrumental for decades in maintaining Green Gables simultaneously as a working farm and as a literary landmark, a tourist destination, and finally the centrepiece of a national park, and it had been their family home until just three years earlier, but none of the Webbs were invited. Thane Campbell to his credit did note, deep into his speech, "There is no doubt ... the house now known as Green Gables, the former residence of her friend Myrtle Webb and still earlier of her Macneill relatives, contributed many suggestions to Lucy Maud's composite conception."[8] It was the only reference to Green Gables' human history that day.

Within a month of the ceremony, the Parks Branch committed publicly to developing Green Gables as a true tourist attraction. It would be furnished to be a museum focused not on the whole Island but on the time of *Anne* and on the life of its author – that is, essentially the form it still has today.[9] Within internal correspondence, Smart noted that there was also "plenty of room" in the house for departmental use. He envisioned setting aside no fewer than six rooms as reserve accommodations for the warden and the tearoom concessionaire, an office for the superintendent, and so on.[10]

Yet even as Smart was planning to utilize the house's considerable size, he downplayed it. He generally referred to Green Gables as a "cottage" – doing so eight times in a single letter to a PEI politician, for example.[11] Thanks to Myrtle Webb's diary, we know that Smart had visited Green Gables at least thirteen times, staying over on a few of these occasions; he certainly knew that although it might be romantic to classify the big, two-storey house as a cottage, it was far from accurate.

In 1949, the Parks Branch began the process of "restoring" Green Gables to a typical rural Island home – that is, to something resembling the form that it had taken until four years earlier. The park ran advertisements announcing that "[t]he old building at Cavendish known as Green Gables ... has been recently reconstructed" and asking whether anyone had period furniture that would be available for sale or loan.[12] But Green Gables had not been "recently reconstructed" – not at all. It was just being reimagined. And why describe it as a "building" (or a "cottage") rather than what it had so clearly been built for, what it so recently had been, and what it was soon to represent again: a *house* or even a *home*? Having Green Gables sit mostly empty in the late 1940s served a useful purpose for the Parks Branch. It created a gap between the home's actual, lived past and the present, with the result that when the agency was ready to develop the site's interior, it could start from scratch. Or pretend to.

---

For two decades Myrtle Webb had been a faithful diarist. She filled forty to fifty pages of her lined notebooks each year, ending one year and starting the next with just a new page or even just a new line. Other than a compendium entry each August, she was remarkably consistent in jotting something down most every day – or having Ernest or one of the girls do so in her stead. This reliability began to slip in the 1940s, but even in 1945, she wrote twenty-five pages' worth of entries. But leaving Green Gables broke that. Myrtle lost interest in keeping a regular record of her life. She did not give up the diary entirely, but she wrote less in the following nine years than she used to write in one. The year 1946 filled a single two-page spread.

Figure 46 | The old parsonage, Cavendish, undated.

Myrtle and Ernest spent their first winter away from Green Gables in Charlottetown at their daughter Pauline's home. They were angry, hurt, and nursing their wounds – and trying to imagine what a new life in their sixties might look like. Ernest visited the park's superintendent, Ernest Smith, that April, telling him that they were considering moving to Ontario and would be willing to sell their Green Gables furnishings back to the park.[13] Nothing came of this offer. They did go to Ontario the following month and spent the rest of the year moving from one of their children's guest rooms to another.

Then Myrtle turned the page of her diary and wrote on the top of the next, "May 1947 The Old Parsonage."

The Webbs had bought the old Baptist manse in Cavendish. It was just a kilometre west of Green Gables and on the same side of the road. There was only one house between them; Bobby would still be their mailman. Their new lot was smaller, with the house close to the road, perfect for an older couple. And it was genuinely a mirror image of Green Gables; it is said to have been made by the same builder, using the same plan, except with the direction of the stairs to the second floor reversed. Since the rooms were the same size as those at Green Gables, all their furniture fit.

With the help of family and neighbours, Myrtle and Ernest threw themselves into getting the new house set up that May. They put down oilcloth and waxed the floor. They painted and papered. They re-established themselves at church. ("Not many out but it was good to see our friends again.") Myrtle set out rhubarb and discovered some black currant bushes on the property. Ernest planted birch and apple trees, and the two of them planted a garden. On 1 June, they took a walk to the shore and declared Cavendish Beach nicer than it had been for years.[14] The move to the old parsonage was a lovely, if bittersweet, adaptation. Having been exiled from their old home, they ultimately decided that what they most wanted was to recreate their old life as fully as possible, and they did so.

They settled into their new old life. Spring turned to summer, and summer to fall. Family visited and returned home. Pauline and Heber had a boy, Larry David. The Liberals won another provincial election. The Webbs' first winter at the parsonage was cold and stormy, but Myrtle kept busy knitting. Her faithful keeping of the diary fell away again, not from melancholy but simply because life was so quiet. "So little to write about," she admitted, "We do the same thing day in day out."[15]

One thing that changed was that Ernest's health began to decline. He had been quite active for the first year after their move, helping neighbours to pick potatoes and haul ice. But he got sick in spring 1948 and then again in the summer and did not fully recover. The day of the dedication of the Montgomery monument at Green Gables passed without mention in the diary. The Webbs had a "very quiet Christmas all by our lonesome."[16]

In 1949, Myrtle's diary recounted her doing chores that Ernest used to do. His bed was moved downstairs. Myrtle's reports of her

Figure 47 | Myrtle and Ernest Webb, undated.

husband's good days – "Ernest better to-day than he has been," "Dad got dressed and had dinner with me," "Dad sat in the sunporch for awhile" – only called attention to how infrequent these days were becoming. By 1950, the diary had devolved into a list of community births and deaths, mostly deaths. Then, in shaky hand, "May 17th Ernest Cecil Webb at 1:30 AM age 69 yr 5 ½ m."[17]

Figure 48 | Myrtle Webb, with cat Peter, undated.

The memoriam in the *Charlottetown Guardian* recalled that Ernest had come to live with Myrtle in Cavendish in 1907 "on the farm familiarly known as 'Green Gables'" and that after the farm was sold to become part of the national park, he had worked as a warden there until his retirement. "During that period his unfailing courtesy in dealing with the public won for him a host of friends." It also noted that Myrtle had tenderly cared for her husband "during his long and trying illness."[18]

## Conclusion

For the next year, the diary carried on as a register of important events. Lorraine and Harold had a girl, Annie Maureen. Keith and Ethel had a boy, Glenn Allen. And then Myrtle returned to the diary in more regular fashion, noting that she had also returned to Cavendish "after seven months of wondering."[19] She presumably meant "wandering," as she had spent the first winter after Ernest's death visiting the children in Ontario. She had even worked alongside Anita for a week as a cook at Willard Hall, a women's residence at the University of Toronto, and toyed with taking a part-time job there.[20] But undoubtedly, she had also spent months "wondering" – about whether she wanted to be back in the parsonage on her own. When she decided that she did, her spring 1951 essentially reproduced her spring 1947, as she filled her diary with reports of readying her home again. She removed the storm windows and set up a hotbed and planted trees and a garden.

She had plenty of family, friends, and neighbours visit (although, notably, there is never a mention of old Green Gables boarders, who seemed to have lost touch over the years). But for the most part, after a lifetime of living with others, Myrtle was on her own. Coming back from a few days in town that May – "It helped put in some hard days of memories of a year ago" – she realized that she had forgotten her keys and had to climb in through a window. She took it as a personal mission to keep her home's extensive lawn cut. Even after going to the hospital that autumn with a bad back, she returned to the parsonage and spent the winter there.[21]

Myrtle appears to have been content enough, but there was not much to write about in her diary, and she told it so: "Not much to write about."[22] In 1952, the diary once again became almost strictly a place to register major occasions. King George VI died in his sleep, and Princess Elizabeth was proclaimed queen of England and the Dominions in February. Keith and Ethel had a baby girl, Anita Gwen. A local couple got married in June and had a baby in September.

One event that Myrtle did not record that summer was the death of Katherine Wyand – a striking omission, especially given how shocking this death was. Wyand was standing in a field in the national park near her home one summer afternoon, "when observed," as the *Guardian* put it, "to be enveloped in flames." The coroner's jury determined that her death was self-inflicted and that she had likely been suffering what would now be called vascular dementia.[23]

Another year passed. Myrtle had an operation in January 1953 and recuperated at Pauline's afterward – "Enjoyed the winter and maybe helped Pauline some." She returned to the old parsonage in the spring. She removed the banking herself, got the garden planted herself, got the house fixed up herself, and sat back and enjoyed a summer with guest after guest after guest. On 2 August, she celebrated her seventieth birthday with two of her children and eight grandchildren running around. She wrote at the end of the summer, "House lonely for I've had someone here since the middle of June."[24]

Myrtle catalogued the births of a few more babies and then, on 2 February 1954, wrote, "We have had a cold and stormy January." After thirty years, almost 10,000 entries, and over 200,000 words, these were her diary's final words.

But not *her* final words: Myrtle lived for another fifteen years. For a time she ran a gift shop out of the old parsonage each summer, selling local handicrafts, and she wintered with one of her children.[25] She eventually moved to Norval, Ontario, to live with Keith's family and to be close to Marion's family and Anita, who also lived in the community. It is ironic that so many of the Webbs ended up making Aunt Maud's old home theirs, as she had made theirs hers.[26]

Myrtle Webb developed dementia and moved to a nursing home in Milton, Ontario. She died in February 1969 at the age of eighty-five and is buried beside Ernest in the Cavendish Cemetery.

---

The 1930 National Parks Act committed the Canadian state to the protection of parks "so as to leave them unimpaired for the enjoyment of future generations."[27] This promise of timelessness is one of the great attractions of the national park philosophy and one of its great successes. But this timelessness is an illusion. Swimming against the relentless current of culture and of nature itself, Parks Canada must constantly exert effort to maintain wanted elements and to make what it sees as improvements to existing ones.

As a result, Green Gables has experienced constant, incremental change since becoming part of the national park. Much of what was the Webb farm is still dedicated to the golf course, but the course does not have the pre-eminence that it once did. More of the course has been hidden from public view – some of it pushed into the back woods of what had been neighbour Fenner Stewart's property to the west – with the result that less of it runs ostentatiously down to the dunes and beach. A green that originally came almost to the front door of Green

Gables now veers respectfully away from it.[28] The homestead is more dominant generally; generations of fans of *Anne of Green Gables* and its author have obliged Parks Canada to make it more central. In keeping with that, more attention has been paid to the house's immediate surroundings. Whereas for decades the house stood nearly alone, with just a clubhouse and tearoom for company, beginning in the 1990s it gradually reaccumulated a barn, outbuildings, fences, and a vegetable garden. Today's Green Gables more expressly simulates the farm where Anne lived in make-believe and that Maud visited in reality.

Parks Canada's illusion of timelessness has historically run backward in time, as well as forward. To justify parks as the best of Canadian nature, the agency downplayed or outright suppressed the sites' human histories. There was no room in site interpretation for mention of the Stoney First Nation at Banff, or subsistence hunters at Point Pelee, or the Webbs at Cavendish – and certainly no room for the people themselves. Thankfully, the agency has come to accept, and is starting to communicate, that these places had histories before they were parks – Keith Webb was even consulted on the 1990s restoration of the Green Gables barns. The next step will be for Parks Canada to accept, and communicate, that these places have experienced history *since* becoming parks and even *because* they have been parks.

When you visit Green Gables Heritage Place today, your tour starts at the Visitor Centre – a grand structure that cost $10 million to build – which opened in 2019 with Her Imperial Highness Princess Takamodo of Japan in attendance. Effort has been made to position the farmstead in the context of its history. The text of one small panel reads, "Shortly after the publication of *Anne of Green Gables*, tourists began visiting Cavendish and the house that belonged to Ernest and Myrtle (Macneill) Webb. By the 1920s, the Webbs were operating their property, now called Green Gables, as a tourist business, accepting summer boarders and hosting teas on the front lawn." There are several photos of when it was the Webb farm, plus one of Myrtle with L.M. Montgomery in a display about the author's female friendships. The Webbs, however, remain distinctly marginal. A larger panel states, "Because of its [Green Gables'] significance to Canada's cultural history, it became part of the new Prince Edward Island National Park." The vague "it became" utterly obscures the process by which the family assisted in the park's early development or how they lost their longtime home. Ernest and Myrtle's grandchildren were dismayed that there was no mention of the Webbs at the centre's opening.

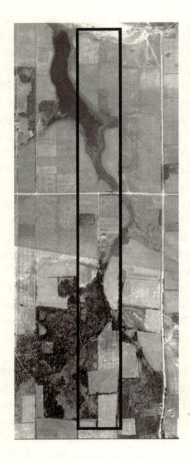

1935                  1958

But perhaps this is only to be expected because Green Gables' real history is so distinct from what is to be memorialized there. Consider this: the Green Gables of *Anne of Green Gables* is one of the most integral settings in all of literature – it appears in the work's title and defines the title character – yet it is barely described in the text. In the 1980s, Parks Canada toyed with repainting the house's exterior to match the book's description of it, but the sole references to a "dimly white" house and its "grey gable end" were insufficient to plan a redesign and violated people's sense of what the house should be.[29] Green Gables Heritage Place is not just a fantasy but a fantasy of a fantasy.

2020

Figure 49 | Photomosaics of the Webb farm / Green Gables in 1935, 1958, and 2020. By 1958, the national park's transformation of the Webb farm was already twenty years old. What had been fields were now golf course or growing back into woods. There was a traffic loop almost to the steps of the Green Gables homestead and a bungalow court on Cavendish Road. In 2020, much of this development remained – although the golf course had been pulled back from both the house and the shore. Despite significant wind damage from post-tropical storms Dorian in 2019 and Fiona in 2022, vegetation is thriving. As the national park moves toward its centennial, nature and development live cheek by jowl more than ever.

Yet the Webbs also helped to create this fantasy of a fantasy. Even as the family planted gardens, hauled ice, produced plays, hosted sing-songs, picked potatoes, cut wood, tramped to the shore, listened to the radio, and grew up or grew old on an ordinary farm on Prince Edward Island, they also welcomed callers, took in boarders, hosted groups and dignitaries, held lunches and campfires, sold books and souvenirs, upgraded their home, built cottages, and ran a tearoom. The story of the Webbs of Green Gables deserves to be remembered because of their importance not to the site's prehistory but to its history. The Webbs made Green Gables.

What the Webbs could not have foreseen is that all their decades of care and curation of the property would ultimately lead to them losing it. This process culminated in their 1945 eviction, but it did not begin with the 1936 sale of the farm or with their mid-1920s decision to take in boarders. Its roots were there from 1909, when they celebrated their purchase of the property with a garden party, where guests "enjoyed a walk through the beautiful path known as 'Lover's Lane' now made famous by the author of 'Anne of Green Gables.'"[30]

# Notes

### PROLOGUE

1 Elaine and Bob Crawford personal papers (henceforth Crawford papers). On Maggie Macneill, see Harold H. Simpson, *Cavendish: Its History, Its People* (Amherst, NS: Harold H. Simpson and Associates, 1973), 245, https://archive.org/details/cavendishitshistoooosimp.
2 This figure is based on the Prince Edward Island National Park settlement list, RG7, series 3, box 12, file 205, Public Archives and Records Office of Prince Edward Island (henceforth PARO); and Cummins Map Company, *Atlas of Province of Prince Edward Island, Canada and the World* (Toronto: Cummins Map Company, 1928), 50–1, https://www.islandimagined.ca/islandora/object/imagined:208774.
3 There are large literatures on *Anne of Green Gables* and Montgomery. Good starting places – besides the novel itself, of course – are Emily Woster, curator, *The Anne of Green Gables Manuscript: L.M. Montgomery and the Creation of Anne*, https://annemanuscript.ca, which has a substantial bibliography at https://annemanuscript.ca/resources-and-links/; the near-definitive biography, Mary Henley Rubio, *Lucy Maud Montgomery: The Gift of Wings* (Toronto: Doubleday, 2008); and Mary Henley Rubio, "Montgomery, Lucy Maud," *Dictionary of Canadian Biography*, http://www.biographi.ca/en/bio/montgomery_lucy_maud_17E.html.
4 *Charlottetown Guardian*, 21 August 1909, 12. The oft-mentioned orchard at Green Gables is referred to as "old" only twice in all the *Anne* books, but the Webbs regularly referred to the grove to the west of their house as "Old Orchard." All cited *Guardian* articles are available at the invaluable Island Newspapers website of the Robertson Library at the University of Prince Edward Island (UPEI), https://islandnewspapers.ca. The *Guardian* was a Conservative organ, and its long-time Liberal competitor, the *Patriot*, has

not been digitized, so this history – like much of the history being researched and written about Prince Edward Island in the twenty-first century – may unconsciously skew Conservative. See Ian Milligan, "Illusionary Order: Online Databases, Optical Character Recognition, and Canadian History, 1997–2010," *Canadian Historical Review* 94, no. 4 (2013): 540–69. Fortunately, the *Guardian* was a far better newspaper than the *Patriot* on local affairs, especially during the 1930s and '40s, and its reporters wrote critically and at length about the establishment of Prince Edward Island National Park, a Liberal project. Heather Boylan, *Checklist and Historical Directory of Prince Edward Island Newspapers, 1787–1896* (Charlottetown: Public Archives of Prince Edward Island, 1987), esp. 54 and 98, https://islandlives.ca/islandora/object/ilives%3A209752#page/1/mode/2up.

5 Name a more famous one. Only the prime minister's official residence in Ottawa at 24 Sussex Drive offers any real competition – except that, thanks to increased security in recent decades, few Canadians can picture what it looks like.

6 A diary such as Myrtle Webb's is typically called an account-book diary, a common format that two scholars have recently characterized as one "that combines traditions of ships' logs, daybooks, commonplace books, and almanacs." Michael Boudreau and Bonnie Huskins, *Just the Usual Work: The Social Worlds of Ida Martin, Working-Class Diarist* (Montreal and Kingston: McGill-Queen's University Press, 2021), 13. There is a large literature on diaries, but most valuable to my understanding of women's, rural, and PEI diaries are Catharine Anne Wilson, "The Farm Diary: An Intimate and Ongoing Relationship between Artifact and Keeper," *Agricultural History* 92, no. 2 (2018), 150–71; Kathryn Carter, ed., *The Small Details of Life: Twenty Diaries by Women in Canada, 1830–1996* (Toronto: University of Toronto Press, 2002); Mary McDonald-Rissanen, *In the Interval of the Wave: Prince Edward Island Nineteenth- and Early Twentieth-Century Life Writing* (Montreal and Kingston: McGill-Queen's University Press, 2014); and Boudreau and Huskins, *Just the Usual Work*. I would be remiss not to point readers to the wonderful Rural Diary Archive project at https://ruraldiaries.lib.uoguelph.ca, which includes over 200 rural Ontario diaries since 1800.

7 Montgomery herself co-wrote a diary with a friend in 1903. See "'... where has my yellow garter gone?': The Diary of L.M. Montgomery and Nora Lefurgey," ed., annotated, and illustrated by Irene Gammel, in *The Intimate Life of L.M. Montgomery*, ed. Irene Gammel, 19–87 (Toronto: University of Toronto Press, 2002).

8 That is about 500 typed pages. By comparison, Montgomery's *selected* journals comprise 1,900 pages of published text, and her complete journals, when all of the volumes are published, will likely be twice that. Montgomery's selected 1889–1942 journals were published between 1985 and 2004. As of 2023, her complete journals up to 1933 have been published. I cite the complete journals whenever possible, the selected journals for the post-1933 period, and the original journals in the University of Guelph Archives when information from this post-1933 period did not make it into the selected journals. I distinguish between Webb's "diary" and Montgomery's "journal" to avoid confusion. But as Kathryn Carter states in discussion of the terms, "Any distinctions between the two are spurious, arbitrarily introduced as a way to separate lesser 'diaries' from more introspective and coherent 'journals' ... In practice, both terms are applied to such a variety of texts and styles that attempts at categorization prove fruitless." Carter, ed., *Small Details of Life*, 5–6.

9 Myrtle occasionally writes supplementary information in the left margin of an entry. My practice is to put this material at the end of the reproduced entry, unless it was obviously meant to define the day (e.g., "Easter"), in which case I place it at the beginning.

10 See Annette Pritchard, "Gender and Feminist Perspectives in Tourism Research," in *The Wiley Blackwell Companion to Tourism*, ed. Alan A. Lew, C. Michael Hall, and Allan M. Williams, 314–24 (West Sussex, UK: John Wiley and Sons, 2014); and, for example, Stroma Cole, ed., *Gender Equality and Tourism: Beyond Empowerment* (Boston: CAB International, 2018).

11 And so, for instance, in an overview text such as Eric G.E. Zuelow, *A History of Modern Tourism* (London: Palgrave, 2016), women appear only as guests, not hosts. On women travellers, see, for example, Sara Mills, *Discourses of Difference: An Analysis of Women's Travel Writing and Colonialism* (London: Routledge, 1991); the database Women's Travel Writing, 1780–1840, https://btw.wlv.ac.uk; and Shelagh J. Squire, "In the Steps of 'Genteel Ladies': Women Tourists in the Canadian Rockies, 1885–1939," *Canadian Geographer* 39, no. l (1995): 2–15. Historian Ian McKay's work on the development of the Nova Scotia tourist trade shows the importance of professional women such as Helen Creighton and Mary Black in demonstrating the trade's economic potential for women, but it does not focus on women on tourism's front lines. Ian McKay, *Quest of the Folk: Antimodernism and Cultural Selection in Twentieth-Century Nova Scotia* (Montreal and Kingston: McGill-Queen's University Press, 1994), chs 2–3 and 260–2.

12  On PEI tourism generally, see Alan MacEachern and Edward MacDonald, *The Summer Trade: A History of Tourism on Prince Edward Island* (Montreal and Kingston: McGill-Queen's University Press, 2022).
13  Notably, see Fred Horne, "Green Gables House Report" and "Human History, Prince Edward Island National Park," both in Parks Canada, *Manuscript Report Number 352* (1979), http://parkscanadahistory.com/series/mrs/352.pdf. See also James De Jonge, "Through the Eyes of Memory: L.M. Montgomery's Cavendish," in *Making Avonlea: L.M. Montgomery and Popular Culture*, ed. Irene Gammel, 252–67 (Toronto: University of Toronto Press, 2002).
14  On the Montgomery and *Anne* brands, see Benjamin Lefebvre, "What's in a Name? Towards a Theory of the Anne Brand," in *Anne's World: A New Century of Anne of Green Gables*, ed. Irene Gammel and Benjamin Lefebvre, 192–211 (Toronto: University of Toronto Press, 2010); Lorraine York, *Literary Celebrity in Canada* (Toronto: University of Toronto Press, 2007), 75–98; E. Holly Pike, "Mass Marketing, Popular Culture, and the Canadian Celebrity Author," in *Making Avonlea: L.M. Montgomery and Popular Culture*, ed. Irene Gammel, 238–51 (Toronto: University of Toronto Press, 2002); and Shelagh Squire, "Literary Tourism and Sustainable Tourism: Promoting 'Anne of Green Gables' in Prince Edward Island," *Journal of Sustainable Tourism* 4, no. 3 (1996): 119–34.
15  For histories of Canadian national parks, see W.F. Lothian, *A Brief History of Canada's National Parks* (Ottawa: Parks Canada, 1987); Paul Kopas, *Taking the Air: Ideas and Change in Canada's National Parks* (Vancouver: UBC Press, 2007); and Claire Campbell, ed., *A Century of Parks Canada, 1911–2011* (Calgary: University of Calgary Press, 2011). My own *Natural Selections: National Parks in Atlantic Canada, 1935–1970* (Montreal and Kingston: McGill-Queen's University Press, 2001) tells the story of Prince Edward Island National Park's creation and early development (ch. 4 and passim), but I did not have access to Myrtle Webb's diary.
16  A useful introduction to Canada's rural history is R.W. Sandwell, *Canada's Rural Majority: Households, Environments, and Economies, 1870–1940* (Toronto: University of Toronto Press, 2016). On rural women, see Jodey Nurse, *Cultivating Community: Women and Agricultural Fairs in Ontario* (Montreal and Kingston: McGill-Queen's University Press, 2022). On rural Prince Edward Island, see Edward MacDonald, *If You're Stronghearted: Prince Edward Island in the Twentieth Century* (Charlottetown: Prince Edward Island Museum and Heritage Foundation, 2000). The print version of MacDonald's indispensable book is unreferenced, but a digital,

referenced version is available on UPEI's Robertson Library website, https://www.islandscholar.ca/islandora/object/ir:ir-batch6-2028. Page numbers here refer to that digital version. Also valuable are William H. McNeill and Ruth J. McNeill, *Summers Long Ago: On Grandfather's Farm and in Grandmother's Kitchen* (Great Barrington, MA: Berkshire, 2009); Jean Halliday MacKay, *The Home Place: Life in Rural Prince Edward Island in the 1920s and 30s* (Charlottetown: Acorn, 1999); and UPEI's IslandLives collection of PEI community histories at https://www.islandlives.ca.

17 L.M. Montgomery, *L.M. Montgomery's Complete Journals: The Ontario Years, 1922–1925*, ed. Jen Rubio (Oakville, ON: Rock's Mills, 2018) (henceforth *LMMCJ, 1922–1925*), 4 August 1923, 165. Montgomery borrowed the Macneill diary to read and transcribe in July 1924. Jennifer H. Litster argues that Montgomery allowed the diary's prosaic descriptions of farming, weather, and nature to influence her next novel, *Jane of Lantern Hill*. Jennifer H. Litster, "The Scotsman, the Scribe, and the Spyglass: Going Back with L.M. Montgomery to Prince Edward Island," in *L.M. Montgomery and the Matter of Nature(s)*, ed. Rita Bode and Jean Mitchell, 42–57 (Montreal and Kingston: McGill-Queen's University Press, 2018).

## INTRODUCTION

1 I write "Macneill," but it could as easily be Mcneill, Macneil, or Mcneil – or any of these with an uppercase "N." The spelling varies among branches of the family and even within pages of Myrtle's diary. Myrtle's name on her own wedding invitation is "Myrtle L. MacNeill," but the Webb family has a trunk on which she signed her name "MLK Macneil."

2 Some of the information in this and the next paragraph is taken from genealogical research that Mary Beth Cavert shared with the Webb family. Thanks to Cavert for sharing it with me. See also "Edward Ellis Locke (1853–1937)," Ancestry website. Locke's property can be seen in J.H. Meacham, *Illustrated Historical Atlas of Prince Edward Island* (Philadelphia: J.H. Meacham and Company, 1880), 33, https://www.islandimagined.ca/islandora/object/imagined:208377.

3 The order of events here is hazy. Some sources have Myrtle born in Havelock, but in Canadian censuses, she always gave Prince Edward Island as her place of birth. In the 1891 census, her birth year is given as 1883, but in 1901, it is 1884. In her diary, Myrtle always writes of having been born in 1883.

4 Myrtle Webb diary (henceforth MW), 8 May 1935. The complete diary, with transcription, can be read at https://greengablesdiary.ca.

5 Alexandra Heilbron, *Remembering Lucy Maud Montgomery* (Toronto: Dundurn, 2001), 47, https://archive.org/details/rememberinglucy moooheil.
6 See, for example, Rand McNally map of Maritimes (1924), Cummins Map Company map of Maritimes (1925), and Arthur Edward Elias map of Prince Edward Island (1929), all in David Rumsey Map Collection, https://www.davidrumsey.com.
7 L.M. Montgomery, *The Alpine Path: The Story of My Career* (1917; reprint, Markham, ON: Fitzhenry and Whiteside, 1997), 73, https://archive.org/details/alpinepathstoryooomont.
8 *LMMCJ, 1922–1925*, 4 August 1923, 163. Notably, Myrtle does not appear in the 1903 diary that Maud wrote with friend Nora Lefurgey.
9 L.M. Montgomery, *L.M. Montgomery's Complete Journals: The Ontario Years, 1926–1929*, ed. Jen Rubio (Oakville, ON: Rock's Mills, 2017) (henceforth *LMMCJ, 1926–1929*), 29 September 1926, 78.
10 L.M. Montgomery, *The Complete Journals of L.M. Montgomery: The PEI Years, 1901–1911*, ed. Mary Henley Rubio and Elizabeth Hillman Waterston (Don Mills, ON: Oxford University Press, 1985) (henceforth *LMMCJ, 1901–1911*), 27 January 1911, 348–9, original emphasis.
11 L.M. Montgomery, *L.M. Montgomery's Complete Journals: The Ontario Years, 1930–1933*, ed. Jen Rubio (Oakville, ON: Rock's Mills, 2019) (henceforth *LMMCJ, 1930–1933*), 7 January 1930, 2.
12 Heilbron, *Remembering*, 37.
13 L.M. Montgomery, *My Dear Mr. M: Letters to G.B. MacMillan*, ed. Francis W.P. Bolger and Elizabeth R. Epperly (Toronto: McGraw-Hill Ryerson Limited, 1980), 27 December 1936, 182.
14 Lorraine Webb, cited in Heilbron, *Remembering*, 53.
15 De Jonge, "Through the Eyes of Memory," 255; editors' note in L.M. Montgomery, *After Green Gables: L.M. Montgomery's Letters to Ephraim Weber, 1916–1941*, ed. Paul Tiessen and Hildi Froese Tiessen (Toronto: University of Toronto Press, 2008), 239n20; Irene Gammel, *Looking for Anne: How Lucy Maud Montgomery Dreamed Up a Literary Classic* (Toronto: Key Porter Books, 2008), 156; Paula M. Graham and Fenner S. Stewart to Mrs H.M. LePage, 1974, Prince Edward Island National Park archival papers, Ardgowan National Historic Site, Charlottetown (henceforth PEINP Ardgowan papers).
16 This story was recounted by Macneill family historian Jean Meggison to Louise Lowther. Thanks to Louise for sharing it with me. The O'Leary connection may explain why Ada was teaching up west when she got pregnant with Myrtle.

17 Montgomery spelled her husband's name "Ewan," but he himself spelled it "Ewen." He was Ewen-with-an-*e* in numerous censuses, in his wedding announcement, on his death certificate, and on his gravestone. Strangely, most Montgomery scholars have adopted her spelling rather than the man's own. Gammel, *Looking for Anne*, 79. In Myrtle's diary, he is usually "Mr. Macdonald," but she refers to him twice as "Ewan" (Maud's spelling in her letters) and once, at his death, as "Ewen" (the funeral announcement's spelling). *Guardian*, 17 December 1943, 7. I will use "Ewen" throughout. Thanks to Mary Beth Cavert for sharing with me her now-published "Ew*n M*donald: Ewen with an E, Macdonald with an A," *The Shining Scroll*, 2023, 2–12.

18 Gammel, *Looking for Anne*, 156. Gammel also posits that Myrtle's September wedding may have served as a model for Anne's nuptials in *Anne's House of Dreams*.

19 *Guardian*, 23 September 1905, 5. Myrtle and Ernest were married by Rev. J.G.A. Belyea. See "Belyea, James Gilchrist Abram (1854–1919)," *Dictionary of Miramichi Biography*, https://archives.gnb.ca/Search/Hamilton/DMB/SearchResults.aspx?culture=en-CA&action=0&page=74.

20 In 1909, the Macneills formally transferred the house to the Webbs and, it would seem, gave them a $4,000, fifteen-year mortgage that they would not need to repay as long as they took care of the elderly brother and sister.

21 Montgomery, *My Dear Mr. M*, 27 December 1936, 182. The degree of trepidation that Montgomery felt when first visiting the Macneill farm after the Webbs had taken it over is evident in *LMMCJ, 1911–1917*, 27 September 1913, 113–16. See also *LMMCJ, 1901–1911*, 27 January 1911, 348–9.

22 Horne, "Green Gables House Report," 5.

23 The following description of the layout relies heavily on ibid., 23–32; notes of Horne interview with Anita Webb, 1978, courtesy of Barb MacDonald, Prince Edward Island National Park; and Brenda Dunn, "Historic Research on Green Gables Site, PEI National Park" (1988), PEINP Ardgowan papers.

24 The following description of the house relies heavily on Horne, "Green Gables House Report," 3–13; notes of Horne interview with Anita Webb, 1978, courtesy of Barb MacDonald, Prince Edward Island National Park; and Ina Reed and Louise Lowther, interview with author, 18 August 2021.

25 Parks Canada, "Green Gables Heritage Place," https://www.pc.gc.ca/en/lhn-nhs/pe/greengables/culture.

26 National Parks Branch, 1949 plans for the house, RG84, vol. 1797, file PEI 56.2, Library and Archives Canada (LAC), https://heritage.canadiana.ca/view/oocihm.lac_reel_t10513/289. Much of LAC's microfilmed archival material has been digitized and is available on the Canadiana Héritage

website. When I have located this LAC material on the website, I link to it. If I do not, either it has not been digitized or I have been unable to locate it.

27 New Glasgow, PEI, subdistrict in Canada, *Census of Canada* (1921), https://www.bac-lac.gc.ca/eng/census/1921. There seem to have been a few larger houses in the subdistrict, but they were duplexes or shared between families. The Webbs' home was also the largest of ninety-one homes in a reconfigured census subdistrict in 1931. Mayfield, PEI, subdistrict in Canada, *Census of Canada* (1931), https://recherche-collection-search.bac-lac.gc.ca/eng/census/index1931. Another means of comparison nationally: the Webb home was larger than all thirty models of Eaton's mail-order homes in this era. See T. Eaton Co. Ltd, *Plan Book of Ideal Homes* (Winnipeg: T. Eaton Co., n.d.), https://www.winnipegarchitecture.ca/wp-content/uploads/2014/10/Eaton-Plan-Book-of-Ideal-Homes.pdf; and Les Henry, "Mail-Order Houses," Canadian Museum of History, https://www.historymuseum.ca/cmc/exhibitions/cpm/catalog/cat2104e.html#1222118.
28 *Guardian*, 7 August 1909, 15.
29 Anne E. Nias, "Interviews with Authors," *Saturday Night*, 28 October 1911. The fictional interview is reprinted in full in Benjamin Lefebvre, ed., *The L.M. Montgomery Reader*, vol. 1, *A Life in Print* (Toronto: University of Toronto Press, 2013), 110–13. On the early recognition of Cavendish as a literary shrine, see also Thomas F. Anderson, "With Our Next-Door Neighbors," *Daily Globe* (Boston), 7 May 1911, SM12, reprinted in Lefebvre, ed., *L.M. Montgomery Reader*, vol. 1, 98–100.
30 Ethel M. Chapman, "The Author of Anne," *Maclean's*, 1 October 1919, 102–5.
31 New Glasgow, PEI, subdistrict in Canada, *Census of Canada* (1911), https://www.bac-lac.gc.ca/eng/census/1911/Pages/1911.aspx; New Glasgow and Rustico, PEI, subdistricts in Canada, *Census of Canada* (1921), LAC. On Prince Edward Island in the 1920s, see MacDonald, *If You're Stronghearted*, ch. 5.
32 *LMMCJ*, 1922–1925, 16 March 1924, 225.

## 1924

1 In the diary's later years, however, an opening "S" may mean Sunday, not a south wind.
2 McDonald-Rissanen, *In the Interval*, 99.
3 On the extent to which Canadians were already engaged with general stores a full century earlier, see Douglas McCalla, *Consumers in the Bush: Shopping in Rural Upper Canada* (Montreal and Kingston: McGill-Queen's University Press, 2015). On the early formation and importance of a local

economy in the Madawaska region of northern New Brunswick, even predating the rise of an export economy in the nineteenth century, see Béatrice Craig, *Backwoods Consumers and Homespun Capitalists: The Rise of a Market Culture in Eastern Canada* (Toronto: University of Toronto Press, 2009). For an evocative portrait of a rural store that operated on the Island from the 1930s to '60s in Fredericton, just 20 kilometres from the Webb farm, see Jack Cutcliffe, "My Father's Country Store," *The Island Magazine*, Fall–Winter 2010, 2–9, https://islandarchives.ca/islandora/object/vre:246.

4 The diary is an imperfect tool for piecing together the Webbs' dealings with local stores. For example, there were several stores in Rustico in this era, and although the family came to favour LePage's store, they would have visited others. Also, Harold Toombs was a family friend, making it impossible to know on which occasions "went to Harold's" indicates a shopping trip. Myrtle writes of Lem Wyand having a store in Mayfield in the late 1930s and the McDonalds having one there in the early 1940s; it is unclear whether these ones replaced Toombs's store, to which there is no reference beyond the mid-1930s.

5 MacDonald, *If You're Stronghearted*, 73.

6 *LMMCJ, 1922–1925*, 26 July 1925, 393.

7 In Montgomery's journal, there is a postcard photo identified as "Lake of Shining Waters, Cavendish, P.E.Island." She has crossed out the first four words and labelled it "Pond." L.M. Montgomery journals, University of Guelph Archives, 13 October 1936. See also Chester Macdonald (Montgomery's son), "Green Gables, etc.," letter to the editor, *Guardian*, 5 September 1945, 4. The pond had been stocked with trout in the 1910s and leased to the Cavendish Sporting Club. *Guardian*, 18 June 1918, 2.

8 MW, 15 May 1924.

9 Having created a transcript of the complete diary, I put it through Voyant Tools, https://voyant-tools.org/, a web-based software for analyzing texts. As in this case, it sometimes proved useful in illuminating things about the diary that were otherwise not visible.

10 Heilbron, *Remembering*, 47, 42; Bob Crawford, communication with Lorraine Burr (née Webb) and Donna Burr, 3 April 2014, Crawford papers.

11 Elizabeth R. Epperly, *Through Lover's Lane: L.M. Montgomery's Photography and Visual Imagination* (Toronto: University of Toronto Press, 2007), 68.

12 *LMMCJ, 1922–1925*, 9 July 1924, 263. On the 1923 storm, see Alan MacEachern, "Storms of a Century: Fiona (2022) & Five (1923)," Active

History blog, 3 October 2022, https://activehistory.ca/blog/2022/10/03/32319/.

13 Horne, "Human History," 129. See also MW, 15 August, 29 September, 2 October 1924.

14 Eight hundred cars arrived on Prince Edward Island by ferry in 1923, 1,400 in 1924, and 2,100 in 1925. Robinson, 20 April 1925, Canada, House of Commons, *Debates*, 14th Parliament, 4th Session, vol. 3, 2238; "Tourist Traffic Brought Island $825,000 in 1925," *The Busy East* (Sackville, NB), May 1926, 28.

15 See, for example, Prince Edward Island Motor League, *Automobile Routes with Road Map and Mileage Chart* (1935), 26, https://www.islandimagined.ca/islandora/object/imagined%3A208296.

16 The *Charlottetown Guardian* was inconsistent as to what it called the Webb home throughout the 1920s and '30s. It sometimes referred to the Webbs (e.g., 8 April 1931, 5), sometimes to Green Gables (e.g., 13 August 1926, 8), and sometimes to both (e.g., 8 August 1928, 5).

17 *LMMCJ, 1922–1925*, 9 July 1924, 263.

18 One summer, during a visit from Montgomery, her young son Chester stole back into the Webb patch and stuffed himself and then his shorts' pockets with berries. He was caught red-handed, with juice running down both legs. Heilbron, *Remembering*, 40.

19 Bob Crawford, communication with Lorraine Wright (née Webb) and Donna Burr, 3 April 2014, Crawford papers.

20 MW, 18 September 1924.

21 The earliest reference I have found to "Spud Island" is in the *Guardian*, 23 September 1902, 11.

22 MW, 27 September 1924.

23 The specific examples mentioned are MW, 29 September, 8 October, 9, 21, 27 January 1925. Of course, it is impossible to know with certainty whether money ever changed hands – perhaps Ernest paid Ham $2 one week and Ham paid Ernest $2 the next. But the absence of any accounting in the diary's back pages and Myrtle's use of verbs such as "helped" rather than "hired" certainly suggest that labour was exchanged rather than bought. On rural labour exchange in Canada, see Catharine Anne Wilson, *Being Neighbours: Cooperative Work and Rural Culture, 1830–1960* (Montreal and Kingston: McGill-Queen's University Press, 2022), esp. 5–6. In the Webbs' case, these arrangements tended to be farm-to-farm, never community-wide; the word "bee" never appears in Myrtle's diary.

24 *LMMCJ, 1901–1911*, 27 January 1905, 122, cited in Jean Mitchell, "L.M.

Montgomery's Neurasthenia: Embodied Nature and the Matter of Nerves," in *L.M. Montgomery and the Matter of Nature(s)*, ed. Rita Bode and Jean Mitchell, 112–27 (Montreal and Kingston: McGill-Queen's University Press, 2018), 113.
25 See Deborah Stewart and David Stewart, "Winter Travel," *The Island Magazine*, Fall–Winter 1979, 19–24.
26 MW, 25 December 1927.
27 See Heilbron, *Remembering*, 53, 177–8.
28 Maude Petit Hill, "The Best Known Woman in Prince Edward Island," *Chatelaine*, May 1928, 8–9, https://lmmontgomery.ca/islandora/object/lmmi%3A17408.

## 1925

1 MW, 12 February 1925.
2 *Through the Years: The Women's Institutes of Prince Edward Island, 1913–1963* (Charlottetown: Women's Institutes of Prince Edward Island, 1963), 63, https://islandlives.ca/islandora/object/ilives%3A155577.
3 *History of Stanley Bridge: Hub of the Universe* (Stanley Bridge, PEI: Stanley Bridge Community Historical Society, 1997), 187, https://islandlives.ca/islandora/object/ilives%3A246007; General Assembly of Prince Edward Island, *Annual Report of the Department of Agriculture ... 1928*, 12, https://islandarchives.ca/islandora/object/leg%3A6892-124.
4 MW, 12 March 1925. Admittedly, the evidence that the party was held at the Webbs' house is circumstantial: Myrtle had been prepping food and decorations at home for days previous, she does not mention it being held elsewhere, and theirs was the local house most often used for big events.
5 On the first appearance of geese, for example, see MW, 24 March 1926, 19 March 1927, 12 March 1931, 7 April 1933.
6 MW, 7 March 1925.
7 MW, 27 April, 26 May, 9–10 November 1925.
8 MW, 11 November, 15 December 1925. On the PEI co-operative movement in this era generally and on "egg circles" specifically, see Marian Bruce and Elizabeth Cran, *Working Together: Two Centuries of Co-operation on Prince Edward Island* (Charlottetown: Island Studies, 2004), esp. 57–86. See also Ian MacPherson, *Each for All: A History of the Co-operative Movement in English Canada, 1900–1945* (Toronto: Macmillan, 1979).
9 Examples of these co-operative activities can be found in MW, 19 March 1926, 3 May 1924, 31 January, 4 May, 10 November 1925. See also *History of Stanley Bridge*, 72–81.

10 Bruce and Cran, *Working Together*, 65; General Assembly of Prince Edward Island, *Annual Report of the Department of Agriculture ... 1919*, 71, https://www.peildo.ca/islandora/object/leg%3A7877#page/72/mode/2up.
11 MW, 27 July, 8 August 1925.
12 There has been a long-standing cultural practice of treating menstruation as shameful and something to be hidden. See Lara Freidenfelds, *The Modern Period: Menstruation in Twentieth-Century America* (Baltimore, MD: Johns Hopkins University Press, 2009), ch. 2.
13 Myrtle had mentioned receiving a complimentary copy of it on 1 September 1925.
14 That the Webbs subscribed to the *Guardian* is something of a surprise since it was the Conservative-leaning newspaper and they were proud Liberals. The Liberal *Charlottetown Patriot* would seem a more natural choice. But the *Patriot* was an evening newspaper, so rural folk could not get it until the following morning. Timeliness trumped tribalism.
15 *Guardian*, 3 November 1925, 3.
16 MW, 9 January 1926. This new organ was not their first. Ernest took "our old organ" to Hunter River on 2 April 1926. The week before buying the new one, Myrtle noted that they had received $124.44 on the sale of cream and had paid some debts.

1926

1 MW, 25 December 1925.
2 MW, 10 March 1926.
3 In line with traditional Maritimes usage, Myrtle usually referred to her hooked work as a "mat" (sixty-four times in the diary) rather than a "rug" (just once).
4 MW, 20 February 1926. That he was playing hockey is suggested by the fact that Myrtle made him shinpads that winter. MW, 29 January 1926.
5 *Guardian*, 22 February 1926, 5.
6 MW, 27 February 1926. Myrtle mentioned skating, hockey, and/or the rink seventeen times that winter.
7 MW, 1932, 1942.
8 For example, on 22 February 1934, Myrtle wrote, "Men at ice and here for dinner"; and on 23 January 1935, she recorded, "A good many at the ice today." Ice was a commodity elsewhere, such as Charlottetown, so it is possible that the Webbs and Ham Macneill charged their neighbours for the privilege, but there is no indication of that in the diary. It may have been free as long as you collected

it yourself. Myrtle sometimes referred to Ernest as "helping" to collect ice for neighbours, and at other times, she mentioned that he had collected it "for" them. See, for example, MW, 11, 15 February 1932, 3, 6, 7 February 1933.

9 The work of chopping down trees and hauling, sawing, and splitting the wood was mostly a family affair, with the occasional assistance provided by neighbours. Ham Macneill and/or Peter Murray helped the Webbs with their wood on 23 and 27 April and on 7, 14, and 15 May 1926. Ernest and Keith helped neighbours in turn. See, for example, MW, 20 December 1925, 9 February 1927.

10 As late as 1941, 84 per cent of Island rural homes were heated principally by wood. See Canada, *Census of Canada* (1941), table 11, https://archive.org/details/1941981941FV91949engfra. Thanks to Joshua MacFadyen for the reference and for the discussion of rural fuel use.

11 Mayfield, PEI, subdistrict in Canada, *Census of Canada* (1931), https://recherche-collection-search.bac-lac.gc.ca/eng/census/index1931. There were some 200 radios on Prince Edward Island in the mid-1920s. MacDonald, *If You're Stronghearted*, 133.

12 Anne's disregard for farm animals may have sprung from Maud's own. As she wrote to pen pal G.B. MacMillan in 1905, "I'm going back to the woods now to get some ferns. Want to come? I could make you useful opening gates and chasing cows. There are always cows back there and I'm horribly scared of them!" Montgomery to MacMillan, 23 August 1905, MacMillan fonds, MG30, D185, LAC, https://heritage.canadiana.ca/view/oocihm.lac_reel_c10689/873. Historian Daniel Samson makes a related point in his insightful analysis of *Anne of Green Gables*. The novel is "escapist fiction," he notes. "But much of what Anne escapes from is the banality and drudgery of farm work." Daniel Samson, *The Spirit of Industry and Improvement: Liberal Government and Rural-Industrial Society, Nova Scotia, 1790–1862* (Montreal and Kingston: McGill-Queen's University Press, 2008), 3.

13 MW, 14 May 1926.

14 *Guardian*, 16 July 1926, 8.

15 MW, 30 September 1926. (Note that it was Marion, not Myrtle, writing in the diary at this point.) The Red Cross program in which nurses went to rural schools and performed dental treatments is described in *Guardian*, 30 October 1926, 2.

16 *Toronto Globe*, 9 August 1926, 5. See also *Guardian*, 7 August 1926, 1, where it was reported that at the banquet Myrtle's mother, Ada – "a relative of the authoress" – had delivered a short sketch of Montgomery's life.

17 *Toronto Globe*, 9 August 1926, 5.

18 *Guardian*, 13 November 1926, 4.
19 *LMMCJ, 1926–1929*, 14 August 1926, 69–70.
20 *LMMCJ, 1926-1929*, 29, 9 September 1926, 78, 74.
21 *LMMCJ, 1926-1929*, 3 October 1926, 79.
22 MW, 2 October 1926.
23 Other Island homes were banked with soil (or later, bales of hay), but a year earlier, Myrtle had mentioned Keith hauling seaweed while Ernest banked. MW, 15 November 1926.

## 1927

1 On the telephone in 1920s and '30s Prince Edward Island, see Walter C. Auld, *Voices of the Island: History of the Telephone on Prince Edward Island* (Halifax: Nimbus, 1985), esp. 56–62, 77–82.
2 MW, 17–18 January 1927. See also *Guardian*, 20 January 1927, 8.
3 That Ernest, often with neighbour Clarence Stewart, also occasionally set up new phone lines for people suggests that he had a knack for the job, which may explain why the Webbs got the telephone as early as they did. There is no indication that Ernest was paid for any work on the lines.
4 MW, 26 February 1927.
5 MW, 26 February, 2 March, 1 April, 17 May 1927.
6 MW, 11–12 November 1927.
7 Simpson, *Cavendish*, 163; *LMMCJ, 1926–1929*, 17 July 1927, 143.
8 MW, 14, 24 March 1927.
9 On the frequency of wallpapering, see Gerald Pocius, *Community Order and Everyday Space in Calvert, Newfoundland* (Athens, GA: University of Georgia Press; Montreal and Kingston: McGill-Queen's University Press, 1991), 94–7.
10 MW, 24 December 1926, 14 June, 1, 11 July 1927. Since Myrtle never mentions removing the old wallpaper, it is tempting to imagine the walls of Green Gables as a palimpsest of changing styles. However, on three occasions in the diary, one of the girls writes about wallpapering and specifically notes that the old paper was torn off first.
11 See Dan Malleck, *Try to Control Yourself: The Regulation of Public Drinking in Post-Prohibition Ontario, 1927–44* (Vancouver: UBC Press, 2012). For a discussion of Prohibition on Prince Edward Island, see Greg Marquis, "Prohibition's Last Outpost," *The Island Magazine*, Spring–Summer 2005, 2–9, https://islandarchives.ca/islandora/object/vre:islemag-batch2-726.
12 *Guardian*, 6 June 1927, 7. See Sharon Anne Cook, "Rowell, Sarah Alice (Wright)," *Dictionary of Canadian Biography*, http://www.biographi.ca/en/bio/rowell_sarah_alice_15E.html.

13 Mrs Merle Johnson of Portage La Prairie "wanted to see around Avonlea and Green Gables." The following day, Myrtle reported that Johnson "did up the Anne country." MW, 30 May, 1 June 1927.
14 *Guardian*, 2 August 1927, 6.
15 Marquis, "Prohibition's Last Outpost"; MacDonald, *If You're Stronghearted*, 121–2. Temperance advocate Sarah Wright, who had visited Green Gables a month earlier, was speaking in British Columbia when the PEI election took place and may well have heard the results around the time that she learned that her husband had died in Ontario on the very same day. *Toronto Globe*, 27 June 1927, 2.
16 Bob Crawford, communication with Lorraine Burr (née Webb) and Donna Burr, 3 April 2014, Crawford papers.
17 Rubio, *Lucy Maud Montgomery*, 367, 369–70.
18 *LMMCJ, 1926–1929*, 13 July 1927, 140–1; 19 July 1927, 148; 26 July 1927, 168. On Maud's earlier expressions of concern for Lover's Lane, see L.M. Montgomery, *L.M. Montgomery's Complete Journals: The Ontario Years, 1918–1921*, ed. Jen Rubio (Oakville, ON: Rock's Mills, 2017) (henceforth *LMMCJ, 1918–1921*), 11 August 1921, 330; and *LMMCJ, 1922–1925*, 9 July 1924, 263.
19 *LMMCJ, 1926–1929*, 14 July 1927, 141–2. Montgomery met Baldwin and his wife in Toronto during their August visit. Rubio, *Lucy Maud Montgomery*, 368–9.
20 Thank you to Kyla Madden at McGill-Queen's University Press for making this point so eloquently. Montgomery likewise noted in her journal that Marion "has not been well." *LMMCJ, 1926–1929*, 31 July 1927, 173.
21 *LMMCJ, 1922–1925*, 21, 28 July 1923, 159, 163. On the Webb children's opinions of the Macdonald children, see Heilbron, *Remembering*, 40, 46.
22 Stuart was attracted, in Maud's opinion, to the wrong girls and failed out of medical school before buckling down and becoming a doctor. But it was Chester who was a constant source of heartache: he had a string of behavioural issues, married secretly in 1933, and generally staggered from one personal and professional problem to another. Rubio, *Lucy Maud Montgomery*.
23 Cited in Heilbron, *Remembering*, 45. See also Rubio, *Lucy Maud Montgomery*, 369. Keith never gained Maud's affection in the same way. "He is a boy I never liked," she wrote in 1928. "But he is his mother's only son and she is dear to me." *LMMCJ, 1926–1929*, 23 December 1928, 242.
24 MW, 31 July, 20, 29 August 1927.
25 MW, 3 September 1927.
26 Neighbour George McCoubrey had sprayed the Webbs' spuds twice that summer to fight late blight and rot. The leading recipe of the day seems to

have involved bluestone, lime, and water. Nevertheless, on 26 September, Myrtle mentions "some rot in Green Mountains."

27 MW, 27, 29, 30 September, 3, 4, 5, 7 October 1927. On that final date, Myrtle wrote, "Dad & Keith away as per usual. Both tired."
28 However, that was likely not the full value of the 1927 crop; Keith hauled two more loads of potatoes that winter. The matter is confused by the fact that the Webbs bought a load of potatoes in November 1927. MW, 4 November 1927, 28 February, 24 March 1928.
29 MacDonald, *If You're Stronghearted*, 88. See also D. Bailey Clark, "'Who Wants a Car Anyway?': Improved Roads, Snowplows, and the Transportation Revolution on Prince Edward Island" (BA honours essay, University of Prince Edward Island, 2022), https://islandscholar.ca/islandora/object/ir:24730.
30 MacEachern and MacDonald, *Summer Trade*, 74–84.
31 *Guardian*, 8 October 1927, 9.
32 MW, 3 November 1926, 26 October 1932; LMMCJ, *1922–1925*, 24 December 1923, 189.
33 Phyllis R. Blakely and Diane M. Barker, "Geddie, John," *Dictionary of Canadian Biography*, http://www.biographi.ca/en/bio/geddie_john_1815_72_10E.html.
34 Rubio, *Lucy Maud Montgomery*, 640n101. Rubio mentions a set of six, without making it clear whether all six ended up at the Webbs' home. Myrtle and Ernest later gave two Geddie chairs to Geddie Memorial Church in Springbrook. *Guardian*, 6 May 1948, 3.
35 *Guardian*, 26 November 1927, 15.

## 1928

1 MW, 25 December 1927.
2 MW, 2 January 1928.
3 MW, 27 February 1928. On rural medicine in this era, see Sasha Mullally, "Unpacking the Black Bag: Rural Medicine in the Maritime Provinces and Northern New England States, 1900–1950" (PhD diss., University of Toronto, 2005).
4 *Guardian*, 10 July 1929, 10.
5 Bob Crawford, communication with Lorraine Burr (née Webb) and Donna Burr, 3 April 2014, Crawford papers.
6 MW, 12, 20 March 1928.
7 MW, 3 May, 7 June 1928.
8 MW, 7 May 1935, 19 June 1928.

9   MW, 5 June 1929. On the later occasion, she referred to "Alfred Kayes," but it was likely an error, as there is no record of anyone by that name on the Island at the time. See David Weale, *A Stream out of Lebanon: An Introduction to the Coming of Syrian/Lebanese Emigrants to Prince Edward Island* (Charlottetown: Island Studies, 1998), esp. 6–9; David Weale, "Going to the Country: Lebanese Pedlars on Prince Edward Island," *The Island Magazine*, Fall–Winter 1985, 11–17, https://islandarchives.ca/islandora/object/vre:islemag-batch2-237; and Frank Zakem, *Zakem-Marji Story: Five Generations* (Charlottetown: Frank Zakem, 2006), 56, https://islandlives.ca/islandora/object/ilives%3A468729#page/60/mode/2up.
10  *Guardian*, 5 April 1938, 4.
11  *Guardian*, 11 July 1928, 4.
12  LMMCJ, *1926–1929*, 23 September 1928, 228; 28 September 1929, 290, original emphasis.
13  *Guardian*, 8 August 1928, 5.
14  MW, 17, 25–27 July, 1, late August 1928.
15  MW, August 1928.
16  Born in 1903, and so a generation younger than Myrtle, Elaine Simpson became particularly close to Marion Webb; they would each name a daughter after the other. Rev. Myron Brinton met Elaine while preaching at Cavendish Baptist Church. Even after moving from Cavendish, they returned for many years to cottage there and for Brinton to serve as a summer minister.
17  Simpson, *Cavendish*, 170.
18  MW, August 1929.
19  MW, 12 October, 1–2, 17–18, 24–28 November 1928.
20  LMMCJ, *1926–1929*, 30 December 1928, 243–4.

## 1929

1   MW, 1, 9 February 1929.
2   Sharon M. MacDonald, "'As the Locusts in Egypt Gathered Crops': Hooked Mat Mania and Cross-Border Shopping in the Early Twentieth Century," *Material Culture Review* 54 (2001): 58–70, https://journals.lib.unb.ca/index.php/MCR/article/download/17903/22068; McKay, *Quest of the Folk*, esp. 160–3.
3   *Guardian*, 17 January 1928, 6; 11 July 1929, 7.
4   *Guardian*, 10 June 1929, 10.
5   MW, 13, 14, 24 May, 10, 14, 24 June 1929.
6   *Guardian*, 22 May 1929, 1.

7   None of these expressions, of course, were Myrtle's own. "It's a sneezer" is cited, for example, in Joseph Wright, *The English Dialect Dictionary* (London: Henry Frowde, 1898), 576, https://archive.org/details/cu31924088038421. "Pet day" also appears in the writings of L.M. Montgomery; see T.K. Pratt, *Dictionary of Prince Edward Island English* (Toronto: University of Toronto Press, 1988), 111.
8   *Guardian*, 29 June 1929, 1.
9   MW, 8 August 1929.
10  The accounting can be found at the back of MW's January 1927 to February 1932 diary. For a PEI teacher's salary in 1929, see Leonard John Cusack, "The Prince Edward Island People and the Great Depression, 1930–1935" (MA thesis, University of New Brunswick, 1972), 12.
11  *LMMCJ, 1926–1929*, 22 September 1929, 285.
12  *LMMCJ, 1926–1929*, 22 September 1929, 286.
13  *LMMCJ, 1930–1933*, 3 December 1932, 292.
14  *LMMCJ, 1926–1929*, 22 September 1929, 286.
15  *LMMCJ, 1926–1929*, 24 September 1929, 287–8. On women and electrification in Canada, see R.W. Sandwell, "How Households Shape Energy Transitions: Canada's Great Transformation," in "Energizing the Spaces of Everyday Life: Learning from the Past for a Sustainable Future," ed. Vanessa Taylor and Heather Chappells, RCC *Perspectives: Transformations in Environment and Society*, no. 2 (2019): 23–30, https://www.environmentandsociety.org/sites/default/files/sandwell_02.pdf. Rev. John S. Bonnell, mentioned in Myrtle's diary entry, was a local boy done good. A native of Charlottetown, he had served as a student pastor in Cavendish in 1920 and '21 and would summer there for decades afterward. In September 1929, he was heading off to minister in Winnipeg. Within a few years, he became the pastor of Fifth Avenue Presbyterian Church in New York – called "the cathedral of Presbyterianism" – and in 1943 he began hosting a radio show that drew millions of listeners. Simpson, *Cavendish*, 162–3; Peter Steinfels, "Dr. John S. Bonnell, 99, Is Dead," *New York Times*, 26 February 1992.

## 1930

1   MW, 6 September, 17 October 1928, 27 February, 1 March, 19 September 1930, 3 January 1931.
2   MW, 16 January 1926, 3 December 1932, 22 December 1928, 19 December 1929, 21 December 1935.
3   MW, 10 May 1930.

4 However, it may have taken the Webbs some time to return to Harold's store. After the events of May 1930, his name does not appear in Myrtle's diary for the remainder of the year. But there are references to ten visits to "Harold's" the following year.
5 *Guardian*, 22 March 1933, 3.
6 MW, 10 December 1930. For that matter, Myrtle also reported that Harold's store had suffered a late-night fire in the summer of 1932, and as a result, "Ernest & I had to go to Rustico for groceries." MW, 2 July 1932.
7 MW, 15, 22 June 1930.
8 MacEachern and MacDonald, *Summer Trade*, 82–4.
9 Canada, Department of the Interior, *Prince Edward Island* (1926), 63, and *Prince Edward Island* (1927), 63.
10 MW, 30 April, 16, 19, 21 May, 10, 18, 26, 27 June 1930.
11 MW, 25 June, 4, 22 July 1930. Dunn, "Historic Research," 2, PEINP Ardgowan papers.
12 On Ernest's sister Louise, see *Guardian*, 20 September 1930, 2.
13 *LMMCJ, 1930–1933*, 6 December 1930, 97.
14 This was Montgomery's interpretation. *LMMCJ, 1930–1933*, 6 December 1930, 97. On Laird and Macdonald's stay, see *Guardian*, 23 September 1930, 6.
15 MW, 18, 30 September 1930.
16 MW, 8, 15 October 1930.
17 *LMMCJ, 1930–1933*, 6 December 1930, 98.
18 MW, 29 November, 2, 3, 25 December 1930

## 1931

1 MW, 2, 9–16 February 1931.
2 The quoted prices are from MW, 28 December 1928, 14 January 1930, 21 November, 15 December 1932, 5, 12 February 1934, 25 February 1936.
3 MW, 17 March 1931. For a description of a PEI poverty social, see the *Guardian*, 2 February 1931, 6.
4 MW, 4 August, 25 February, 13 March 1930, 5 April 1931. The hooked mat may have been a gift. But considering that the McGarrys were not friends, family, or even regular boarders – there is no previous mention of them – and that she sent the mat to them by express mail, it was more likely a commercial arrangement.
5 *Guardian*, 8 April 1931, 5.
6 *LMMCJ, 1930–1933*, 8 April 1931, 127.
7 *LMMCJ, 1930–1933*, 18 April 1931, 130.

8 *LMMCJ*, 1930–1933, 26 April 1931, 132.
9 MW, 10, 18, 22 May 1931. This was likely Anita writing.
10 MW, 24 May 1931. This was likely Anita writing.
11 See MW, 20–1 August, 4 September 1931.
12 MW, 9 July 1931. See the number and range of activities throughout July 1931.
13 McNeill, *Summers Long Ago*, 34. There is a reason why cartoonist Seth's book about his father's memories of Prince Edward Island in the Great Depression is entitled *Bannock, Beans, and Black Tea* (Montreal: Drawn and Quarterly, 2004).
14 Rubio, *Lucy Maud Montgomery*, 418.
15 Guardian, 10 November 1931, 10.
16 MW, 1 November 1931; *LMMCJ*, 1930–1933, 31 October 1931, 200. H.S. Bishop was the United Church minister – and drove a car.
17 *LMMCJ*, 1930–1933, 13 November 1932, 280.
18 *LMMCJ*, 1930–1933, 19 December 1931, 207–8.
19 MW, 11 April 1932.
20 MW, 15 April 1932.

## 1932

1 MW, 14 May 1932, 13 February 1935, 1, 3 April 1936. By 1936, Anita was writing her own diary. When noting Hauptman's death, she asked, "Is capital punishment just?" Anita Webb diary (henceforth AW), 3 April 1936, in possession of Brenda Jones, daughter of Pauline Jones (née Webb).
2 See Joshua MacFadyen, "The Fertile Crescent: Agricultural Land Use on Prince Edward Island, 1861–1971," in *Time and a Place: An Environmental History of Prince Edward Island*, ed. Edward MacDonald, Joshua MacFadyen, and Irené Novaczek, 170–81 (Montreal and Kingston: McGill-Queen's University Press; Charlottetown: Island Studies, 2016).
3 Myrtle's diary mentions Keith getting mud from the Sou West River (New London), Campbellton (near Stanley Bridge), "Alf Moores" (Cavendish), and "McEwens" (unknown). MW, 24–26, 29 February, 18–19, 21–22, 24, 26, 30–31 March, 6, 9 May 1932. Myrtle also has Ernest spreading mud on 14 May 1932.
4 MW, 21 March 1925, 27 April 1933.
5 *LMMCJ*, 1930–1933, 9 November 1931, 201; 4, 19 December 1931, 206, 208; 26 February 1932, 231; 12 March 1932, 238; 3, 13 May 1932, 247–8. Myrtle's health was one of Maud's seven "distinct and separate" worries in this period. *LMMCJ*, 1930–1933, 26 February 1932, 231.

6 *LMMCJ, 1930–1933*, 12 March 1932, 238.
7 *LMMCJ, 1930–1933*, 13 May 1932, 248.
8 MW, 18 May 1932.
9 MW, 8 September 1927.
10 MW, 2 July 1932.
11 MW, March 1932.
12 MW, 19 August 1924.
13 MW, 16 September 1932.
14 *LMMCJ, 1930–1933*, 13 November 1932, 275–6.
15 *LMMCJ, 1930–1933*, 13 November 1932, 280. Maud could be self-absorbed, but her concern for Myrtle was genuine. On the first day of 1933, she told correspondent G.B. MacMillan that although two friends had died the previous year, "a third very dear friend, who was exceedingly ill for over a year and whose doctor says she could not possibly recover has made a most remarkable recovery and is quite well again." Montgomery to MacMillan, 1 January 1933, MacMillan fonds, MG30 D185, LAC, https://heritage.canadiana.ca/view/oocihm.lac_reel_c10690/454.
16 *LMMCJ, 1930–1933*, 18 November 1932, 290. With Maud's concern for Myrtle reduced, she did not write of her in her journal for the next year.
17 See MW, 26 October, 1, 21 November, 3, 15, 23 December 1932, among others.
18 MW, 25 December 1932.

### 1933

1 MW, 18 November 1932.
2 MW, 15 January 1941.
3 MW, 7 March 1933.
4 *Guardian*, 19 January 1929, 16; 3 April 1929, 3.
5 MW, 10 March 1933.
6 The Webb-Lowther wedding, as well as their two showers, are described in the *Guardian*, 1 April 1933, 11.
7 *LMMCJ, 1930–1933*, 22 March 1931, 124. Marion's old suitor, Elmer Fyfe, was Keith's best man.
8 *Guardian*, 22 June 1933, 6.
9 MW, 9, 11, 16 May, 6, 8, 14, 26, 28 June, 13 September 1933.
10 The character descriptions are from the play itself. Arthur Lewis Tubbs, *Valley Farm* (Boston: Walter H. Baker & Co., 1903), 2–3, https://vaudeville.library.arizona.edu/wp-content/uploads/azu_ms489_b1_f7_005_w.pdf.
11 MW, 9 June 1936.

12 *Guardian*, 14 July 1933, 1, 3. New Brunswick premier Leonard Tilley, son of a Father of Confederation, congratulated the Italians and particularly their leader, "Mussolini – whose name will go down in history as a man whose outstanding ability and patriotism have brought his country to the forefront of the nations of the world." On the Italians' return flight later that month, one of the seaplanes had a broken water pump and took an unscheduled stop in Victoria, Prince Edward Island. Harry T. Holman, "Italians Land in Victoria," *Sailstrait*, blog, 22 November 2016, https://sailstrait.wordpress.com/2016/11/22/italians-land-in-victoria.
13 MW, 1, 21 July 1933.
14 In 1936, Myrtle noted that the arrival of the *Gaspesia* steamship in Summerside always brought visitors to Green Gables. That same year, the local newspaper noted that forty of forty-one tourists aboard the *Gaspesia* were women. MW, 14 September 1936; *Guardian*, 22 July 1936, 11.
15 LMMCJ, *1930–1933*, 14 October 1933, 323.
16 *Guardian*, 8 September 1933, 8. The *Charlottetown* had been launched in 1931 but was overhauled in 1933.
17 "Big crowd, not much fun for some." MW, 18 February 1935.
18 L.M. Montgomery, *The Selected Journals of L.M. Montgomery*, vol. 4, *1929–1935*, ed. Mary Rubio and Elizabeth Waterston (Toronto: Oxford University Press, 1998) (henceforth LMMSJ, *1929–1935*, 16 September 1933, 18 December 1933, 25 February 1934, 237–42, 247, 255; Rubio, *Lucy Maud Montgomery*, 427–31.
19 MW, 28–30 December 1933, 2 January, 25 February 1934. On that winter, see Charles H. Pierce, "The Cold Winter of 1933–34," *Bulletin of the American Meteorological Society* 15 no. 3 (1934): 61–78, https://doi.org/10.1175/1520-0477-15.3.61; and Environment Canada, "Top Weather Events of the 20th Century," https://www.ec.gc.ca/meteo-weather/meteo-weather/default.asp?lang=En&n=6A4A3AC5-1. Green Gables was a drafty house in a relatively exposed location. In 1940, Lorraine would write in her diary that it was "–4° and blowing a gale. Too cold to hook." Lorraine Webb diary (henceforth LW), 17 January 1940, in possession of Donna Burr, daughter of Lorraine Vessey (née Webb).
20 MW, 14 January 1934.

## 1934

1 At one point, Haszard sold her work at the Island's Tourist Office in Charlottetown. *Guardian*, 1 December 1932, 1.

2   Haszard's mother was a Moore and had two sisters, Amelia ("Amy") and Minnie, who do not seem to have married.
3   LW, 8 September 1939.
4   MW, 30 April 1930.
5   MW, 4 January to 26 December 1933. Quotation from MW, 20 April 1933.
6   Myrtle was happy to report that "Little Harold a very good boy." MW, 17 April 1934.
7   MW, 3 January 1936 (one of the Webb girls, likely Anita, was the author of this entry); *Guardian*, 21 November 1939, 1.
8   "Elmer Blaney Harris," *Wikipedia*, https://en.wikipedia.org/wiki/Elmer_Blaney_Harris. See also *Guardian*, 14 May 1934, 3.
9   See one such handbill for the 1934 *Anne of Green Gables* film at https://www.imdb.com/title/tt0024831/mediaviewer/rm4273135872; and the pressbook at http://auctions.emovieposter.com/Bidding.taf?_function=detail&category_id=9824&Auction_uid1=6237215. See also *Guardian*, 11 January 1935, 3. The Green Gables of the handbill, at least, is based on a 1930s postcard of the Webb home. Photographs of rural Prince Edward Island and of the Webb home were purportedly used in developing sets for the film. *Globe* (Boston), 2 December 1934, 46.
10  Lorraine writes in her diary of playing these sports many evenings in the summer of 1938.
11  MW, 18 July 1933.
12  MW, 20, 28 July, 11, 16 August 1933.
13  This plotting was accomplished using Voyant Tools, https://voyant-tools.org/.
14  Prince Edward Island Motor League, *Automobile Routes*, 26, https://www.islandimagined.ca/islandora/object/imagined%3A208296; MW, 26 July, 26 August, 5 September 1934. Coincidentally, Wyand also had a cottage burn down that August.
15  *Guardian*, 13 October 1934, 13. The report of Marion's wedding shower did not appear until several weeks after the report of her wedding. *Guardian*, 31 October 1934, 6.
16  LMMSJ, 1929–1935, 3–4 October 1934, 305–6.
17  MW, 28 September 1934.
18  MW, 25–30 December 1934.

## 1935

1   On the film's Charlottetown showing, see *Guardian*, 11 January 1935, 3; 14 January 1935, 4. The former article contains the same text as an article in

the *Toronto Globe*, 3 December 1934, 5. This may have been a case of plagiarism or of both papers using the same public relations puffery. As the former article also demonstrates, some advertisements for the film used a sketch of the Webbs' Cavendish home. Myrtle notes that the Prince Edward Theatre manager, A.R. Cooper, invited the family specially. See MW, 8 January 1935. The film was such a hit on the Island that it returned for a second engagement that summer. *Guardian*, 5 July 1935, 6.
2 *Guardian*, 12 March 1935, 2.
3 Anita, in MW, 7 April 1935.
4 MW, 13 April 1935.
5 *Guardian*, 26 April 1935, 1.
6 MW, 1 June 1935; *Guardian*, 7 June 1935, 3.
7 AW, 6, 27 October 1936. Irving had at this point served only sixteen months of a twenty-four-month sentence, so it is unclear what the eighteen-month figure given by Anita refers to.
8 MW, 14 April 1925, 23 May 1926, 8, 11 May 1927, 16 April 1930, 1 May 1931, 6, 11 May 1932, 8 May 1933, 11 May 1935.
9 MacDonald, *If You're Stronghearted*, 144–6; and Clark, "'Who Wants a Car?'" 22–6.
10 MW, 19, 22 June 1934.
11 MW, 12, 14, 17, 19, 21 April 1935. Anita was the author of these entries.
12 MW, 27 April 1935.
13 MW, 24, 25, 27 March 1936. See also MW, 22 April 1938, 28 April 1939.
14 MW, 16, 25–27 June, 2, 10, 13, 15–16 July 1935.
15 Ian McKay, "Tartanism Triumphant: The Construction of Scottishness in Nova Scotia, 1933–1954," *Acadiensis* 21 no. 2 (1992): 5–47.
16 MW, 10 June, 3 July 1936; AW, 25 November 1937.
17 MW, undated [August 1935].
18 Postcard, "Mother" [Myrtle] to Murray, undated [early August 1935], Crawford papers.
19 MW, 9 December 1930, 12 April 1931.
20 *Guardian*, 30 October 1935, 3.
21 MW, 29, 31 December 1935, 1–2 January 1936. This was the third year that the Macneills had gotten "their" books, suggesting the possibility that Maud sent her gifts to two sets of close Cavendish friends in one parcel. See MW, 14 January, 28 December 1932.

## 1936

1 Previous mentions of Ernest grave digging occur in MW, 19 January, 21 March 1925, 18 February, 19 December 1928, 15 January 1931, 8, 18–19 April 1932, 29 January, 11 February, 6 April 1933, 9 March 1934, 29 January, 27 March, 28 May, 21 September 1935.
2 LMMCJ, 1901–1911, 28 January 1912 (but recounting events of the past year), 384–5.
3 MW, 11 March 1930, 11 March 1935. Myrtle does say that Ernest found John F. Macneill "pretty miserable and fussy" after one 1933 visit. But that was not long after his wife died, and he had been (and presumably still was) quite sick himself. It was the sort of assessment that she had made a decade earlier about Aunt Margaret. MW, 15 April 1933.
4 Montgomery biographer Mary Rubio's description of John F. Macneill as "irascible" and "autocratic" is seemingly based on her subject's opinion of him. Rubio, *Lucy Maud Montgomery*, 31, 45.
5 MacDonald, *If You're Stronghearted*, 150.
6 MW, 2 June 1934, 24 June 1935.
7 In recent years, the Webbs had also grown shallots, cucumbers, pumpkin, parsnips, and cauliflower. In 1936, they may have planted some or all of these vegetables too.
8 MW, 22 April 1936.
9 AW, 20 June 1936.
10 See Office of the Lieutenant Governor, Government of Prince Edward Island, "The Honourable Bradford LePage," https://www.lgpei.ca/former-governors/bradford-lepage. LePage's brother owned the general store that the Webbs frequented in Rustico. Coincidentally, LePage's second cousin was the founder of the Royal LePage real estate company and had just helped L.M. Montgomery to buy a home in Toronto.
11 After all, the Banff and Jasper parks were larger than all of Prince Edward Island. On the opinion of Parks Branch staff regarding Maritimes landscapes and on their selection and establishment of Prince Edward Island National Park, see MacEachern, *Natural Selections*, chs 2 and 4.
12 See Williamson and Cromarty's report on PEI sites, 28 July 1936, RG84, vol. 1777, file PEI 2, vol. 1, 5, LAC, https://heritage.canadiana.ca/view/oocihm.lac_reel_t10502/63.
13 AW, 24 June 1936.
14 General Assembly of Prince Edward Island, *Expenditure on Teachers' Salaries ... 1935–36*, 5, https://www.peildo.ca/islandora/object/leg%3A3057. For the full 1937 year, she would be paid $386. General Assembly of Prince

Edward Island, *Expenditure on Teachers' Salaries ... 1936–37*, 5, https://www.peildo.ca/islandora/object/leg%3A6585.

15  MW, 14, 21, 28 July, 31 August 1936.
16  MW, 15, 12 July 1936.
17  B.W. LePage to F.H.H. Williamson, 27 March 1937, RG84, vol. 1777, file PEI 2, vol. 3, LAC.
18  PEI Executive Council minutes, 21 September 1936, RG7, series 3, box 12, no. 2640, PARO. See MacEachern, *Natural Selections*, 84–5.
19  MW, 23, 25 September 1936. See also *Guardian*, 25 September 1936, 1.
20  L.M. Montgomery, *The Selected Journals of L.M. Montgomery*, vol. 5, *1935–1942*, ed. Mary Rubio and Elizabeth Waterston (Toronto: Oxford University Press, 2004) (henceforth *LMMSJ, 1935–1942*), 27 September 1936, 93.
21  See A.W.H. Needler, "Irish Moss Industry in the Maritime Provinces," circular, Fisheries Research Board of Canada, July 1947, 1–5, https://waves-vagues.dfo-mpo.gc.ca/library-bibliotheque/26356.pdf.
22  *LMMSJ, 1935–1942*, 23 October 1936, 107.
23  *LMMSJ, 1935–1942*, 10 October 1936, 97. It is unclear on what basis Montgomery informed correspondent G.B. MacMillan two months later that the government "is going to build a new house for the Webbs." Montgomery, *My Dear Mr. M*, 27 December 1936, 183.
24  *LMMSJ, 1935–1942*, 10, 11, 15 October 1936, 97–100.
25  Alberta Land Surveyors' Association, "R.W. Cautley," https://albertalandsurveyhistory.ca/index.php?title=R.W._Cautley.
26  MW, 23–25 December 1936.
27  See MacEachern, *Natural Selections*, 19–20.
28  Thane Campbell to T.A. Crerar, 12 November 1936, RG84, vol. 1777, file PEI 2, part 2, LAC, https://heritage.canadiana.ca/view/oocihm.lac_reel_t10502/690. The Parks Branch had originally budgeted $25,000 for Dalvay but ended up getting it for $15,000. On the Dalvay sale, see MacEachern and MacDonald, *Summer Trade*, 85–6, 88.
29  Bank of Canada, Inflation Calculator, https://www.bankofcanada.ca/rates/related/inflation-calculator/.
30  For example, whereas the Webbs received $6,500 for their property, which had been assessed for tax purposes at $3,200 ($3,300 or 103% more), Rev. John S. Bonnell would ultimately be awarded $1,500 for a property assessed at $500 ($1,000 or 200% more), W.A. McDonald $4,750 for one assessed at $1,250 ($3,500 or 280% more), and Sydney Ranicar $2,750 for one assessed at $1,250 ($1,500 or 120% more). Prince Edward Island National Park settlement list, RG7, series 3, box 12, file 205, PARO.

31 In 1938, the provincial government set up the Higgs Commission to put valuations on expropriated properties. The commission ultimately priced land from $6 per acre for sand dunes to $65 for extra good land. If Green Gables had been expropriated, rather than sold, at $46.50 per acre, that would have meant it was considered only "good land." Prince Edward Island National Park, Higgs Commission reports, RG7, series 14, subseries 2, PARO.
32 AW, 31 December 1936.

## 1937

1 MW, 30 November 1936. Mary Vipond, *Listening In: The First Decade of Canadian Broadcasting, 1922–1932* (Montreal and Kingston: McGill-Queen's University Press, 1992), 38. This figure is based on 1931 statistics.
2 LW, 16 May 1937.
3 Rubio, *Lucy Maud Montgomery*, 519.
4 *LMMSJ, 1935–1942*, 31 January 1937, 143; also 20 December 1936, 118; 11 June 1937, 169–70.
5 MW, 17 April 1937.
6 Myrtle Webb to F.H.H. Williamson, 11 March 1937, RG84, vol. 1777, file PEI 2, vol. 3, LAC, https://heritage.canadiana.ca/view/oocihm.lac_reel_t10502/1172.
7 Williamson to Myrtle Webb, 17 March 1937, RG84, vol. 1777, file PEI 2, vol. 3, LAC, https://heritage.canadiana.ca/view/oocihm.lac_reel_t10502/1167. Webb's reference to "Green Gables" in this letter is the earliest instance that I have found of a family member calling the home by that name. On 17 June 1939, Anita wrote in her diary, "Left Green Gables on our way to Toronto."
8 MW, 27, 30 April 1937. See also *Guardian*, 12 May 1937, 10.
9 On Wyand's property, see Prince Edward Island National Park, Higgs Commission reports, RG7, series 14, subseries 2, file 754, PARO.
10 AW, 5–8 May 1937.
11 MW, 8 May, 1–2, 8 June 1937; LW, 2 May 1937.
12 MW, 12 June 1937, with the amount jotted in the back of the May 1937 to August 1941 diary.
13 AW, 12 May 1937.
14 LW, 11 May 1937. Manitoba Historical Society, "Memorable Manitobans: James Smart (1888–1957)," http://www.mhs.mb.ca/docs/people/smart_j.shtml.

15 Myrtle Webb to Williamson, 6 May 1937, RG84, vol. 1777, file PEI 2, vol. 3, LAC, https://heritage.canadiana.ca/view/oocihm.lac_reel_t10502/971.
16 James Smart to Ernest Webb, 12 May 1937, in possession of Brenda Jones. See also Smart to R.A. Gibson, 29 May 1937, and memo, 4 January 1938, RG84, vol. 23, file PEI 336, LAC; and MW, 14 May 1937. In the coming years, Ernest's position was described interchangeably as "warden" and "caretaker." To avoid the impression that his duties were changing, I will use "warden" throughout.
17 R.W. Cautley to Williamson, 29 May 1937, RG84, vol. 1777, file PEI 2, vol. 3, LAC, https://heritage.canadiana.ca/view/oocihm.lac_reel_t10502/941.
18 Williamson to E.C. Webb, 3 June 1937, RG84, vol. 1777, file PEI 2, vol. 3, LAC, https://heritage.canadiana.ca/view/oocihm.lac_reel_t10502/939. Parks Branch internal correspondence always refers to the tourist operation of "Mrs. Webb," yet the letter saying to cease the operation was directed to Ernest.
19 Memo for clerk of the Privy Council, undated [1937], RG84, vol. 1777, file PEI 2, vol. 3, LAC, https://heritage.canadiana.ca/view/oocihm.lac_reel_t10502/939.
20 Williamson to Gibson, 25 October 1937, RG84, vol. 1784, file PEI 16.112.1, LAC.
21 Smart to Gibson, 13 June 1937, RG84, vol. 1777, file PEI 2, vol. 3, LAC, https://heritage.canadiana.ca/view/oocihm.lac_reel_t10502/929.
22 MW, 5 June 1937. The latter was probably *Captain Spanky*, an ill-fated spinoff of *Our Gang* (aka *The Little Rascals*).
23 Webbs to Marion Laird, 6 June 1937, Crawford papers.
24 Ibid.
25 Ibid.
26 The Gillings, for example, who had stayed at Green Gables every summer since 1928, stayed at Simpson's place this summer. MW, 7 August 1937. On Wyand, see RG84, vol. 1784, file PEI 16.112.1, LAC.
27 A.L. MacKay to Williamson, 11 April 1938, RG84, vol. 1784, file PEI 16.112.1, LAC, https://heritage.canadiana.ca/view/oocihm.lac_reel_t10509/396.
28 There is no record of what Myrtle earned from this work preparing meals. She states on one occasion that she was paid $1.75 for making tea for a carload of park staff. MW, 25 July 1937.
29 LW, 16 August 1937; MW, 25 July, 2, 6, 10, 15, 16, 20, 24 August 1937.
30 MW, 29 July 1937.
31 *Guardian*, 24 August 1937, 1; 26 August 1937, 1; 28 August 1937, 1; MacEachern, *Natural Selections*, 89.
32 *LMMSJ, 1935–1942*, 15 September 1937, 204.

33 LW, 15 September 1937.
34 Ernest was not given thanks for stepping into this role. On one occasion, he asked permission to lay fenceposts on what had been a Mr Bernard's property. Parks Controller Williamson warned, "This is, in effect, recognizing that Mr. Bernard has a right to the land, which, of course, he has not." Williamson to Cautley, 21 June 1937, RG84, vol. 1784, file PEI 16.112.1, LAC.
35 MW, 16 October 1937. See also MW, 27, 28, 30 September, 1, 8, 13, 14, 30 October, 3, 4, 6, 10, 12, 17, 22, 24 November, 6, 7 December 1937.
36 MW, 5–6, 24 July, 25–26 November 1937. Quotation from 6 July.
37 MW, 23–24 September, 8 November 1937, 5 January 1938.
38 *Guardian*, 2 December 1937, 3, and two articles on 27 November 1937, 13. See also Rosemary Curley, "Wildlife Matters: A Historical Overview of Public Consciousness of Habitat and Wildlife Loss on Prince Edward Island," in *Time and a Place: An Environmental History of Prince Edward Island*, ed. Edward MacDonald, Joshua MacFadyen, and Irené Novaczek, 109–39 (Montreal and Kingston: McGill-Queen's University Press; Charlottetown: Island Studies, 2016), esp. 124–5.
39 MW, 20 December 1937; Myrtle Webb to Marion Laird, 21 December 1937, Crawford papers.
40 MW, 23 December 1937.
41 Myrtle Webb to Marion Laird, 21 December 1937, Crawford papers.
42 MW, 25 December 1937; AW, 1 January 1938.

## 1938

1 AW, 3–5, 11 January 1938.
2 Quoted in *Guardian*, 21 February 1938, 7.
3 MW, 11 March 1938.
4 *Guardian*, 1 April 1938, 1; 5 April 1938, 4; and 2 April 1938, 1.
5 *Guardian*, 5 April 1938, 4; 1 June 1938, 1.
6 Myrtle Webb to Marion Laird, 2 June 1938, Crawford papers. Even with Wyand's situation resolved, tension with the Webbs remained. "Went to the shore for a look around," Myrtle wrote of a hot day in August. "Mrs Wyand pretty snappy." MW, 6 August 1938.
7 The Parks Branch had actually selected Green Gables as the golf course's site in January of that year. See Williamson to Gibson, 13 January 1938, RG84, vol. 150, file PEI 313, part 1, LAC. On the early history of golf courses in Canada, see Elizabeth Jewett, "Behind the Greens: Understanding Golf Course Landscapes in Canada, 1873–1945" (PhD diss., University of Toronto, 2015).

8 Thompson's early vision for the course can be seen in plans dated 10 June 1938, RG84, vol. 151, file PEI 313.7, part 1, LAC, https://heritage.canadiana.ca/view/oocihm.lac_reel_t10432/435.

9 *Globe and Mail*, 20 July 1939, 1; General Assembly of Prince Edward Island, *Public Accounts of the Province ... 1936*, 7, https://www.peildo.ca/islandora/object/leg%3A2979; General Assembly of Prince Edward Island, *Public Accounts of the Province ... 1937*, 32, https://www.peildo.ca/islandora/object/leg%3A6567; General Assembly of Prince Edward Island, *Public Accounts of the Province ... 1938*, 13, https://www.peildo.ca/islandora/object/leg%3A6466. The province had been reimbursed in full the $6,500 for the Webb farm and the $15,000 for Dalvay. The $21,500 "Dominion Refund" is cited under provincial revenue in General Assembly of Prince Edward Island, *Public Accounts of the Province ... 1937*, 7, https://www.peildo.ca/islandora/object/leg%3A6567.

10 Myrtle Webb to Marion Laird, 2 June 1938, Crawford papers; MW, 27 June 1938.

11 MW, 18, 23 August, 2 September 1938.

12 Lorraine told her diary, "Two little ponds made on no.11 fairway & are they pretty!" LW, 12 September 1938.

13 *LMMSJ, 1935–1942*, 26 September 1938, 281.

14 On Ernest Smith, see MacEachern, *Natural Selections*, 95–6; and *Guardian*, 29 October 1938, 6. Lorraine Webb initially believed that she had wangled a landscaping job for her boyfriend, Arthur Wright, and told him to hurry from Ontario. But after talking to Superintendent Smith, she had to telegram Wright and tell him not to come. "Don't think I was ever so disappointed." LW, 3, 6 August 1938.

15 James A. Barclay, in his biography of Thompson, does not call the golf architect an alcoholic, but he does say that Thompson was "more than a social drinker" (47), that he was a heavy drinker later in life (71), that he was a "secret drinker" who kept whiskey stashed "for emergencies" (146), and that his life was likely cut short by "lubrication" (15). James A. Barclay, *The Toronto Terror* (Chelsea, MI: Sleeping Bear, 2000).

16 MW, 27–31 September 1938. None of the Webb diarists – Myrtle, Lorraine, or Anita – deal directly with Thompson's drinking. On this occasion, Lorraine writes, "Mr. Thompson arrived – as usual." LW, 27 September 1938.

17 MW, 10 November 1938; American Society of Golf Course Architects, "Norman H. Woods," https://asgca.org/architect/nwoods/.

18 MW, 29 September 1938.

19 *Guardian*, 29 October 1938, 6.

20 MW, October–November 1938.

21  LW, 8 November 1938.
22  MW, 7, 11 November 1938.

## 1939

1   MW, 6, 20, 27 January 1939.
2   Smart to Williamson, 7 June 1938, RG84, vol. 151, file PEI 313.7, LAC.
3   MW, 6 December 1938, 4, 11–17 January, 3 May 1939. The Parks Branch may well have been backing away from using the barn as a clubhouse anyway, but the damage to its roof sealed its fate.
4   LW, 17 January 1939.
5   Smart to Williamson, 28 October 1938; Gibson to Williamson, 4 November 1938; and memo to Williamson, 7 February 1939, all in RG84, vol. 150, file PEI 313, LAC.
6   Ernest Webb to Superintendent Smith, 11 January 1939, box 1, Yankee Gale monument file, Prince Edward Island National Park papers, Dalvay (henceforth PEINP Dalvay papers). These files were stored at the park's Dalvay office in 1995, when I was doing research for my PhD. Park staff and I attempted to relocate them in 2021 but were unsuccessful. In April 1939, Myrtle reported that two locals had driven over the golf course – "drunk but knew better." MW, 8 April 1939.
7   MW, 4 November 1939, 11 May 1940.
8   *LMMSJ, 1935–1942*, 4 March 1939, 310.
9   Rubio, *Lucy Maud Montgomery*, 555–8.
10  AW, 3 September 1938.
11  MW, 12, 30 May, 1–2 June, 6 July, 2 November 1939.
12  Myrtle Webb to Marion Laird, 12 June 1939, Crawford papers. Almost as bad in Myrtle's books was the fact that, in the three days that Thompson stayed with them, he never once was in time for a meal.
13  Myrtle Webb to Marion Laird, 12 June 1939, Crawford papers.
14  *Guardian*, 15 June 1939, 1.
15  AW, 4 July 1939.
16  AW, 19 July 1939; *Guardian*, 20 July 1939, 1, 3; *Evening Patriot*, 19 July 1939; Mollie Gillen, *The Wheel of Things: A Biography of L.M. Montgomery* (Don Mills, ON: Fitzhenry and Whiteside, 1975), 181. An Associated Screen News cameraman also captured footage. See Robert J.C. Stead to Williamson, RG84, vol. 22, file PEI 109, LAC. A silent clip of the preliminaries of the golf match can be seen in National Film Board Archives, "Shot ID: 6388," https://archives.nfb.ca/stockshot/6388/.
17  LW, 19 July 1939.

18 Canada, *Annual Departmental Reports*, cited in MacEachern, *Natural Selections*, 243; Superintendents' *Annual Reports* (1937–39), PEINP Dalvay papers. From the outset, Green Gables was a much more popular destination than Dalvay, with three to four times as many registering there. See also Deirdre Kessler, *A Century on Spring Street: Wanda Lefurgey Wyatt of Summerside Prince Edward Island, 1895–1998* (Charlottetown: Indigo, 1999), 313, https://archive.org/details/centuryonsprings0000kess.
19 Blake Sinclair to Williamson, 3 October 1939, RG84, vol. 182, file PEI 313.7, LAC, https://heritage.canadiana.ca/view/oocihm.lac_reel_t10433/742.
20 MW, 1, 3, 27 August 1939.
21 MW, 7, 11, 17 August 1939.
22 MW, 14, 21 July, 24 August 1939, 5 July 1941.
23 MW, 24 August 1939.
24 MW, 10 September 1939.
25 AW, 6 September 1939.
26 MW, 23 September 1939.
27 On Maud and Ewen's mental and physical health in these years, including their prescription drug addiction, see Rubio, *Lucy Maud Montgomery*; Kate Macdonald Butler, "The Heartbreaking Truth about Anne's Creator," *Globe and Mail*, 20 September 2008, https://www.theglobeandmail.com/incoming/the-heartbreaking-truth-about-annes-creator/article17971607/; Vanessa Brown and Benjamin Lefebvre, "Archival Adventures with L.M. Montgomery; or, 'As Long as the Leaves Hold Together,'" in *Basements and Attics, Closets and Cyberspace: Explorations in Canadian Women's Archives*, ed. Linda M. Morra and Jessica Schagerl, 233–48 (Waterloo, ON: Wilfrid Laurier University Press, 2012); and Alanna Mitchell, "Lucy Maud Montgomery's Agonizing Drug Addiction," *Maclean's*, 12 February 2020, https://macleans.ca/society/health/lucy-maud-montgomerys-secret-drug-addiction/. Anita was living with Montgomery at the time, but her diary is silent as to Maud's physical and emotional state.
28 MW, 13 October 1939.
29 That summer, Lorraine had been disappointed to learn that her Cavendish School teaching position had been given to someone else for the 1939–40 school year. LW, 29–30 June 1939.
30 *Guardian*, 2 December 1939, 3.
31 MW, 28 November 1939.
32 Williamson to Smith, 14 May 1940, and surrounding file, RG84, vol. 150, file PEI 313, LAC, https://heritage.canadiana.ca/view/oocihm.lac_reel_t10430/1560; *Guardian*, 15 July 1993.

## 1940

1. See, for example, MW, 24 April 1938, 22 June, 10 December 1939.
2. The Webbs soon bought a new radio for $35. The price that they received for cattle in this era was in the $40 range. MW, 10 November 1941, accounting of August 1941.
3. MW, 8–11 February, 26 March 1940.
4. What's more, Myrtle and Ernest occasionally visited Premier Campbell's home socially. See MW, 26 September 1942.
5. MW, 23 April 1940.
6. MW, 23 May 1940.
7. Sandwell, *Canada's Rural Majority*, 201.
8. Blake Sinclair to Williamson, 3 October 1939, RG84, vol. 182, file PEI 313.7, LAC, https://heritage.canadiana.ca/view/oocihm.lac_reel_t10433/742; MW, 7, 9 November 1939.
9. MW, 7 May 1940; LW, 21–23 May 1940.
10. MW, 2 August, 17–26 September 1941.
11. MW, 30 May 1940.
12. MW, 13 April, 8 May 1940.
13. MW, 17, 23 May 1940.
14. MW, 12, 8 June 1940.
15. MW, 2 July, 9–10 August 1940, 19 May 1941.
16. MW, 6 July 1940.
17. Attendance was actually up somewhat across the Canadian park system as a whole in 1940. MacEachern, *Natural Selections*, 243.
18. *Guardian*, 31 December 1940, 7.
19. MW, 25 May, 13 October 1940.
20. Rubio, *Lucy Maud Montgomery*, 567–8.
21. *Guardian*, 7 December 1940, 8.
22. "[A]nd so that's the way we spent our 35th anniversary." MW, 19 September 1940.
23. Keith Webb to Marion and Murray Laird, 20 December 1940, Crawford papers.
24. Ina Reed and Louise Lowther, interview with author, 18 August 2021; Keith Webb to Marion and Murray Laird, 20 December 1940, Crawford papers.

## 1941

1. MW, 25 December 1940.
2. Myrtle Webb to Marion Laird, 1 January 1941, Crawford papers.

3 It is unclear why Pauline went to Ottawa (other than to visit Lorraine) and to Toronto just then. While in Ontario, she sent home a letter with what Myrtle calls an "important announcement." MW, 11 February 1941.
4 Among cases cited in the *Charlottetown Guardian* in the 1930s, the sentences handed down for "assault on female" ranged from twenty days to two years, whereas most of those found guilty of "assault on female (wife beating)" were fined or had their sentence suspended. (However, one husband did receive a thirty-day sentence.) See *Guardian*, 10 June 1931, 11; 15 August 1934, 7; 11 June 1935, 3; 20 September 1935, 11; 13 November 1935, 7; 11 August 1936, 3; and 15 June 1938, 6. On domestic violence in this era, see Joan Sangster, *Regulating Girls and Women: Sexuality, Family, and the Law in Ontario, 1920–1960* (Toronto: University of Toronto Press, 2001), ch. 3.
5 See the Clarks' wedding announcement in the *Guardian*, 22 March 1937, 6. MW, 5 February 1943 and newspaper clipping dated 18 May 1950.
6 MW, 3 April, 25 March, 25 May 1941.
7 On the Air Training Plan, see Ted Barris, *Behind the Glory: The Plan that Won the Allied Air War* (Toronto: Macmillan of Canada, 1992); and Spencer Dunmore, *Wings for Victory: The Remarkable Story of the British Commonwealth Air Training Plan in Canada* (Toronto: McClelland and Stewart, 1994).
8 *Guardian*, 17 April 1941, 1–2. On the Air Training Plan on Prince Edward Island, see MacDonald, *If You're Stronghearted*, 192–200.
9 As many as 12,000 aircrew trained on the Island during the war. MacDonald, *If You're Stronghearted*, 197.
10 *Guardian*, 2 June 1941, 1; 4 June 1941, 6. See Find a Grave, "Leading Aircraftman Glen M. Cameron Fletcher," https://www.findagrave.com/memorial/146649717/glen-m._cameron-fletcher; and Find a Grave, "Leading Aircraftman Bonar Lloyd Robertson," https://www.findagrave.com/memorial/14819312/bonar-lloyd-robertson.
11 The Island Motor Transport company operated the route. See *Guardian*, 2 July 1941, 9; 30 April 1943, 5; and 25 September 1945, 7.
12 MacEachern, *Natural Selections*, 243. Myrtle wrote that 1941 was "the wettest summer since 1900." MW, 12 August 1941.
13 Smart to Gibson, 19 July 1941, RG84, vol. 150, file PEI 313, LAC, https://heritage.canadiana.ca/view/oocihm.lac_reel_t10430/1399.
14 Smart to Smith, 18 May 1941, RG84, vol. 1780, file PEI 16.2, LAC, https://heritage.canadiana.ca/view/oocihm.lac_reel_t10505/402; Smith to Smart, 8 June 1941, RG84, vol. 1780, file PEI 16.2, LAC, https://heritage.canadiana.ca/view/oocihm.lac_reel_t10505/382.

15 MW, 15 June, 25 July 1941.
16 MW, 6 July, 1 August 1941; *Guardian*, 1 August 1941, 1. Ralston was staying at Campbell's summer home in Stanley Bridge. See *Guardian*, 24 July 1941, 9.
17 Canadian Virtual War Memorial, "Sergeant John Rainsford Keith," https://www.veterans.gc.ca/eng/remembrance/memorials/canadian-virtual-war-memorial/detail/2709910. There is a photo of Keith's memorial stone at the British and Commonwealth Military Badge Forum, https://www.britishbadgeforum.com/forums/showthread.php?p=538445.
18 Myrtle had welcomed Havelock visitors to Green Gables previously. She refers to visits by Minnie Alward, the daughter of Carrie Alward (née Keith), and by Julia Fowler Hicks of Havelock. MW, 26 May 1924, 31 August 1925.
19 MW, 2–3, 16, 24, 26, 29, 30, 31 August, 5, 6, 13, 17–26 September 1941.
20 "Kenneth Brookman (ca. 1917–43)," Ancestry website.
21 Commonwealth War Graves, "Flight Sergeant Richard Collinson Hovers," https://www.cwgc.org/find-records/find-war-dead/casualty-details/1082305; Find a Grave, "Flight Sergeant Richard Collinson Hovers," https://www.findagrave.com/memorial/15269750/richard-collinson-hovers.
22 "Gordon Leslie Hatherly (1919–98)," Ancestry website.
23 MW, 19 October, 8–9 November 1941, 23 January, 14 March 1942; Commonwealth War Graves, "Pilot Officer Maurice Edward Charles Bird," https://www.cwgc.org/find-records/find-war-dead/casualty-details/2622457; "Maurice Edward Charles Bird (ca. 1916–41)," Ancestry website.
24 With L.M. Montgomery by this point no longer keeping a journal, there is no direct evidence that Pauline went to Ontario to assist her. But just weeks after Anita returned to live with Maud in early March 1942, Pauline returned to the Island.
25 MW, 8 December 1941.

## 1942

1 MW, 24, 31 January, 3–6 February, 2, 4 March 1942.
2 Rubio, *Lucy Maud Montgomery*, 575–7. On L.M. Montgomery's death, see also Macdonald Butler, "The Heartbreaking Truth"; Brown and Lefebvre, "Archival Adventures"; and Mary Beth Cavert, "Anita Webb and Aunt Maud, December 13, 1911 – March 4, 1996," *The Shining Scroll*, part 2 (2011): 17–19 at 18, https://lmmontgomery.ca/islandora/object/lmmi%3A4137. Anita had stopped keeping a diary in 1940.

3 MW, 28 April 1942. "Mr. Macdonald in a terrible state," according to Myrtle.
4 *Guardian*, 29 April 1942, 1. The newspaper identified the author as "Mrs. Ewan Macdonald ... who wrote more than a score of books under the name of Lucy Maude Montgomery" – that is, her name, which the paper misspelled.
5 National park staff on Prince Edward Island and in Ottawa must surely have known of Montgomery's death and presumably approved of the use of Green Gables.
6 MW, 30 April, 1 May 1942. Montgomery's funeral is described in the *Guardian*, 30 April 1942, 1.
7 Superintendent Smith, *Annual Report* (1942), PEINP Dalvay papers; Smart memo, May 1942, RG84, vol. 150, PEI 313, LAC.
8 MW, 7–8 January, 8 May, 11–20 June, 12 July 1942.
9 MacEachern, *Natural Selections*, 243.
10 MW, 12, 21 August 1942.
11 Clarence Hope, *Anecdotes of an Airman* (n.d.), 74. Maud called Anita (and presumably the other Webb girls) her "niece." Montgomery, *After Green Gables*, 258.
12 Mary Beth Cavert, "L.M. Montgomery and Cultural Memory: The Value of Paratext in Montgomery Books," *The Shining Scroll*, part 1 (2012): 22–7 at 26, https://lmmontgomeryliterarysociety.weebly.com/uploads/2/2/6/5/226525/the_shining_scroll_2012_part_1.pdf.
13 MW, 4, 10 August, 6 September, 11 October 1942.
14 MW, 20 September, 17, 25 October, 11 November 1942.
15 MW, 23 November 1942.
16 MW, 1 January 1943.

## 1943

1 MW, 23 January 1943.
2 MW, 29 March, 21 May, 21 June 1943.
3 MW, 13 February 1943.
4 *Guardian*, 17 May 1943, 2. The *Charlottetown* frigate was replacing a corvette of the same name that had been sunk by a U-boat in the St Lawrence River in 1942.
5 MW, 1 May 1943. The *Guardian* made no mention of local sightings that month.
6 Michael L. Hadley, *U-Boats against Canada: German Submarines in Canadian Waters* (Montreal and Kingston: McGill-Queen's University

Press, 1985), 172–4. On little evidence, a legend has developed that Islanders that day witnessed a battle between a Canadian warship and a German submarine. *Guardian*, 13 May 1995, 14 June 2010.
7 MW, 6 July 1943. See also *Guardian*, 17 July 1943, 10; 7 August 1943, 3.
8 RG84, vol. 150, file PEI 313, LAC.
9 MW, June 1943.
10 MW, 13 August 1943.
11 MW, 16 August 1943.
12 *Guardian*, 1 October 1943, 3, describes a farewell party that was held in North Carleton for Keith and the kids.
13 MW, 14 December 1949. See also *Guardian*, 28 December 1949, 3.
14 Ina Reed and Louise Lowther, interview with author, 18 August 2021.
15 Ibid. The Webbs had gotten Nickey as a "boxer bull pup" in 1940. MW, 4 September 1940.
16 *Guardian*, 20 December 1943, 7; *Globe and Mail*, 14 December 1943, 21. The *Globe and Mail* refers to "his wife's death a few years ago," but it had actually been only eighteen months.
17 Ina Reed and Louise Lowther, interview with author, 18 August 2021.

## 1944

1 MW, 23 December 1943.
2 Ina Reed and Louise Lowther, interview with author, 18 August 2021.
3 MW, 3 April 1944.
4 MW, 18–25 March 1944; Ina Reed and Louise Lowther, interview with author, 18 August 2021.
5 The closest thing to war news previously that year was a reference in May to three planes on nighttime training out of Charlottetown going down off Newfoundland. See MW, 13 May 1944; and *Guardian*, 18 May 1944, 1.
6 Keith left Pickering for Georgetown, Ontario, in 1945 to manage a farm owned by the Eaton family. He eventually moved, bought a greenhouse, and opened a flower shop in Marion's hometown of Norval.
7 Ina Reed and Louise Lowther, interview with author, 18 August 2021.
8 MW, 9–26 July, 26 September, 14 October 1944, 15 April, 16 September 1945.
9 LW, 26 December 1938, 19 November 1940, 9 January, 12 February 1941 (the final entry of her diary).
10 Heilbron, *Remembering*, 54; *Guardian*, 25 August 1944, 3. Discussing Lorraine in passing two years later, the *Guardian* would note, "Mrs. Vessey was Miss Webb of the Famous Anne of Green Gables district of Cavendish and the National Park." *Guardian*, 30 July 1947, 12.

11 RG84, vol. 182, file PEI 313, LAC; B. Graham Rogers, Supervisor, Prince Edward Island Travel Bureau, to Controller Smart, National Parks Branch, 10 May 1945, RG84, vol. 1780, file PEI 16, LAC.
12 MW, 26 August 1944.
13 MW, 19 September 1944.
14 See MacCallum's obituary in the *Guardian*, 7 January 1957, 5.
15 MW, 16, 1–11 September 1944.
16 "Howard John Hurst (1922–2006)," Ancestry website. Hurst had visited Green Gables in September 1944 and would return in May 1945.
17 Canadian Meteorological and Oceanographic Society Archives, "RCAF Met Ob Course 1944," photo, https://cmosarchives.ca/Metphotos/T4/MetOb1944.html.
18 Environment Canada, Historical Climate Data, Charlottetown, 25 November 1944, https://climate.weather.gc.ca/.
19 MW, 19, 24–25 December 1944.

## 1945

1 MW, 7 January, 16 February 1945. Keith had decided to leave Pickering and start work at Georgetown.
2 MW, 19, 20, 29 March 1945.
3 MW, 12–14, 26 April, 4 May 1945.
4 MW, 28 April, 4–5, 7, 9 May 1945.
5 The closest Myrtle came to describing the war that summer was noting that passenger train travel in Canada was impossible because there were so many servicemen heading home. She also noted the visit to Green Gables of a pair of airmen. MW, 27 June, 3 July 1945.
6 MacEachern, *Natural Selections*, 243.
7 Kessler, *Century on Spring Street*, 331.
8 MW, 15–21 January 1945.
9 For example, the Stanley Bridge co-operative creamery went out of business as soon as the park came in because of reduced milk production. Horne, "Human History," 54.
10 MW, 9 December 1945; Myrtle Webb (on behalf of "Mother & Dad") to Anita Webb, 26 December 1945, Crawford papers.
11 MW, 10 December 1945. Myrtle's phrasing is not without ambiguity. One might interpret this passage to mean that the Webbs' focus was on Ernest's job and that, without his pay, they felt obliged to move for financial reasons. If this was the case, they were not being evicted so much as unable to continue to afford living there. But such a reading does not bear weight:

they had not been paying rent at Green Gables, so living elsewhere could hardly have been less expensive. The simpler reading of Myrtle's words is that they were told that because Ernest would no longer be an employee of the park, they were no longer welcome to live there. Of course, the only reason one has to parse meaning from Myrtle's few words is that the Parks Branch did not put its directive in writing.

12 The federal government had moved to compulsory retirement at the age of sixty-five a decade earlier. See J.E. Hodgetts, William McCloskey, Reginald Whitaker, and V. Seymour Wilson, *The Biography of an Institution: The Civil Service Commission of Canada, 1908–1967* (Montreal and Kingston: McGill-Queen's University Press, 1972), 150–1; and *Globe and Mail*, 28 April 1939, 1.

13 Robert J.C. Stead to B. Graham Rogers, 25 January 1946, RG84, vol. 172, file PEI 28, LAC.

14 Myrtle Webb to Anita Webb, 26 December 1945, Crawford papers. The account that follows is cobbled together from this letter and one by Myrtle (on behalf of "Mums and Dad") to "family," 17 December 1945, Crawford papers. Myrtle wrote this second letter to all the Ontario children because she did not have the time or energy to write each child separately, and she hoped that they would be seeing one another. She dated the letter 7 December, but internal evidence makes clear that it was the seventeenth.

15 Smith "felt rather terrible about the whole thing," according to Myrtle in "Mums and Dad" to "family," 17 December 1945, Crawford papers. This letter indicates that Sterling Campbell, a twenty-eight-year-old veteran of the RCAF, was already rumoured to have been given the warden position for the Cavendish end of the park. He took up the job in the new year. See *Guardian*, 15 February 1946, 3; 9 April 1941, 10. Despite Smith's assurances, Campbell did live in Green Gables for a time, although not straightaway. Acting Superintendent J.H. Atkinson to Smart, 9 June 1948, RG84, vol. 1797, file PEI 56.2, LAC, https://heritage.canadiana.ca/view/oocihm.lac_reel_t10513/366.

## CONCLUSION

1 Paula M. Graham and Fenner S. Stewart, "Green Gables House ... 1974: Important Donations," PEINP Ardgowan papers. Graham and Stewart (nephew of the Fenner Stewart who had been the Webbs' next-door neighbour) claim that Montgomery donated the typewriter shortly after the park's creation, whereas Mary Rubio states that Montgomery gave it to her friend Rev. Edwin Smith and that it was eventually donated by his widow

to the park in the 1950s at the earliest. Rubio, *Lucy Maud Montgomery*, 270, 622n56.
2 *Guardian*, 12 January 1946, 1.
3 Acting Superintendent J.H. Atkinson to A.B. LePage, 3 June 1948, RG84, vol. 1797, file PEI 56.2, LAC, https://heritage.canadiana.ca/view/oocihm.lac_reel_t10513/368.
4 See, for example, Mary E. Passmore to H.S. Robinson, Associate Superintendent, National Parks Branch, 14 June 1948, RG84, vol. 1797, file PEI 56.2, LAC, https://heritage.canadiana.ca/view/oocihm.lac_reel_t10513/365.
5 *Guardian*, 30 July 1947, 3; 14 June 1948, 9; 1948 petition, RG84, vol. 1797, file PEI 56.2, LAC, https://heritage.canadiana.ca/view/oocihm.lac_reel_t10513/337.
6 This point is made in Carole Gerson, "Seven Milestones: How *Anne of Green Gables* Became a Canadian Icon," in *Anne's World: A New Century of Anne of Green Gables*, ed. Irene Gammel and Benjamin Lefebvre, 17–34 (Toronto: University of Toronto Press, 2010), 22–3.
7 Parks Canada, "L.M. Montgomery's Cavendish National Historic Site, Green Gables Heritage Place Draft Management Plan, 2022," https://parks.canada.ca/lhn-nhs/pe/greengables/gestion-management/ebauche-draft.
8 *Guardian*, 13 September 1948, 1, 3, 8, 11. For the text of the cairn's plaque, see *Guardian*, 10 September 1948, 4. Perhaps the most remarkable thing about this memorialization is that there were follow-up "rededication" ceremonies in the fall of 1949 and 1950. Thane Campbell spoke at both, and the 1950 one drew 300 people. *Guardian*, 26 September 1949, 5; 2 September 1950, 3.
9 On plans for the site, see *Guardian*, 25 October 1948, 1; 2 November 1948, 2; 7 February 1949, 5; 18 June 1949, 12.
10 Smart to Gibson, 16 October 1948, RG84, vol. 1797, file PEI 56.2, LAC, https://heritage.canadiana.ca/view/oocihm.lac_reel_t10513/355; Smart to Gibson, 23 February 1949, RG84, vol. 1797, file PEI 56.2, LAC, https://heritage.canadiana.ca/view/oocihm.lac_reel_t10513/287.
11 Smart to J.L. Douglas, MP, 16 October 1948, RG84, vol. 1797, file PEI 56.2, LAC, https://heritage.canadiana.ca/view/oocihm.lac_reel_t10513/356.
12 See, for example, *Guardian*, 30 June 1949, 3.
13 Cited in "Notes Taken from Green Gable File," PEINP Ardgowan papers.
14 MW, May–June 1947, quotation in MW, 18 May 1947.
15 MW, 19 April 1948. There was of course other news. In September 1947, four young men drowned at Cavendish Beach, and Superintendent Ernest Smith resigned, faulting the Parks Branch for not providing him with

sufficient lifesaving staff. Smith moved to Nipigon, Ontario, and his son was killed while sledding the following winter. In December 1948, Myrtle's old friend Mima died. Anita got a job as a cook at the University of Toronto in February 1949. Myrtle's onetime friend and Keith's onetime mother-in-law, "Ellice, Mrs Harry Lowther," died in December of that year.

16  MW, 25 December 1948.
17  MW, 21 March, 3, 13 April 1949, 17 May 1950.
18  *Guardian*, 26 June 1950, 3. See also *Guardian*, 19 May 1950, 5.
19  MW, 1 May 1951. Her return was reported in *Guardian*, 21 April 1951, 5.
20  MW, 1 May, 22 November 1951.
21  MW, 16, 19 May 1951; *Guardian*, 27 October 1951, 5.
22  MW, 10 January 1952.
23  *Guardian*, 11 July 1952, 5; 15 July 1952, 5. Wyand had been sick enough in 1951 that her family asked whether her bungalow camp lease could be transferred to her daughter's name. That did not happen, but with her death, the lease shifted to her estate, which could then assign it to her daughter. See Atkinson to Smart, 6 April 1951, RG84, vol. 1784, file PEI 16.112.1, LAC, https://heritage.canadiana.ca/view/oocihm.lac_reel_t10509/219; Superintendent G.B. McGillivray to Smart, 28 June 1952, RG84, vol. 1784, file PEI 16.112.1, LAC, https://heritage.canadiana.ca/view/oocihm.lac_reel_t10509/124; Acting Director J.A. Hutchinson, memo, 22 August 1942, RG84, vol. 1784, file PEI 16.112.1, LAC, https://heritage.canadiana.ca/view/oocihm.lac_reel_t10509/100; and Smart to Deputy Minister Hugh Young, 11 July 1952, RG22 vol. 242 file 33.21.2, part 2, LAC.
24  MW, undated [winter 1953]; *Guardian*, 20 January 1953, 3; MW, 28 August 1953.
25  *Guardian*, 18 June 1955, 3.
26  Marion and Murray's Norval home has received historic designation, in part because of its association with Montgomery. City of Brampton, "Notice of Intention to Designate," https://www.heritagetrust.on.ca/fr/oha/details/file?id=32. Efforts are also underway to make the Norval manse, where Montgomery lived for a decade, the Lucy Maud Montgomery Museum and Literary Centre, whose website is at https://lmmontgomerynorval.com/. Norval is also home both to the Lucy Maud Montgomery Garden and to the Spirit of Maud Theatre Company. Carole Gerson, "Patterns of Commemoration in Montgomery's Afterlife: 'We Are Not Anne of Green Gables; We Are L.M. Montgomery,'" *Journal of L.M. Montgomery Studies*, 27 September 2023, doi.org/10.32393/jlmms/2023.0008.
27  Canada, House of Commons, National Parks Act, 20–21 George V, c. 33 (1930), http://parkscanadahistory.com/publications/national-parks-act-1930.htm.

28 In the 1970s, Parks Canada staffer Fred Horne went so far as to call Green Gables "a rather incongruous wooden monument in the middle of a golf course." Horne, "Green Gables House Report," 24. The course's evolution since the 1930s is described in detail in John Smith and Jamie Harris, "Green Gables Golf Club: The Winds of Change and the Sands of Time," *Dormie*, April 2015, 2–7, https://www.stanleythompson.com/downloads/april-3.pdf.
29 *Globe and Mail*, 3 October 1985.
30 *Guardian*, 21 August 1909, 12.

# Index

Page numbers in italics indicate references to images.

A.E. Toombs Music Store, 39
*Anne of Green Gables* (1934 film), 105, *106*, 110
*Anne of Green Gables* (novel), xvii–xviii, 15, 43, 46, 105, 122–3, 181, 213–14, 216, 217n3
Armenian genocide, 39
Atkinson, J.H., 205
automobiles, 34, 112, 119, 137, *138*, 141, 163; and tourism, 77, 107, 226n14
autumn at Green Gables, 48, 57, 71, 79–80, 92, 109, 151–2, 183, 193–4
Avonlea, xviii, 15
Avonlea branch, Women's Institute, 32, 198, 203
Avonlea Lodge, 136, 141
Avonlea lunch counter, 63

Bailey, Temple, 59
Baldwin, Stanley, 53
Bayview, 4, 15, 37, 117, 176, 193
Bernard, J.A., 204
Bideawee (Bidawee), 114–16.
 *See also* Green Gables: cottages
Bingham, Fred, 76
Bird, Maurice, 173–6

Bishop, H.S., Rev., 87, 236n16
boarders at Green Gables, 26, 33, 36, 52–3, 63, 69–70, 90–1, 98, 187, 194–5; as correspondents, 75, 109–10, 144, 177, 211. *See also* Green Gables: tourist operation; *specific boarders*
Bobby (Bobbie), the mailman, 81, 162, 172, 208
Bonnell, John S., Rev., 71, 172, 234n15
Brackley, 172
British Commonwealth Air Training Plan, 170–1
Brookman, Kenneth, 174–5

Campbell, Thane, 124–5, 131–2, 139, 150, 172, 204–5
Canadian Girls in Training, 170
Canadian War Services, 170
Canadian Women's Press Club, 69
Cape Breton Highlands National Park, 147
cats, *6*, 43, 55, 71, 88, 92, 94, 133, 190, 210
cattle, 43, 137, 140
Cautley, R.W., 129, 137–9

Cavendish, xviii, 4, 16, *20*, 27–8, 30, 53, 89, 103–5, 119, 172, 198–9; sense of community, 32–3, 36, 36, 41, 60–1, 75–6, 107–8; tourism, 15–17, 45–6, 63, 69, 108, 122, 141–2
Cavendish Baptist Church, 65, 82
Cavendish Beach, 63, 64, 94, 141, 171
Cavendish Cemetery, 65, 89, 118, 179, 183, 190, 212
Cavendish Hall, 38, 60–1, 68, 112, 128, 130
Cavendish Players, 68, 96–7
Cavendish Road, *21*, 23, 112–13, *124–5*, 153
Cavendish Rural Telephone Company, 48
Cavendish School, 44–5, 74, 91, 123, 189
Cavendish Senior Dramatic Club, 60–1
Cavendish United Church, 49, 82, 179, 194
Chamberlain, Neville, 145–6
Charlottetown, 91, 184, 202, 207; trips to, 22, 39, 95, 112, 130, 140, 153, 155–6, 179, 198
*Charlottetown* (ferry), 99–100
Charlottetown Business College, 74
*Charlottetown Guardian*, 15, 38–9, 146, 217n4, 228n14
Charlottetown Hospital, 183
*Charlottetown Patriot*, 146, 217n4
Charlottetown Police, 169
chickens, 35–6, 81, 86
Christmas at Green Gables: 1920s, 31, 40, 59; 1930s, 75, 80, 87, 94–5, 109–10, 117–18, 130, 144, 152, 161–2; 1940s, 168, 177, 182–3, 190, 195
church union, 49

Clark, Fred, *20*, 100–1, 169
Clark, George, 76, 169
Clark, Nellie, 75
Clark, Sadie, 169
Clark, Thyra, 75–6
Clark, Wilbur, 75
Clifton, 68
Coffin, Eric, Rev., 194–5, 202
Collier, Miss, 75
Committee of Dispossessed Landowners, 142–3, 146
Confederation Week (1939), 156
co-operative movement, 35–6, 48, 227n8
Cornwall, 68
Cosy Corner rink, 41
Crerar, T.A., 131, 150, 153, 156
Crociera aerea del Decennale, 97–8
Cromarty, W.D., 122
Czechoslovakia, 151

Dalvay-by-the-Sea, 131–2, 156, 172
D-Day (6 June 1944), 191
deaths: of community members, 29, 35–6, 58–9, 65, 118–19, 211; of family members, 28, 78, 109, 117, 167–8, 178, 189, 195, 209, 212
Depression. *See* Great Depression
diaries, 218n6, 219n8; of Charles Macneill, xxvi; of Anita Webb, 112, 137; of Lorraine Webb, 103, 133; of Myrtle Webb, xix–xxvi, 19–21, 35, 37, 43, 68–9, 107, 173, 206, 212
Dieppe, 182
dogs, 43; Happy, 202; Nero, 140–1; Nickey, 189, *199*, 202
domestic violence, 169
Dominion Seed House, 120
Down syndrome, 133–4, 141

# Index

Dunkirk, 164
Dunning, Charles, 124

Eaton's catalogue, 50
Eden, Anthony, 145
Edward VIII, King, 129–30
Edwards, Miss, 44–5
egg circle, 35, 82, 118. *See also* co-operative movement
elections: federal, 38, 163, 197; provincial, 51–2, 114, 154, 208
electrification, 163–4, 234n15
Elizabeth, Queen (Queen Mother), 155–6
Elizabeth II, Queen, 211

Farmer's Institute, 36
Fenton, T.C., 137–9
Fleming, Dolph, 49, 60
Fleming, James, Dr, 60, 83
Fletcher, Glen, 171
flowers, 23, 58, 137, 165, 172
food, 45, 77, 86, 91, 102, 120, 191–2; berries, 27–8, 123, 192; seafood, 23–4, 76–7
Fortune Bridge, 105
fossil fuels, 42, 71, 95, 152
Fyfe, Elmer, 79–80, 237n7

Geddie, John, 58
general stores, 22, 225n3–4, 235n6. *See also* LePage, E.C.; Toombs, Harold
Gillings, Mr and Mrs, 69, 98, 244n26
George V, King, 112
George VI, King, 138, 140, 155–6, 211
Graham, W.A.: Seaside Farm (tourist operation), 108
Gray, Will, 59

Great Depression, 72, 74–5, 81, 89–90, 103, 113, 122
Green, Irving, 110–12
Green Gables, *xviii*, xxv, 10, *5*, *17*, *106*, *126*, 134, 152, *204*; association with *Anne of Green Gables*, xviii, 15–16, 45–6, 51–2, 70, 106–7, 122–3, 142; attendance at, 157, 166, 172, 180, 197; barns and outbuildings, 11–13, 25, 139, 152–3, 213; commemoration, 204, 208; cottages, 78, 85, 92, 114–16, 143; fame of, 15, 26, 46, 105–7, 122–3; farm, 15, *20*, 22, 29, 45, 57, 191–2; farm livestock, 15, 43, 137; filled with people, 14, 32–4, 67, 83, 111, 161, 170; gardens, *11*, 12–13, 23, 77, 120, 149–50, 165, 179, 187, 241n7; house electrification, 164; house exterior, 51, 120–1, 151–2; house heating, 42, 48, 95, 238n19; house indoor plumbing, 135, 164; house layout, *12–13*, 13–14; house maintenance, 34, 50–1, 78, 120–1, 187, 197; house renovations by National Parks Branch, 151–2, 155, 164; house renovations by Webbs, 5, 13–14, 34, 78, 164; landscape change, *214–15*; and L.M. Montgomery, 5, 26, 70, 92–3, 128, 160, 178–9; Marion's lane, 150; name, xix, 27, 51–2, 70, 114, 134, 226n16, 243n7; National Parks Branch plans for, 122, 139–40, 153–4, 201, 203–6, *205*, 207, 213–14; property, xvii, *xxi*, 14–15, *20*, 96; sale for national park, 130–2; Second World War, 161, 173–6, 181–2, 184; tearoom, 157–9, *158*, 165–6, 172, 182, 198, 203;

tourist operation, 26–7, 36–7, 44–5, 52–3, 56, 63, 77–8, 85, 91, 98–9, 107–8, 114, 123, 134–5, 139, 187. *See also* Green Gables Golf Course; Haunted Woods; Lover's Lane; Macneill's Pond
Green Gables Golf Course, *148–9*, 157, *185*, *214–15*; clubhouse, 152–3, 190, 213; landscaping, 150, 154–5; planning, 140, 147–9, *148–9*; redesign, 212; Second World War, 179, 182, 186, 193–5
Green Gables Heritage Place, 10, 33–4, 204, 213–14
Groskorth, Otto, 181

Harrington, 68
Harris, Elmer, 105
Harris, Misses, 36
Harvey, D.C., 204
Haszard, Helen, 102–3, *104*
Hatherly, Gordon, 174–5
Haunted Woods, *127*, 189
Hauptmann, Richard, 88
Havelock, New Brunswick, 3, 173, 193–4, 251n18
Herd, Joyce, 75
Hiscott, Sadie, 169
Historic Sites and Monuments Board, 204
Hitler, Adolf, 145, 151, 196
HMCS *Charlottetown*, 184
HMCS *Skeena*, 155–6
Holman, Roy, 184
hooking, 27, 40–1, 67, 82, 102–3
Hope, Clarence, 181
horses, *24*, *30*, 33, 43, 119; Daubin, 43; Laddie, 137; Queenie, 119, 137; Sport, 43
Hovers, Richard, 174–5

Howe, C.D., 156
Hunter River, 22, 61, 68, 111, 143; meeting or taking trains at, 52, 58, 154, 166, 178, 189, 194; shopping at, 22, 40, 42, 152, 162, 189, 190; taking goods to, 57, 81
Hurst, Howard, 194–7
Hussey, Fred, 194–5

ice harvesting, 41, 102, 151, 228n8
*Inner Silence, The*, 105
Irish moss, 126–8
Italian Air Fleet, 97–8

Jackson, Peter, Rev. and Mrs, 49
Jenkins, Jack, 105
*Johnny Belinda*, 105
Jones, Heber, 161–2, 184–5, *186*, 196, 202
Jones, J. Walter, 204
Jones, Larry, 208
Jones, Terry, 192, 196, 198

Kays, Albert, 62
Keith, Beatrice, 173, 193–4
Keith, Charles B., 3
Keith, Rainsford, 173
King, William Lyon Mackenzie, 47–8, 163, 197
Kochaly, Absolom, 39, 63

labour exchanged, 29–30, 57, 66, 226n23
Laird, Austin, *20*, 108, 111, 153
Laird, Elaine, 149, 180
Laird, Ian, 130, 133, 195
Laird, Murray, 54, 80, 83, 86–7, 99, 108–9, 116, 149, 180, 195
Laird, Pat, 116, 130, 133–4, 141, 180–1, 191

Lake of Shining Waters.
    See Macneill's Pond
Leaskdale, Ontario, 47
Lea, Walter, 114
LePage, A.B., 203
LePage, B.W., 121–2, 124–5, 203
LePage, E.C.: general store, 22, 74, 112
LePage, Reuel and Enid, 39, 97, 110, 117, 122, 184
Lindbergh, Charles, 88
livestock, 43, 86, 137, 140, 145
L.M. Montgomery's Cavendish National Historic Site, 204
Locke, Edward, 3
Lord Tweedsmuir, 163
Lou S. Darling catalogue, 22–3
Lover's Lane, xviii, 15, 25–6, 27, *104*; in *Anne of Green Gables*, 43; L.M. Montgomery and, 5, 26, 53, 58, 71, 72, *115*, 128
Lowther, Edward, 118
Lowther, Ellice, *8*, 29, 88, 96, 103, 111, 188
Lowther, Harry, 29, 34
Lowther, Margaret, 96, 109, 111, 120, 167–8

MacCallum, Grant, 194
Macdonald, Chester, 54, *55*, *56*, 58, 79, 101, 178–9, 189, 231n22
MacDonald, Edward, 22, 57
Macdonald, Ewen, Rev., 10, 46–7, 169, 178, 223n17; death, 189–90; health, 109, 166–7, 178, 248n27; marriage to L.M. Montgomery, 15, 167
Macdonald, Luella, 101
Macdonald, Stuart, 54, 178–9, 190, 231n22

MacKay, Jennie, 44
MacKendrick, May, *8*
MacKendrick, Will, *8*
MacMillan, G.B., 7
Macneill: spelling of surname, 221n1
Macneill, Ada. *See* Simpson, Ada
Macneill, Albert, 65
Macneill, Alec, 118
Macneill, Alexander, 15
Macneill, Charles, xxvi, 221n17
Macneill, David, 3–4, 8–10, *9*, 58
Macneill, Ham, *20*, 23, 29, 120, 130, 132. *See also* Macneill's Pond
Macneill, John F., 32, 118–19
Macneill, Lucy, 15
Macneill, Maggie, xvii
Macneill, Margaret, 3–4, 8–10, *9*, 16, 25, 28
Macneill, May, 118
Macneill, Myrtle. *See* Webb, Myrtle
Macneill, Sadie, 23, 126, 167
Macneill's Pond, xviii, *xxi*, *125*; ice and fish harvested from, 23–4, 41, 102, 142, 152, 177; identified as Lake of Shining Waters, xviii, 23, 122, 124–5, 225n7
mail delivery, 50, 75, 79–81, 109, 144, 177
Manion, Robert, 163
Maritime provinces, 67, 74, 114, 184
Marshall, Miss, 75
Mayfield, 4, 22, 38, 47, 51, 76, 97, 99, 197
McClelland and Stewart, 31, 158–9
McCoubrey, George, 201–2
McCoubrey House, 108
McCoubrey, Ira, 140–1
McCoubrey, J.N., *20*
McCoubrey's rink, 41
McFarlane, Spanky, 140

McGarrys, 82
McNeill, Lorne, 108
McNeill, William H., 86
Meighen, Arthur, 38
modernity, xxvi, 153
Monopoly game, 133
Montgomery, Lucy Maud, xxvi, 5, 15, 46, 58, 73, 217n3; *Anne of Green Gables*, xvii–xviii, 7, 15, 217n3; *Anne's House of Dreams*, 114; books for the Webbs, 31, 59, 80, 86–7, 94, 110, 118, 130, 144, 152, 158–9; brand, xxv, 54, 158–9, 165, 179, 201, 203–6, 220n14; on Cavendish, 27–8, 30, 63, 70–1, 118–19; death, 178–9; *Emily Climbs*, 37; friendship with Myrtle Webb, 5–7, 6, 23, 46–7, 54, 72, 101, 133, 213; on Green Gables, 10, 70–1, 92–3; health, 47, 160, 167, 248n27; journals, xix–xx, 219n8; "Journey's End" (Toronto home), 90, 154, 156, 178, 181; on Katherine Wyand, 63, 90; on Lover's Lane, 15, 26, 53, 72, 115, 128; marriage to Ewen Macdonald, 10, 15, 47, 109, 160, 167; *Mistress Pat*, 116; on the national park, 125, 128, 142, 150; *A Tangled Web*, 86; visits to Prince Edward Island, 27, 52–4, 70–1, 92, 94, 128, 149–50, 160; and Anita Webb, 154, 156, 168–9; and Marion Webb, 54, 79–80, 96, 99, 109; and Webb children, 54, 231n23; worries about her sons, 101, 160; worries about Myrtle Webb's health, 66, 83–4, 87, 90, 92–3
Moore, Miss, 55, 85, 102–3
Mount Pleasant, 171

movies, 39, 140, 153. See also *Anne of Green Gables* (1934 film)
mussel mud, 82, 88–9

national parks, xxv–xxvi, 121–2, 220n15; inviolability, 147, 200, 212; Second World War, xxvi, 172, 179–80, 197. See also Prince Edward Island National Park
National Parks Act, 212
National Parks Branch, 121–2, 124–5, 129, 131, 134–5, 137–9, 201–6. See also Parks Canada; *specific staff members*
nature observations, 19, 34–5, 68
New Glasgow, 61, 62, 66, 68, 90, 105
Norrises, 69, 70, 98
North Cape, 184
North Carleton, 111, 116, 118, 120, 133, 149, 167–8, 176–8; Lowther farm, 29, 96, 187–9
North Shore, 16–17, 41, 58, 89, 142, 179; site for national park, 122, 125, 142
Norval, Ontario, 47, 94, 212, 253n6, 257n26; Marion Webb's married life in, 109, 116, 130, 133, 156, 176; Marion Webb's trips to, 54, 79–80, 83–4, 99

Old Home Week, 39
old orchard, xviii, 12, 217n4
old parsonage, the, *207*, 208–12
O'Leary, 3, 8–10, 24, 59, 65, 78–9, 126
Ottawa, 164–5, 176, 192–3
*Our Town*, xxvi

Page, L.C., 73
Park Corner, 46, 179

# Index

Parks Canada, 212–14
Paterson, W.A., Rev., 111
plays, 38, 60; *Among the Breakers* (1928), 60–1; *Mrs. Briggs* (1928), 60; *The Road Back* (1929), 67; *Valley Farm* (1933), 96–7
potatoes, 29, *30*, 57, 81
poverty, 16, 27, 45, 59, 81, 103, 119
prices, 26, 35, 57, 67, 81, 94, 119, 131–2, 137
Prince County Hospital, 69, 87, 168, 180
Prince Edward Island, xx, 220n16; agriculture, 29, 35–6; ethnic diversity, 62; Great Depression, 81, 89, 112–13; newspapers, 217n4; politics, 51–2, 115, 131, 136, 142–4, 154, 203–4; poverty, 59; Prohibition, 51–2; roadwork, 57–8, 112–13; Second World War, 170–1, 184; tourism, 16, 46, 77, 103, 166, 172
Prince Edward Island National Park, *136*, 199–200, *214–15*; attendance, 157, 179, 180, 197; expropriation process, 140–3, 146; opening, 156–7; preparation and planning, 129, 135–40; Second World War, 161, 166, 172, 179, 186, 193, 197; site inspection for, 121–2, 125, *124–7*; today, 212–13; wildlife in, 143–4
Prince Edward Island Railway, 52, 57–8, 80, 109, 130, 137, 168
Prince Edward Island Travel Bureau, 70, 166, 201
Prince Edward Theatre, 110
Prince of Wales College, 91, 97
Prohibition, 51–2, 100–1

Quigley, William, Rev., 118
quilting, 14, 43, 69, 94, 110, 119–20, 170, 190

radio, 19, 41–2, 59, 129–30, 133–4, 137–8, 144, 163, 176
Ralston, J.L., 171–2
Rennie Seed, 120
roadwork, 57–8, 112–13
Robertson, Bonar, 171
Rogers, B. Graham, 166, 201
Roosevelt, Franklin D., 196
Royal Air Force personnel, 173–4, *174*, 182
Royal Canadian Air Force personnel, 171, 173, 181–2, 195, 197
Rubio, Mary, 53, 86
Ruddy, E.L., 191
rural history, 220n16
Rustico, 4, 24, 57–8, 61–2, 68, 74, 84, 89, 197; shopping in, 22, 142, 152, 191

Second World War, 162–4, 166, 170, 173, 176–7; beginning, 159–60; end, 196; news of, 182–4, 191, 195–7; rationing, 179; servicemen, *175*, *176*
Shediac, 98
Shirley, Anne (actress), 105
Simpson, Ada, 3, *4*, 15, 32, 37, 42, 117, 176, 181–3
Simpson, Annie, 84, 103–5, 123
Simpson, Cecil, *4*, 37, 41–2, 117, 176, 181–2
Simpson, Claude, Dr, 90, 180, 184
Simpson, Earl, 103–5
Simpson, Elaine, *4*, 233n16
Simpson, Harold, 103

Simpson, Jerry, *20*, 60, 74, 75, 90, 102, 108; exchanging labour, 38, 82, 100; opposition to national park, 142; Sunnyacre Farms (tourist operation), 16–17, 26, 36, 45, 108, 141
Simpson, Leona, 117
Simpson, Mabel, 161
Simpson, Miriam, 117
Simpson, Nellie, 103
Simpson, Wallis, 130
Simpson, Walter, 4, 39
Sinclair, Peter, 124–5
singsongs, 82–4, 190
skating, 41, 66, 80, 117, 130
Smart, James, 137–9, 147, 151, 172, 203, 205–6
Smart, Katherine, 203
Smith, Ernest, 149–51, 153, 164, 166, 194, 200–2, 207, 256n15
snowshoeing, 40, 162, 196
spring at Green Gables, 23, 34–5, 112–13, 120–1, 137, 196
Stanley Bridge, 32, 36, 41, 79
Stead, Robert J.C., 201
Stewart, C.F., Mrs: Kirklawn (tourist operation), 108
Stewart, Clarence, 121
Stewart, Fenner, *20*, 28
Stewart, J.D., 51
Stewart, Stirling, 165
Stirling, John, Rev., 178
subsistence, xxvi, 22–3, 28, 35–6, 42, 73, 123, 191–2. *See also* Green Gables: farm
summer at Green Gables, xvii, 15, 26; 1920s, 36–7, 52–3, 56, 63, 69–70; 1930s, 78, 84–5, 91, 98, 107–8, 114, 116, 141–2, 157–8; 1940s, 165–6, 172, 180, 186–7, 193, 197

Summerside airport, 170–4, 180, 194
Swindlehurst, Ethel, 191, 196, 211

Takamodo, Princess (Japan), 213
telephone, 48, 74
Thompson, Jones, & Co., 147–50, *148–9*, 164
Thompson, Stanley, 147–53, 155, 164, 172
Tignish, 171
Timmins, Mrs, 98, 114
Toombs, Harold, *20*, 68, 75–6; general store, 22, 76
Toombs, Lena, 76
tourism, xxv, 36, 56, 107; Americans, 56, 76–7, 172; arts and crafts, 102–3, *104*; in Cavendish, 15–17, 26, 45–6, 63, 69, 108, 122, 141–2; on Prince Edward Island, 16, 46, 58, 76–7, 122, 166, 172, 187; Second World War, 16, 166, 172–3, 197. *See also* Green Gables: tourist operation
trains. *See* Prince Edward Island Railway

U-boats, 184
*U-262*, 184

Vessey, Annie Maureen, 211
Vessey, Donna, 198
Vessey, Harold, 192–3, 211
Victory in Europe (ve) Day, 196

wages, 29, 49, 65–6, 70, 89, 123, 139, 154, 194
Ward, Dorothy, 123
Webb, Anita Gwen, 211
Webb, Anita Maud, 44, *55*, 69, 83, 91, 111, 116, 141, *174*, 181, 212;

automobile, 137, *138*, 141; birth, 10; housework, 66, 68, 73, 91, 121, 145; keeping her own diary, 112, 123, 132, 138, 144, 159; maintaining the diary, 84, 111, 118, 120; at L.M. Montgomery's home, 154, 156, 167–9, 178, 181; in plays, 60, 68, 88; work in tearoom, 166, 172, 180, 197; work outside home, 74, 128, 150, 182, 194, 211. *See also* Webb family

Webb, Ernest, xvii–xix, 9, *9*, 26, 35–6, 38, 71, 82, 170, 178; death, 209–10; farmwork, 29, *30*, *33*, 40–3, 48, 57, 66, 78, 87, *100*, 118, 137, 177–8; Green Gables renovations, 10, 11, 14, 33–4, 77–8, 114; housework, 94, 190, 198; ill-health, 145, 180, 194, 208; marriage to Myrtle Webb, 75, 92, 99–100, 110, *113*, 161–2, 183, 188, 198, *199*, *209;* maintaining the diary, 64–5, 83–4, 168, 176; at old parsonage, 208–9; in plays, 61, 67–8, 97; travel, 59, 78, 111, 154; wedding, *8*, 9–10; work in cemetery, 65–6, 89, 118–19; work on roads, 57–8; work on telephone, 48–9, 74; work with national park, 128–9, 131–2, 139, 143, 153, 162, 200–2, 244n16; work with neighbours, 29, 32, 37, 38, 57, 66, 82, 100, 119. *See also* Webb family

Webb family, xvii–xix, *xxii*, 16, 95, *187*; children, 10, 16, 24, 37, 44, 54, 73, 75, 212; as Liberal supporters, 38, 47–8, 52, 114, 154, 163, 197. *See also specific family members*

Webb, Glenn Allen, 211

Webb, Ina Austina, 111, 168, *187*, *188*, 187–91

Webb, Ina Rosamund, 10, 111

Webb, Keith, 10, 54, 73, 91, 213; children of, 111, 120, 168, 176, 188, 190–1, 211; death of Margaret Lowther, 167–8; health, 65–6; in North Carleton, 29, 96, 137, 187–8; in Ontario, 187–8, 190–1, 212; recreation, 40–1, 196; wedding to Ethel Swindlehurst, 191; wedding to Margaret Lowther, 96; work on farm, 11, 22–3, 35, 40–1, 47, 66, 74, 87–9; work outside home, 29, 84, 87; work with neighbours, 29, 38, 50, 57, 66, 68. *See also* Webb family

Webb, Lorraine, 16, *17*, 25, 45, 53–4, 101, 116, 133, *134*, 198; birth, 10; craft art, 102–3; health, 66, 85; housework, 91, 121, 157, 191; keeping her own diary, 103, 133, 138, 141, 152–3; maintaining the diary, 120, 129–30, 133, 138, 183; marriage to Harold Vessey, 192–3; in plays, 60–1; at Prince of Wales College, 91, 97–8; in Second World War, 164–5, *175*, 176, 182, 190, 192–3; as teacher, 123, 150; work in tearoom, 141, 157; Arthur Wright, 133, 192–3. *See also* Webb family

Webb, Louise, 120, 120, *187*, *188*, 187–91

Webb, Marion, 9, 16, 40, 42, 51, 79, 91, 191, 212; birth, 10; children of, 116, 130, 133–4, 141, 149, 180, 195; courtship with Murray Laird, 79, 83–4, 86–7, 99; craft art, 102; health, 40, 52–3, 69, 75, 85, 116, 180, 196; housework, 23, 66, 73, 85, 91; maintaining the diary, 46–8,

84; L.M. Montgomery, 53–4, 79–80, 96, 99, 108–9; in plays, 38, 60, 97; wedding to Murray Laird, 108–9. *See also* Webb family

Webb, Myrtle, xvii, 79–80, 211–12; birth, 3, 7–8; as diarist, xix–xxvi, *xxiii*, 19–21, 34–5, 44, 56, 58–9, 68–9, 78, 85, 98, 185, 206, 211–12, 219n9; in community, 15, 32, 38, 82, 140–1; cooking, 45, 48, 86, 90, 107, 126–8; death, 212; early life, 3–5; eviction from Green Gables, 200–2, 254n11; farmwork, 35, 61–2; friendship with L.M. Montgomery, 5–7, 46–7, 54, 72, 101, 133, 213; hooking, 40–1, 67, 82; housework, 21–2, 28, 40, 107, 121, 170, 179, 190, 208; ill-health, 24–5, 50, 60, 66–7, 69, 73, 82–4, 87–90, 93–4, 145, 168, 177, 183, 211–12; marriage to Ernest Webb, 59, 78, 92, 94, 99–100, 140, 161–2, 166, 180, 182, 188–9, 198; menstruation, 37; as model for Anne of Green Gables, 7–8; movies, 39, 140, 153; music, 40, 65, 82; nature observation, 19, 34–5, 68; at old parsonage, 208–10; photographs of, *xxii, xxiv*, 4, 5, 6, 9, 10, 24, 72, *113, 175, 187, 199, 209, 210*; in plays, 60–1; reading, 31, 37, 75; travel, 39, 46–7, 64, 78, 111, 118, 130, 133–4, 176, 193–4, 198, 207, 211; walking, 24, 42, 46–7, 84, 94, 130, 133–4, 145, 162, 170, 208; wedding, *8*, 9–10; work with national park, 129, 141, 143, 150, 156–9, 172. *See also* Green Gables: gardens; Green Gables: tearoom; Green Gables: tourist operation; Webb family

Webb, Pauline, 16, *17, 27*, 44, 45, 50, 111, *174, 175*, 201–2, 207, 211; birth, 10; children of, 192, 196, 208; housework, 91, 121, 126, 147, 157, 179; in Ontario, 176, 182; wedding to Heber Jones, 162, 184–5, *186*; work in tearoom, 157, 166, 172, 180. *See also* Webb family

Wellington, 171

Wheatley River, 48

Wilder, Thornton, xxvi

Williamson, F.H.H., 122, 134–5, 139

Windsor girls, the, 75

winter at Green Gables, 30–1, 40, 48–9, 66, 81, 101–2, 133, 170, 177–8, 195–6

Woman's Christian Temperance Union, 51, 57, 135

women: diaries, 218n6; electrification, 234n15; tourism, xxv, 91, 98–9, 219n11

Women's Institute, 31–2, 34, 39, 45, 67, 76, 86, 198, 204

wood: cutting, hauling, and sawing of, 31, 41–2, 61–2, 66, 74, 152

Woods, Norman, 147, 151, 156

Wright, Arthur, 133, 192–3

Wright, Sarah, 51

Wyand, Allan, *20*

Wyand, Katherine, 63, 90, 103; death, 211; friend of Webbs, 46, 75, 91, 108; opposition to national park, 135–6, 139–40, 142, 144, 146; tourist operation, 63, 91, 108, 141; work with national park, 146, 204

Wyatt, Wanda, 198

York, 74, 192

Young People's Society, 37, 83, 107, 110–11, 136, 144